FLIGHT FOR DISCOVERY

Aviation Advocate!
Inspiration. Motivation. Plane Stuff.

"Sometimes truth is scarier than fiction"

By Karlene K. Petitt PhD

at

Flight To Success

www.KarlenePetitt.com

FLIGHT FOR DISCOVERY

KARLENE K. PETITT PHD

Johnny, Enjoy the journey!
xo Karlene Petitt

JET STAR PUBLISHING INC.
SEATAC WA

Copyright 2022 Karlene Petitt
All rights reserved. No part of this publication may be reproduced or transmitted in any form or by any means, electronic or mechanical, including photocopy, recording, or any information storage and retrieval system, without permission in writing from the publisher.

Requests for permission to make copies of any part of this work should be submitted online at Karlene.Petitt@gmail.com

The thoughts, opinions, and attitudes expressed in this work are my own, and do not represent those of my employer.

ISBN: 978-1-944738-13-6
www.JetstarPublishing.com

DEDICATION

Flight For Discovery is dedicated to Lee Seham, Attorney at Law. There is nobody more masterful with the written word, has more knowledge of the AIR21 statute, aviation and employment law, and exemplifies what a good human should be. Lee is honest, kind, compassionate, and gives more than he takes. His talents extend beyond the courtroom, and he can brighten the darkest days with his humor. I am honored to have shared the most challenging journey of my life with him, and to call him my friend.

Foreword

As an airline pilot with 40 years in the industry, I've seen some serious changes—some good, some bad. Advancements in technology and evolution in Crew Resource Management (CRM) have exponentially improved safety on the flight deck. But one area of concern keeps me and other "old school" pilots, such as author Karlene Petitt, up at night: the direction of pilot training and safety culture.

Like me, Ms. Petitt gained her wings in an era when the pilot candidate was expected to virtually memorize the flight manual on any given plane. The pilot could draw the electrical system blindfolded, find and push the Bus Isolation switch in a black cockpit, and tell you off the top of one's head the max speed for a cracked cockpit window.

These days, not so much. "Train to proficiency" has become the norm. Get a pilot "just good enough," then cut them loose. Red light goes on, push a button, get a banana. Or at least, that's what it feels like to us old-timers.

Pilot-Author Karlene Petitt has dedicated her professional aviation life to calling attention to just this issue, not without repercussions. Regardless of where your opinion falls on the Pilot Training School of Thought spectrum, the fact that airline flight training has been reduced to the lowest common denominator cannot be ignored. This may indeed vastly reduce the average flight training footprint and increase schoolhouse efficiency. But does this minimalist approach do anything to uphold safety? Or rather, as some pilots such as the author portend, reduce safety margins to near-dangerous levels, all while FAA bureaucrats look the other way?

The question should be asked if management is shortchanging pilot training with a singular goal—to ultimately replace the pilot with automation. That is the main theme of Ms. Petitt's *"Flight For"* series. She aims to present to the reader, through entertaining and dramatic fiction, this most critical and contemporary of topics. In pursuit of safety, Captain Darby Bradshaw was subjected to an abusive psychiatric evaluation for reporting safety concerns, and through perseverance she fought her way back to the flight deck. Now in pursuit of justice, she uncovers the extent of how far airline management would go to oppose safety. This novel has a flavor of an aviation legal thriller—with the potential for safety compromise in pursuit-of-a-buck that is forever the temptation for airline CEOs the world 'round.

Read this for entertainment, but also as a cautionary tale. As Ms. Petitt has always intimated in her writing, the truth is out there—and frightfully closer to nonfiction than one cares to realize.

B777 Captain Eric Auxier
"Cap'n Aux"
Phoenix, Arizona USA
January 1, 2022
Pilot-Author-Airways Magazine Columnist
Capnaux.com

Flight For Discovery

Prologue

Washington DC
January 12, 2016

NOBODY EVER BELIEVED *it could happen, but in less than ten years the aviation industry will be nothing that it is today,* George Wyatt thought while staring at the Northwest 747 in retirement, behind the glass. Unfortunately, the pilot job would be nothing but a memory. Just a sacrifice, and life was full of them. He was glad, however, to have had the opportunity to fly a plane, something his grandchildren would never see.

With one meeting over and the next scheduled 90 minutes later, Wyatt had taken the opportunity to visit the Smithsonian. A simple pleasure he rarely gave himself—that of doing nothing. He had wandered around the museum for an hour killing time while considering the next step. Everything was in place. The meeting that morning had been a success, and the remainder of the day should be nothing but a formality. *Should* being the operative word. He could only hope. Wyatt knew the game well. Hell, he had played it for the better part of his adult life. He had also been well taken care of. Now it was time to pay back the privilege he'd received for so many years. The stakes were higher than he could have ever imagined.

He ambled down the street and hesitated outside a pub, the very spot he had spent many evenings during his D.C. layovers so many years before. His eyes sparkled at the memories. He glanced at his watch, then stuck his hands into his pockets and continued down the street, putting as much distance between himself and the bar that had brought him so much pleasure back in the day.

Wandering down Pennsylvania Avenue, he could have been a tourist if it had not been for his suit. He was anything but, and he blended well with the D.C. society. He turned right on 15th Avenue and headed toward this much-anticipated event. A meeting that would impact the bottom line of Global Air Lines for years to come. The truth was, he didn't care about the airline as much as they thought. This was about him. It had always been about him. Negotiations began early in his Air Force career, simply because of the family he had been born into. The deal was sealed when they learned he could be trusted.

Wyatt had spent the better part of his day listening to discussions regarding the Aviation Rule Making committee's recommendations on mental health. The committee had been brought together in response to the Germanwings pilot who, four months earlier, intentionally crashed his plane into a mountain, killing everyone on board. The ARC, as they called it, was staffed with enough airline owned officials to guide the results of their report toward the airlines' suggested outcome.

Today's meeting had been a handful of airline representatives, the Deputy Flight Surgeon, and the FAA Administrator. The group was tasked to appease the public with this bill. That was the easy part because people believed what the media told them. They also believed what they wanted to believe. More like what they needed to believe. When aviation safety was involved, the public had no option but to convince themselves they were safe every time they boarded an airplane or they would be landlocked. They chose to believe that they were being protected by policy makers and airline executives who purported to place safety above all else. If passengers ever learned the truth, they would never get on a plane again. That belief system is what made it so easy to convince them they were safe, simply because someone told them it was so.

The challenge now was to convince FAA Administrator, Michael Hackman, to support their decision. His support was a roll of the dice at this point. If he went for it, all they had to do was package it in a manner the public would not question. If he did not go along with it, there would be an unfortunate chain of events. The outcome would be the same, regardless.

Wyatt had been given the green light to offer Hackman the moon, or at least a slice of it. This was always the dangerous part, and what made Wyatt the most nervous—not knowing if whomever he was negotiating with had principles. He chuckled out loud at the thought. There were not too many in the airline industry that had ethics of any sort.

Yet, the balance of offering an opportunity for conformity always made him uncomfortable, despite having been in this position many times before. Only once had he been challenged. That pilot never challenged anyone again. But this time, he was dealing with the FAA Administrator. Not that it really made any difference to those in power.

Earlier that morning Michael Banks, the FAA's deputy flight surgeon, had thrown his two cents into the hat during their meeting. He had explained the difference between mental health testing and simulator evaluations. Banks advised Hackman that currently no psychological testing was necessary for airline pilots because they were routinely evaluated as to how they handled stress during tests of their flying skills. *Like hell they were,* Wyatt thought.

He paused a moment at the street corner, observing a fender-bender just ahead. He looked both ways and stepped briskly across the street to avoid the commotion and any potential media, then continued down the street. He knew better than anyone that instructors today were nothing more than administrators. There was not much teaching in the current training environment, with an exception or two. Not at his airline, at least.

Due to automated aircraft, minimal training was provided, compliments of the FAA. The thought of assigning instructors the task of assessing how pilots handled stress was an interesting concept that had brought a smile to his eyes at the suggestion. Almost as humorous as the idea proposed by Michael Banks, Deputy Flight Surgeon, that a pilot would fly his plane into a mountain simply because he was stressed. If that were the case, nobody was safe. Pilots dined on a diet of daily stress. It went with the job.

Training on the cheap worked well for his airline and served a useful purpose. Any change could stir up problems they did not need. He was thankful for Banks' assistance from a medical perspective, albeit as ridiculous as it was. Due to Banks' powerful position, nobody had the nerve to suggest he was ill-advised. What Wyatt couldn't figure out is if someone had purchased that response from him, or if he believed what he had said. But then, maybe the suits at the table that morning believed him too, because they needed to believe him. That path of agreeing with someone was far easier to navigate than speaking out in challenge and then scaling the wall without a rope.

Banks had been helpful years earlier with Global's efforts to remove a pilot through their Section 8 process. A process used to identify a mentally unstable pilot. When the judge ordered the airline to no longer use Banks for mental health evaluations, Global moved him to Washington. A little smoke was created by a reporter highlighting the fact that Banks went to the head of the FAA medical department after he had taken bribes during his tenure with Global Air Lines. The one thing about smoke—if you don't fan the flames it dissipates. That's exactly what happened.

Arriving across the street at the Old Ebbitt Grill, Wyatt looked up at the structure and a slow smile spread across his face. He breathed deep, looked both ways and strode across the street. It had been a long time since he'd been here. This bar had a history of Presidential visits from those who were both famous and notorious. He wondered which group he and his dining companion fell into this evening. This was the oldest saloon in Washington, and once upon a time had been a boarding house. The stories this building could tell would make most men blush and send others to prison. He reached for the door.

Wyatt walked through the entrance and approached the hostess. "George Wyatt. I'm meeting Michael Hackman."

"Oh, yes," the hostess said. "Mr. Hackman requested I seat you. He's running a few minutes late. Please follow me."

Of course he is, Wyatt thought as she guided him to a table in a dark corner of the room. Wyatt no sooner sat, than a platter of crab cakes arrived.

"Compliments of Mr. Hackman," the waiter said. "What can I get you to drink?"

"What does Hackman drink?" Wyatt asked.

"House bourbon. It's nice."

"I'll give it a try," Wyatt said, placing a crab cake onto a plate.

He was famished and there was no sense letting them cool while he waited for his guest. He stuck his fork into the cake, knowing that it was he who was Hackman's guest. Hackman's delay and his offering was a direct message of who was in charge. Wyatt didn't care.

His bourbon materialized quickly, of which he intended to nurse until Hackman arrived. He thanked the young man and glanced toward the door. Hackman wielded power that one day Wyatt, too, would have. *The power I deserve,* he thought as he sipped his drink. The waiter was correct, it was nice.

Michael Hackman's claim to fame as the Federal Aviation Administrator was the implementation of Safety Management Systems, known as SMS. While the world believed SMS was an end-all safety measure for the traveling public, it was implemented to improve efficiency and profitability for the airlines. Unfortunately, nobody really understood what the hell SMS was. It didn't matter anyway because each airline could create their own program. This was one of the greatest quackeries of regulations, and Hackman had pulled it off to the benefit of the airlines.

Halfway through the crab cakes with Wyatt's glass close to empty, Hackman finally approached the table. Wyatt stood quickly, dropping his napkin as he did.

"Sorry, I'm late," Hackman said shaking Wyatt's hand. His eyes flashed to Wyatt's glass, and then to the waiter as he sat.

"Thank you for the crab cakes," Wyatt said. "I've managed to save a couple for you." He sat and reached to the floor to pick up his napkin.

"My favorite," Hackman said as he sat. He lifted a cake and added, "Even cold."

Hackman's disposition was rushed, and he spoke rapidly. For Hackman's sake, Wyatt hoped this meeting was more than an obligatory brush off.

"Your committee put together quite a report. Covered all bases, even with AsMA," Hackman said with a mouthful.

The Aerospace Medical Association (AsMA) was a professional organization with over 2,500 physicians, nurses, and scientists, that engaged in the clinical practice of Aerospace Medicine, research, and education. That morning AsMA had sent Michael Hackman the list of their recommendations for pilot assessments on mental health. The most significant recommendation being the proposal for in-depth psychological testing of all pilots to detect serious mental illness as part of their routine periodic pilot aeromedical assessments. Meaning, the pilots would receive a cognitive test during their first class physical, that would be administered in addition to the physical evaluation. What was once a one-hour event would become two days. The expense immeasurable for more reasons than one.

The suggestion from the medical team was—*it would be neither productive nor cost effective and did not warrant a recommendation.* Basically, it didn't work.

They had done their job well, Wyatt thought. He had initially wondered who had gotten to them, but in fact they were correct. Those tests were worthless in the determination of an unstable pilot.

"You'll have the entire report in a couple months," Wyatt said, and tipped his drink emptying the glass.

The waiter arrived with two bourbons and a platter of oysters. Once he was out of earshot, Hackman said, "I'm looking forward to that." He lifted his glass, his eyes never leaving Wyatt's as he sipped. Then he asked, "Why don't you want us to test the pilots?"

Wyatt chuckled. "Hell, those tests don't assess whether a pilot's going to crash a plane. Any kid who plays video games could pass. But a pilot? Not part of the brain they normally use."

"You might lose your cadre of pilots?" Hackman asked with a grin.

"Hell, I'd lose my second in command," Wyatt said, "and probably our Regional Director and a few chief pilots, too."

Hackman laughed. "Understood. It would cost millions as well." He leaned back and rested an arm over the back of his chair. "What do they want?"

"They want you to support the rule making committee's report for mental health. Then make a public statement telling them that psychological tests are ineffective because they reveal a pilot's mental health for only a moment in time without providing insight into whether the pilot will suffer problems later."

Hackman reached for an oyster without a response. He added a dollop of horseradish and an equal amount of cocktail sauce, squeezed lemon onto it, and then slid the creature off the shell and into his mouth.

Wyatt did not push for a response. Lifting his glass, he asked, "Any plans when you leave the administration?" He sipped his bourbon, his eyes held on Hackman watching for a sign.

"None, yet," Hackman said reaching for another oyster. He went through the same ritual as before, and then he asked, "And you?"

"I've got a few years until they kick me out for being too old," Wyatt said. "Vice President of Flight Operations works well for now."

Wyatt was 55 and he could retain his position until he was 65. Two million a year, which would only increase, served him well. He was also home every night. Both of which would not be a reality if he flew the line. Wyatt was extremely content in his current position. Yet, they had been grooming him from the beginning of this godforsaken career. There was no turning back. He knew too much, and if he wasn't an asset, he would become a liability. Liabilities were removed at Global Air Lines.

"Maybe I can extend the retirement age for you," Hackman said.

"No thanks. Sixty-five is old enough," Wyatt responded with a feigned shudder. "So, what do you think?"

"I think they're asking a lot," Hackman said. "If we have another crash by a mentally unstable pilot, then I'm done if I don't support mental health testing for all pilots."

"Probably," Wyatt said, with a shrug, lifting an oyster. He slipped the goo into his mouth.

Hackman did not respond, and Wyatt knew better than to fill the space with chatter. It would be up to Hackman to play the next card. The clock ticked slowly now for a man who arrived rushed. So much so, time appeared to have stopped.

"Retirement feels like a lifetime away," Hackman finally said. He sipped his bourbon. As he lowered his glass, added, "But I'm really only looking at fifteen months."

There it was, Wyatt thought. Hackman's cards were placed face up on the table. He chose his words carefully. "Time goes by quickly, doesn't it?" Wyatt said.

"That it does."

Wyatt allowed Hackman to sit with that thought for a moment. Then he added, "Chances are, nothing's going to happen in that short amount of time."

"Why not kill the psychological tests all together?" Hackman asked. "Wouldn't that solve everyone's problem?"

"Airlines need them for… let's just say discriminate discipline."

Hackman nodded and sipped his drink. He set his glass on the table and folded his hands. Lowering his voice he said, "I actually wouldn't mind sitting on a board of directors someplace after retirement."

They were not only in the same book, but on the same page. Global could legally buy Hackman's support with the promise of a lucrative position on their board. He would be guaranteed a salary for years to come without any liability, without worry, and there would be no way to track the bribe that was directly in front of his face.

"Nice retirement plan," Wyatt said. "Any ideas where?"

"None," Hackman said, checking his bet.

Wyatt now allowed the seconds to tick by and then said, "Global will have a position open in January 2018."

"How much?" Hackman asked.

"They'd start you at 430K."

"Hmm," Hackman said. He glanced at his watch, wiped the corner his mouth with the napkin and set it on his plate.

"It might get you out of the line of fire at Boeing," Wyatt said.

Hackman stared at him for a never-ending moment, his dark eyes unnerving. This could be the beginning for Wyatt or the end of Hackman.

Hackman broke their gaze and reached for his glass. He stared into the liquid, swirling it ever so slightly as he lifted his glass. If Wyatt wasn't mistaken, there was distinct tilt toward him before he drank.

Returning the empty glass to the table Hackman said, "Tell them the bourbon *is* perfect."

Chapter 1

Seattle Washington
October 5, 2018

Darby swirled her finger in the fruit dip, and then stuck it into her mouth and sucked. "Yummy!" she said and placed the bowl in the fridge. The fruit plate was ready, and the vegetables were waiting to be washed and chopped. She pulled a plastic platter from the top shelf and set it on the counter.

Today was a celebration with Kathryn, Jackie, and Linda for finishing her training. More than that, this was a celebration of life. Her life, for surviving the Global attack. Darby pulled a knife from the drawer and set it by the cutting board, then moved to the sink. Celebration or not, she was simply looking forward to spending quality time with her friends. She began rinsing the vegetables.

Kathryn Jacobs worked for the FAA and was Darby's go-to friend on everything safety. But more than that, she was Darby's best friend. They had been through so much together, and Kathryn had come close to losing her job at the FAA for her involvement with Darby's safety report. Hell, Kathryn had all but quit standing on principle. At the end of the day, she was promoted. Yet, Kathryn was still unable to solve the issues at Global Air Lines. Together they had navigated the slippery slope of an FAA/airline pilot relationship and shared truths while protecting each other in the process.

Jackie was another one of Darby's dearest friends, who now was on her second marriage, with a two-year-old, married to the Department of Transportation Secretary, John McCallister. Jackie was a retired flight attendant from Global, and Darby had adored working with her, and loved her like a sister. She'd been there for Darby through the toughest times with a sympathetic ear.

Her friend Linda had reinvented herself from housewife to psychiatrist. She had helped Darby maintain her sanity when Global challenged it. Linda had lost the life that she had known as a wife of an airline pilot. Now highly educated, married to a surgeon instead of a pilot, she created a new life for she and her daughter. It was through Linda's guidance that Darby had come to realize her life would not be over if Global got away with grounding her, it would have just been different.

It had been difficult for Linda losing her first husband and never being able to ask him why he intentionally crashed his plane and killed so many and himself. Her search found her in a classroom earning a degree. The answers never came.

Jackie's first husband had been drugged and unable to stop his plane from going down. Darby swiped a tear with the back of her hand, for all their loss, and then placed all the vegetables on the towel and patted them dry.

Pain and death had drifted through their lives over the years now lingering like low hanging fog. All due to Kathryn's psychopathic husband, Bill Jacobs, who had attempted to run the union and control the aviation industry. He now sat in prison with none other than the former President of the United States, Drake. No doubt plotting something together. She could not fathom the depth of depravity those two could sink to if left on their own. Darby moved a red bell pepper to the board and then stabbed her knife into it, cutting deep.

She had been confident that the executives at Global Air Lines would not get away with taking her down, but she had had her moments of doubt. Her friends gave her the strength at the lowest times of her life to fight, and fight she did. She had courage, but courage alone does not diminish fear or win a battle. It was more than fighting for a job or livelihood; she had been fighting for her life and the lives of every passenger.

Lifting a carrot, she stared at it and wondered if it was true what they said about having the same effect on women that oyster had on men. She glanced at the knife and then grinned. *Perhaps if it wasn't cut,* she thought. She took a bite just as the doorbell rang.

Grabbing a towel, she wiped her hands and headed to the front door. Pulling it open she smiled. "A package for me?" she said to her favorite FedEx delivery guy. "I don't remember ordering anything."

"This must be important," he said handing it to her. "It's from the other Washington."

Darby took the package, signed for it, and thanked him. She carried the box into the kitchen and set it on the table. She began to open it.

"God dang it!" she said when she realized it was the 759-page report she had sent to the FAA medical department in complaint of Dr. Wood, the criminal psychiatrist that provided Global a false report. *Now what?* she wondered, removing the enclosed letter. She read and her eyebrow raised. She reached for her phone, and dialed the number on the bottom of the page.

"Is Mr. Fredricks in?" Darby asked.

"May I ask who's calling?"

"Darby Bradshaw. I'm in receipt of a package from him, and he stated if I have any questions to call."

"Please hold."

Darby plugged in her headset and returned to her vegetables as she waited. She lined up the carrots and was lifting the knife when he answered.

"Ms. Bradshaw what can I help you with?"

"I want to know why you are allowing Dr. Wood to continue to evaluate airline pilots," she said, chopping the ends off the carrots.

"He doesn't work for us," Fredricks said. "He's not an AME. He's an MD and licensed in the state of Illinois."

"I understand that," Darby said, stabbing the knife into the cutting board. "But he is certifying pilots on behalf of the airlines. Or decertifying them without cause. Did you read that report he wrote about me? That guy is a friggen quack. He's nothing short of a hitman."

"We can't regulate him."

"Why not?" she asked. Before he could respond she said, "You're saying that if Global Air Lines employed a naturopath to evaluate a pilot's mental health, and put him in an airplane, that's okay with you?"

"That's between your airline and their approved doctor," Fredricks said. "That pilot also has to be certified by an aviation medical examiner. What your airline does in addition to that medical certification is not our business."

"It should be," Darby said. "I guess I should not be surprised. I was told that Wood was the FAA's big gun."

"I can assure you he is not our big gun," he said with a chuckle. "We don't have a big gun."

"The ALPO medical department's doctor emailed me and said that I would never get my medical back because Dr. Wood was the FAA's big gun. He also said the FAA preferred private practice doctors over the Mayo Clinic."

"Miss Bradshaw, did you get your medical back?"

"Sir, I never lost it."

"My case in point," he said. "This is frustrating to me as well. I recommend that you take this to the Illinois medical board. They are the only agency that can decertify him."

"I have called multiple times in the last two years. They are overloaded, understaffed, but he's scheduled to be investigated," she said mimicking the broken record. "All the while the quack is impacting aviation safety and the FAA is doing nothing."

"The process takes time," Fredricks said. "I wish you the best."

He ended the call and she wanted to scream. Instead, she lifted the knife and chopped the carrots in half with one whack. Then she grabbed her phone again and searched her contacts, then pressed dial.

"Illinois medical department, how may I help you?"

"Darby Bradshaw calling for Donna Ginsberg," she said, now standing with a hand on her hip drumming her red nails on her jeans.

A few moments later a woman said, "This is Donna."

"Donna, this is Darby Bradshaw. I have called you numerous times over the previous two years regarding Dr. Wood. I'm just checking on the status."

"Just a moment," she said. "Um, your case has still not been assigned."

"Are you kidding me!" Darby said, with all the displeasure she felt.

"I'm sorry things aren't working as rapidly for *you* as you wish, but we have hundreds of cases and not enough investigators to cover them all."

Rapidly for me? Darby thought, her blood pushing 100 degrees centigrade. "I personally know of at least three complaints against Dr. Wood. Are you telling me they would be investigated by different investigators? Or have you placed all Woods complaints together and are waiting to assign one investigator?"

"I am not at liberty to discuss our process."

"Your process?" Darby said. "You have hundreds of complaints against doctors, are years out, and you don't see a problem with your process?"

"There is nothing I can do," she said. "I'm sure we'll get to him soon."

"Ms. Ginsberg, are you familiar with the Germanwings accident, where the pilot intentionally crashed the plane into the mountains killing everyone on board?"

"Yes, but what does that have to do with Dr. Wood?"

"I'll tell you what it has to do with Dr. Wood," Darby snapped. "He is a criminal taking money in exchange for writing false diagnoses to remove pilots from duty. What happens when the pilot who *should* be removed is the highest bidder? What happens when he pays Dr. Wood all his money to ensure he's reinstated, because after he's dead he won't need it. What happens to the Illinois medical department when that pilot crashes his plane and kills hundreds of people, or thousands if he takes out a city, and the investigation reveals that *your* department has known for years about him and has had dozens of reports against this very doctor, and you did absolutely nothing?"

Chapter 2

THERE WAS ONLY one thing better than sitting in a hot tub with friends drinking champagne—it was the reason why. "I love you guys," Darby said, as she filled their glasses. "You've all been with me through so much. I'm not sure how I would have survived it without you."

Darby set the champagne bottle on the stone wall to the right of their fruit and vegetable tray and glanced at her friends. It was amazing, despite all that had happened in their lives, they had survived stronger than ever. They had become connected through life's challenges. *The tapestry of life,* she thought.

She sank into the water holding her glass high, careful not to create a hot tub champagne mixture. "Toast?" she said.

Her friends raised their glasses and they all said, "Congratulations."

"To good things to come," Darby added, clinking her glass with theirs. "For all of us."

They sipped their champagne and then settled into a conversation about Kathryn's, Linda's, and Jackie's kids. Darby loved being Aunt Darby to Kathryn's twin daughters and she had fun babysitting Jackie's baby. She had taught Jackie's older son how to drive a stick shift, and it did not go unnoticed that he had a major crush on her. Linda's teenage daughter and Darby had also become good friends.

Darby loved them all, but sometimes it saddened her not to have a family of her own.

While the women began discussing the topic of potty-training Darby drifted to what had brought them here today. She had just passed her Boeing B777 type-rating after not having flown for two years, compliments of Global Air Lines grounding her for a company ordered, doctor administered, bought and paid for, bipolar diagnosis. A month later she was fine.

Prior to her training on the new aircraft type, Darby had been warned that the Director of Training had put a hit out on her. He had called her instructor and asked him to "take an extra close look" at her. That was the code to fail her. *Thank God for integrity,* Darby thought.

Darby's mental health issue had started less than a month after she presented the SVP of flight operations, George Wyatt, and his VP, Rich Clark, a safety report. She had written an ethnographic study on Global's flight operations outlining examples of federal regulatory violations, a negative safety culture that did not support safety management systems, fatigue violations, and basically everything you would not expect from an airline because the behavior opposed safety in the most blatant manner, and placed passenger lives at risk.

It had taken her three months to get a meeting with Wyatt and Clark. Her captain representative had warned her they would give her a Section 8 if she followed through with the meeting. At the time, she was unaware that the Section 8 process would remove her from flying. Yet, that knowledge wouldn't have prevented her from coming forward regardless, because she knew it was illegal to retaliate, no matter how they did it. That was before she learned Global was above the law.

After their meeting, Clark had requested she talk to Ms. Abbott who was supposed to be an HR safety investigator looking into the safety issues in her report. As it turned out, Abbott was the manager of the pass travel complaint department and an equal opportunity investigator who was clueless about anything safety. She was nothing but a pawn who had made false assertions about the meeting they'd had. Abbott's reward was a promotion two months after Darby had been pulled from the flight line.

It took a year before Darby even knew why they had pulled her because nobody would tell her. A year later Global's hitman, Dr. Wood, had diagnosed her as bipolar. That's when she'd learned of Abbott's report. During the entire time, Darby had never lost her first-class medical certificate, even with a disqualifying diagnosis. Two months after she "became" bipolar, she had gone to the Mayo Clinic where a panel of ten specialists said she was not bipolar.

Two years of hell, and Darby returned to Global.

"No more baby discussions," Jackie said. "I'm a free woman tonight and this is a celebration for Darby."

Darby refilled her glass and clinked it to Jackie's. Then she relayed the conversation with Ginsberg at the medical board, and her effort to remove Dr. Wood.

"After my diatribe," Darby said, "Ms. Ginsberg said that she would see to it that he would be on the agenda for next week's meeting."

"Thank God, for that," Kathryn said.

"What's next?" Linda asked. "I mean with the lawsuit."

"We're getting ready for court," Darby said. "Which I pray will never happen."

"I can't believe Global hasn't yet offered a settlement," Linda said.

Darby had filed the AIR21 complaint, known as the whistleblower law, to get reinstated. Unfortunately, the legal system took time… too much time. But then, so did the contractual grievance process.

The mental health evaluation should have taken no more than three months. Hers took two years. Sadly, her union, ALPO, the Air Line Pilots Organization, had been involved in the game, but playing on the corporate team. Due to their unethical involvement, there were times she was not sure if she would survive. The only advice ALPO had provided would have sunk her permanently had she followed it. She never did.

There was a 90-day limitations period to file the AIR21 complaint that forced her to file at the same time she filed the grievance. If she had waited for the grievance process and lost, she would have exceeded the statute of limitations for an AIR21, and that would have left her without any legal rights or a job. She was now into this game for over a hundred thousand in attorney fees, and the real expense had not even begun.

If the judicial system worked a judge would tell Global that what they did was illegal and order them to make her whole and reimburse her with reasonable attorney fees. The term *reasonable* was interesting and speculative at best.

The only reason Darby got her job back prior to the grievance and AIR21 completion was because she followed the process to completion, as outlined in the pilot working agreement. Her attorney, Robert Allen, provided the best advice—*do what you're supposed to do and honor the contract*. Had she not made that effort, she would still be twisting in the wind.

"We're in the middle of discovery and depositions are next," Darby said. This was an entirely new world she had embarked upon. An exhausting world.

"What could they possibly gain by going to court?" Linda asked.

"Nothing," Darby said with a shrug. "I suppose if I hadn't gotten my job back, they'd fight to keep me off property."

"I get that," Jackie said. "No expense spared to keep your crazy ass from holding *them* accountable."

Darby splashed her, and Jackie squealed. She was correct, however. Now, there was no reason for them to fight her. She had beat them in the first round. She won. She had returned. Why they were continuing the process as if they were going to court, she had no idea.

"The firm they hired is going to cost millions," Kathryn said. "What the hell are they trying to prove anyway?"

"None of this has ever made *any* sense," Darby said. "All because I gave them a safety report. Do you think Rich Clark's ego was just so friggen big he couldn't handle that there might be a better way to train pilots and improve safety?"

"I think a lot had to do with a *girl* telling him," Jackie said.

"No doubt. God, I wish he would come to the current century," Darby said with a theatrical roll of her eyes. "But…I do love the triple seven!" She glanced toward the sky as an American 757 flew into the distance.

"When do you actually get to fly?" Jackie asked. "I mean the real plane."

"I start my operating experience the day after tomorrow," Darby said. "We're flying from Los Angeles to Tokyo, then Minneapolis. Back to Tokyo, and home."

"What the hell," Linda said, choking on her champagne. "I'm sorry for the profanity, but are you telling me that after not having flown for two-years, and you're on a brand-new airplane, that you're flying for the first time with passengers on board?"

Darby grinned. "Well, when you say it like that… yep. Maybe with 350 passengers." Then she sang, "This is how we do it baby…"

Then she did her best to convince Linda it was going to be okay. When she thought she had accomplished that task, she noticed Kathryn was staring into her empty glass and asked, "Kat, can I top you off?"

Kathryn startled and looked up. "Yes. Thanks." And then she asked, "I'm just curious if your attorney has given any indication if they are willing to talk settlement?"

"That would be so great," Jackie said.

"It would be really nice to get this off my plate, so I could focus on flying and get on with my life."

Litigation was not for the weak or poor. It consumed all her time, energy, and bank account. Mostly, it was a huge distraction that was unappreciated while she was learning a new plane. But there was no way they could put any of this on hold, nor would she quit.

"Is there a chance?" Linda asked. "For a settlement."

"There is," Darby said. "Maybe sooner than later. If the judge lets us depose the CEO, I think it might be on the sooner side."

"Why does the judge have to approve for you to depose the CEO?" Jackie asked. "That doesn't seem fair. You should be able to talk to anyone."

"Because there's something called the Apex Doctrine that prohibits deposing executives who are high up in the company," Darby said.

"The Apex Doctrine was designed to protect high-level corporate executives," Kathryn said. "We see this all the time with airlines and manufacturers. The theory is, that Walter Croft as the CEO is too high up in the company to have any first-hand knowledge of Darby's case. Therefore, there is no reason to depose him. As if why would he know anything?"

"I'm not even going to touch that statement," Darby said with a chuckle, refilling Kathryn's glass.

"Like I said, that hardly seems fair," Jackie said, reaching past Darby for a strawberry.

"We have a conference call with the judge a week from Monday.

He'll decide if we get to or not," Darby said. "I think because Croft asked for my safety report prior to Clark throwing me into the looney bin, gives him some sort of knowledge. But how much, I just don't know."

"Why would they settle if you get to depose him?" Linda asked.

"Maybe to keep him from saying something he shouldn't," Jackie offered.

"Exactly," Darby said. "I was listening to a call between my attorney and one of their attorneys, Wendel Kowalski and—"

"Wendel?" Jackie said giggling. "Seriously?"

"Yep, and it's fitting," Darby said. "The guy is schmoozer and he's kind of whiny, too."

"You've met him?" Linda asked, reaching for a second bottle.

"Nope," Darby said. "But on the call Wendel said something about *me* offering Global a settlement. My attorney said Global would have to make the offer if that's what they wanted, and he could present it to me. Then Wendel said he really, really, didn't want us to ask the judge to depose the CEO."

"Of course, he doesn't," Kathryn said with a grin.

"Then he promised to give my attorney *anything*, information wise, that we wanted if we dropped the request. My attorney politely conveyed that would *not* be an option. We were going to depose the CEO, if allowed. Wendel said something about if we won that ruling, then it would be over."

"That would be great!" Jackie said.

"It would," Darby said. "He also said pilots were hard to deal with because a hundred thousand dollars doesn't mean anything to us."

"Sounds like he's got you pilots figured out," Linda said with a wink.

"What did your attorney say to that?" Jackie asked.

"Well… he actually said something to the effect of not knowing about that price tag, but this was about safety and that I had bigger balls than any guy he knew."

Jackie and Linda spewed champagne as they laughed.

Kathryn's eyes widened and she said, "I really like Robert Allen." She extended her glass toward Darby, and they touched glasses. "To Robert."

"Wait. Don't leave us out," Jackie said.

She and Linda both extended their glasses, too.

"The funny part was…," Darby continued, "that Wendel scolded Robert and told him he couldn't say that about my balls."

Darby was kind of proud of her balls. She was most certain that regarding the different standards between men and women, that it was far better for a woman to have big balls than a man to have little tiny girl balls.

"I still can't believe they did this," Linda said. "But after what Bill did, nothing surprises me regarding sociopaths."

"At least Bill was a smart sociopath," Darby said. "Rich Clark is an idiot."

"We could call Bill a lot of things, but not an idiot," Kathryn said in agreement. "His mind was sharp, too sharp. He almost got away with it."

"Yeah, but he didn't because you stopped him," Darby said. "That can only mean one thing." She exchanged a knowing glance with Kathryn, as they had had this discussion many times before. The world would be safe because Kathryn was far more intelligent than Bill Jacobs, and she used her powers for good not evil.

"But you stopped Clark," Jackie said to Darby.

"Only from killing my job. The reality is, I don't think I'd have a job or even have an AIR21 case, if he wasn't such an idiot in how he handled his little plot," Darby said. "He seriously is a complete baboon."

"How could he have possibly stopped you?" Linda asked Darby selecting a slice of cheese from the platter.

Grinning at Linda, Darby said, "Let me count the ways."

Chapter 3

ALBERT EINSTEIN SAID that the only two things that are infinite are the universe and human stupidity, and he wasn't sure about the universe. Prior to her meeting with Wyatt and Clark, Clark had tried to get Darby to meet with an equal opportunity investigator. Darby had no idea why they had requested that at the time, but she had refused. Her concerns were about safety. They finally gave her the meeting, but they were surprised as hell that she had given them a written report during that meeting. More than likely, they were surprised because her union attorney had advised her against giving them anything in writing. Thankfully, Darby hadn't listened.

Days after her providing them the report, Clark asked if she would speak to an HR safety investigator because they were taking her concerns seriously, and she did. As it turned out, that investigator, Abbott, was not an aviation safety investigator, she was with EEOC and was the manager of the Pass Travel Complaint Department. They pulled Darby a month after the Wyatt and Clark meeting, allegedly for something she had said to Abbott. Yet, they had never told her what that "something" was. She did not find out for over year when she read her medical report.

"Remember that letter from the instructor that I found in my medical report about my being *emotionally unstable and a threat to the safety of the aircraft,"* Darby said with air quotes—a talented move while holding a champagne glass. "And the allegation that I was restricted to the jumpseat due to safety while on duty?"

"Oh God, that was so ridiculous," Linda said.

"Especially since you didn't learn of it until you read it in your medical report over a year later," Kathryn added. "They would have been legally required to divert, and at the very minimum bring you in and counsel you at the time."

"That quack never even told you about it either," Jackie said. "Such BS."

"Yeah, but…" Darby said, holding up a finger as she tipped back her glass and finished her champagne. She set the glass on the ledge. Linda refilled it and Darby continued.

"I'm still not sure when that check airman actually wrote that letter," Darby said. "But it was signed and apparently put in my file *before* I met with Clark and Wyatt, so says Dr. Wood's medical report. The Regional Director Dodson, and Clark also argued about not meeting with me for months before Clark finally gave in. But out of the blue they did. What was with that?"

"I don't know," Jackie said.

Darby stared her way for a moment to determine if that were a serious statement or the champagne talking, but then she figured it didn't matter.

"I may never know," Darby said. "But if Clark had any brains in his evil little head… either one of them, he could have used that letter to deny my meeting with them, and therefore preventing me from reporting to him in person. He could have sent me to an evaluation based on that letter. I would not have given them the report, *and* there would be no protected activity."

"Oh my God," Linda said, covering her mouth. "If they had

used that as the reason to give you a mental health evaluation, that would have been a far more plausible than what the manager of the pass travel department said."

"Exactly," Darby said. The thought still chilled her as to how close she had come to being skewered.

"Then you wouldn't have given them the safety report before they retaliated," Kathryn added.

"Technically, my giving them notification that I *wanted* to report safety concerns is also protected, but that would have been harder to prove," Darby said. "Therefore, I rest my case." She stood, steadying herself on the edge of the tub, and took a bow. Accepting her glass of champagne she added, "I was wrong. Rich Clark's not an idiot, he's a fucking idiot."

"Yeah, but didn't they promote him to a senior vice president in flight operations after Wyatt retired?" Jackie asked.

"That they did," Darby said, grabbing a carrot stick, sinking back into the tub. "Therefore, I'm not really sure who he has naked pictures of."

"Maybe you can find them in discovery," Jackie said.

"If the judge rules in your favor with the CEO, then this might be over before you know it," Linda said. "Let's hope for that."

Darby smiled and nodded. She could only hope. She dipped the carrot into the ranch dressing. "You know, all I ever wanted them to do was apologize and hold Clark accountable."

"They kept you out for two years with a false medical diagnosis and *never* apologized?" Linda said. "I guess I didn't realize that. I thought they would have at least apologized after you returned. If nothing else to cover their tracks in a feigned effort to prove it wasn't intentional."

"And one more reason they're not that smart," Darby said. "It's amazing how far an apology could have gone. Even for their defense." She stuck the carrot stick into her mouth.

"Your research identified major flaws with pilot training worldwide," Kathryn said. "It also proved that your report was accurate."

"I wonder if that's why they did this," Linda said.

Darby and Linda's eyes locked. That was something that had already crossed Darby's mind.

"I can only can hope that everyone reads my book," Darby said, and then added, "Shameless marketing about to happen. But if everyone reads *Normalization of Deviance a Threat to Aviation Safety*, at least they would understand the industry problems and perhaps why Global did this to me, or rather what they were trying to keep quiet."

"Shameless marketing aside," Linda said, "I think they wanted to silence you because of that book."

"We may never know," Darby said. "But what I do know is that it would have been so much easier to solve the problem instead of trying to kill the messenger."

"Good luck with the judge," Linda said.

"I don't want to be a killer of hope," Kathryn finally said, "but I suspect they will take this process through to the very end. They will waste your time, spend your money, push you to the edge of the cliff, and then if they haven't broken you, or found anything tangible that they can hang their hats on to screw you over, they'll offer a settlement on the courtroom steps."

Darby, Linda, and Jackie, stared with mouths open. Then Darby began to laugh.

"Okay, Kathryn Comedowner," Darby said. "Based on your theory, the worst case is that I've got a hell of a year ahead of me."

Chapter 4

NEW YORK, NEW YORK
LAW OFFICES OF GOLDMAN, GOLDMAN, AND EPSTEIN
OCTOBER 5, 2018

IT WAS NOT unusual for their law firm to receive a client this large. It was unusual when they said, "No expense spared. Do whatever it takes to shut this down." Their firm was given the green light to hold nothing back. Not that they ever would, but 'no expense spared' gave them the open door for billable hours. They also had been offered a three-million-dollar bonus if they could shut this down without going to court. Something that should have been in the bag with Wendel Kowalski.

Todd Epstein took a drag on his cigarette as he reread Darby Bradshaw's initial AIR21 complaint on his laptop, shaking his head. He suspected that the only way in hell Global could win would be outside a courtroom. The question for their firm was how to maximize profits before they received their bonus.

Double mahogany doors at the far end of the room opened and Todd looked up from his laptop.

"Please," Dean Goldman said with disdain, glaring at Todd's cigarette as he entered. He strode to the credenza and turned the fan to high. A fan that had been placed in the room for this exact reason.

Todd dropped his cigarette into his coffee cup. "Sorry, the time got away from me." He knew the rules regarding no smoking in this office. But being a partner gave him room to push the limits every so often. "Where's Frank?" he asked.

"He'll be here in a few minutes," Dean said. "Did you hear about Kowalski?"

"I did," Todd said, leaning back in his chair. "Were we wrong to select him?"

"No," Frank said, from the doorway. "He just found his match with Robert Allen."

Frank Goldman entered the room and closed the door. He set his briefcase on the table, and then headed for the coffee pot. He poured himself a cup and returned to the table.

Behind his back, he was referred to as the old man. The old man had started this law firm, but it was Dean who grew it. Now they had over a hundred offices scattered across the country with thousands of employees. Frank still did everything by paper.

Todd pushed his cup aside with the floating cigarette, stood and walked to the credenza. He poured himself a fresh cup of coffee. "Can I get you one?" he asked Dean.

"Black. Thanks."

Todd handed Dean his coffee and returned to his seat. Frank was opening his briefcase and removed a couple folders. He tossed them in front of Dean, who then handed one to Todd.

"Okay, who else do we place on this team?" Frank asked clasping his hands on the table, looking between Dean and Todd with his perpetual scowl.

"I'm concerned about Kowalski," Dean said. "He should have gotten Allen to agree to drop the Croft deposition."

"Why the hell would Allen drop anything regardless of what anyone said?" Todd asked.

"Kowalski told him that if Bradshaw won the ruling to depose Croft, this would be settled. Why not make the effort?" Dean said.

Todd leaned back and sipped his coffee. With a smile he said, "We're talking billable hours and none of us want this thing to end too soon."

"Robert Allen wouldn't have backed down regardless," Frank said, looking over the top of his glasses at Dean. "That discussion was insignificant. Allen's father was one of the best aviation attorneys I've ever met and he would he be proud of his son. Our boys have a tough road ahead. Kowalski did fine."

"Regardless," Dean began, "Kowalski hasn't had much trial experience. I'm just not sure…"

"Hell, this isn't going to trial," Todd said. "If anyone can convince them to keep it out, Kowalski can. He's at least good for that."

"Agreed," Frank said.

Nobody mentioned that Wendel was married to Frank's daughter, and despite his failures, he was thrown the big cases. Most of which won themselves. This, however, was not a slam dunk.

"We need the rest of the team to balance out his weaknesses," Frank added.

"We also need strength in the courtroom," Todd said. "Just in case." He liked Wendel well enough, but also knew there was no way he could handle this if it went to court. He'd bet his bonus that would never happen, but when dealing with egos and emotions, things often failed to make sense. That group at Global were a little full of themselves.

"I put together a list of options," Frank said. "First page in your file."

Todd opened the folder and read the names. One stood out, and he typed it into the company database on his laptop. He read his credentials to confirm what he'd heard about the man. "What about

Johnson Von Dietrich from our D.C. office?"

Frank leaned back and steepled his fingers. "I like it. Tough. Aggressive. He would balance the softness in Wendel."

"Good cop, bad cop," Dean added. "I like it, too."

"When Kowalski's power of manipulation doesn't work, Von Dietrich would be the right amount of pit bull," Frank said. "He's also good in trial. Lots of experience."

"Hopefully we won't get there," Todd said again, knowing their firm could not afford a loss of this magnitude. Global Air Lines cannot lose. He had warned his partners this could be a timebomb. Now he was nothing but a broken record.

"Won't matter," Frank said. "If we go to court, that three million will be doubled well before it starts. No expense spared."

"We can't afford this loss," Todd said. "Global doesn't have a case. It's simply he-said, she-said."

Dean pulled his attention away from the folder. "What do you mean they don't have a case? *Everyone* has a case if they have enough money and connections."

Todd shrugged and returned his attention to the folder before him. There was no arguing with the old man when he had his mind set. But then again, he was correct.

"The company is claiming they were investigating a sexual harassment claim," Todd said. "I think we need a woman on the team."

"You were reading my mind," Frank said. "I've added some names, photos, and bios on the female attorneys in our system."

Todd flipped the pages and began looking through the photos. He smiled at the sight. If you had to employ a woman, she might as well be good looking—a strategy in itself. "I think a blond would be best."

"Couldn't agree more," Frank said.

"What about Nancy Dawson?" Dean asked, removing the photo. "Cute, but not too flashy. Just sexy enough to get her way."

Todd looked at her photo and read the bio. "Wasn't she the attorney that was screwing Von Dietrich during the Boeing trial?"

"Ah shit," Frank said. "She was. Nearly cost us that case."

Dean leaned back in his chair. "I'm just thinking aloud here. But what if we brought in a pregnant attorney. Not too far along, but …"

"That could work. Trial is on the books at the end of March," Todd said. "Let's see if anyone has notified the company of maternity leave." He logged into his company email and sent a message to HR and flagged it as urgent.

"I'm not sure a pregnant attorney is what we need," Frank said.

They often selected the women to question the opposing male subjects for a reason. The men were naturally more receptive and less argumentative with a good-looking woman. A woman could get a man to say anything she wanted him to. "I'm just not sure pregnant will have the best effect."

"It could be a better effect in this case," Dean said. "She could draw sympathy. Could have the mother effect. Allen would even go easy on her, and Geraghty would give her leeway."

"I agree with Dean," Todd said. A ding indicated that he had a message from HR. They had one female attorney who qualified. "Karen Sherwin is scheduled to take leave at the beginning of her eighth month." He flipped through the pages and found her photo and nodded in approval. "Court is scheduled to begin March 25, 2019. This might work. She'd be six months pregnant."

"At least she wouldn't be screwing Von Dietrich," Dean said.

"I like it." Frank leaned back and folded his arms. "So, we concur, the team to represent Global Air Lines is— Karen Sherwin, Wendel Kowalski, and Johnson Von Dietrich."

Chapter 5

Los Angeles Airport
October 6, 2018

IF GLOBAL AIR Lines management had not deemed crying to be a threat to aviation safety, tears of joy would have filled her eyes at this very moment. Her battle had been long, and Darby hadn't known if she would ever fly again. She walked down the exterior stairs to the ramp below, gripping the railing as she went. To fall after all she had been through would be irony's sadistic stab at humor.

She walked around to the tug and stood ten feet in front of her aircraft and looked up. The Boeing B777 was beautiful. An overwhelming feeling of appreciation embraced her. Closing her eyes, she said a silent prayer of gratitude for being giving a second chance at life. Flying was her life and she'd almost lost it. The morning sun felt warm until a breeze picked up out of the West that brought her skin alive. Her goosebumps, however, were more from excitement than the chill. Life felt so good to be back.

"You ready to get started?"

The question was more of a command and came within two feet of her. She opened her eyes, startling a bit, and glanced at her captain. She gave him a broad smile. Thankful to be wearing aviator sunglasses, he had no clue her eyes had been closed. She looked up to the blue backdrop and then to her plane. "Absolutely," she replied.

Darby followed him around the right side of the aircraft, and then circled the left engine checking blades, probes and thrust reverser panels. Her escort was not only the captain, but a check airman. She would be flying with him for the next six days. When all went well, she would receive his blessing by signing her off. The final step in training. Until another three months when her currency lapsed on her landings, or six months later in recurrent training. She would be visiting the simulator multiple times a year for the remainder of her career to play *bet your license* that her instructor was legit.

They examined a wing and ensured the static wicks were in place, and position lights were illuminated without cracked lenses. The captain emphasized everything she'd learned online, but now she could see it firsthand. *Online* being on her computer, not like the old days when it meant on the flight line.

Where a picture was worth a thousand words—the real thing was priceless.

This wasn't her first walkaround for a widebody Boeing. Everything they looked at was nothing she hadn't seen before. Technically it was different because it was a triple seven. But the flaps, lights, and assessment of damage was the same between each aircraft. This process with the check airman was nothing more than a check-the-box-task.

She had done hundreds of walkarounds in her career. But never a day went by that she did not feel in awe of the aircraft, or the appreciation of the engineers who were able to get hundreds of thousands of pounds airborne. She was humbled each time she walked below the magnificence of what most mere mortals called a plane. Maybe it took standing on the ramp in the shadow of a wing too high to touch, smelling jet fuel, and listening to the roar of engines in the distance, to fully embrace this feeling. She doubted anyone could really know what this felt like unless they walked in this path.

Darby wore three stripes on her shoulder today. She could have been flying as a B757 captain, but with the pending lawsuit and not having flown for two years this was a good way to merge back into her career. That's not the only reason she took the first officer bid. She bid this airplane because she had been warned by an attorney, after she'd been grounded, that management would do one of two things to her—either keep her out just long enough to give her minimum training and then mess with her in the simulator, or pay a doctor to say she was crazy.

Being proactive, she bid a new plane to get a full training program. Unfortunately, she wasn't senior enough to hold a captain position on this widebody. Darby suspected the plane didn't care how many stripes she wore. At the end of the day, Global management had paid that doctor to call her crazy. She never imagined that could be possible in today's world in the United States. Unless Global came clean, she would also never know the price tag for such a purchase.

Despite the director of training placing a hit on her during her initial training, all her instructors had been both professional and supportive. She also gave them no excuse for concern with her performance. She worked hard and having been an instructor in another life, she knew what she needed to know and did it.

They finished the walkaround and climbed the stairs. The captain punched the code into the lock, and they entered the jetway. Darby checked the water level to ensure they had enough for their eleven-hour flight. Then she selected the lavatory button to confirm the waste had been emptied. Once that was done, they headed upstairs to the bunk room.

They passed by an area with a sink and a mirror, not bigger than a small hall closet. Then with one step they were into a sleeping compartment the size of a small nursery with twin beds that were not more than elevated mattresses a couple inches thick, side by side, with a curtain separating them. There was no room for furniture in this bedroom, other than two seats, one at the end of each mattress. The curtains wrapped around the front of the sleeping compartment to provide an element of privacy to the entrance.

They confirmed there were enough blankets and pillows for all crewmembers, and then the captain asked her to preflight the emergency equipment for him.

After she was done with the preflight, they were heading out and he hesitated, looked at the sink, and said, "And don't…" Mid-sentence he stopped and looked at her with a huge grin and a slight blush. He waved a hand and said, "Never mind."

"Seriously?" Darby said, knowing exactly what was coming next. "Guys are peeing in that sink?"

He laughed. "They're not supposed to."

They finally got into the flight deck. Normally the crew not flying conducted the exterior preflight while the flying crew prepared the flight deck. However, Darby and her instructor arrived an hour early to get the exterior preflight out of the way. She'd been signed off for that, now all she had to do was demonstrate she could configure this big bird and safely conduct a takeoff and a landing, hopefully in that order, and manage all procedures between city pairs.

The flight deck felt familiar because the simulator was a replica of the B777. They pushed all the buttons that needed to be configured, and those that were already in position she simply confirmed. The rest of the flight crew arrived as did the flight attendants. The lead flight attendant poked his head in and introduced himself. The other first officer offered to get coffee, as he handed them each a large bottle of water.

While everyone was openly friendly toward her, the elephant was in the room. Rumors were running rampant among the airline employees. Did they believe the company? Did they think she was crazy? Did they know what happened? Too many questions to be answered, and Darby pushed them all to the back of her brain.

No worms would be allowed to work their way into her head during this flight. She had also decided to ignore any looks or comments. She would simply do the best job she could with a smile on her face. While they were working, she would say nothing about what happened. If the opportunity arose, and the time was right, she would tell them exactly what had happened. But *only* if they asked. Until then, they could assume whatever they wanted. She had a plane to fly.

Today they were flying to Tokyo. It had been far too long since she'd been there and was really looking forward to the layover. The second best thing about flying was the destinations she experienced. Tokyo had always been a favorite. She loved the food, loved the people, and relished the deep bathtub in her crew hotel.

In no time, they were ready to go. They received a pushback and start clearance, started engines, performed checklists, and then began their taxi. Everything was clicking into place as it should.

"Global ninety-two, cleared into position runway two-four left," an air traffic controller said.

She responded to ATC as the captain advanced the power just enough to make the turn onto the runway and into position. He aligned the aircraft with the runway and said, "You've got the plane."

Darby placed her left hand on the thrust levers and slid her feet up to the top of the rudder pedals and applied brake pressure. The captain took control of the radios.

"Global ninety-two, cleared for takeoff, runway two-four left."

The captain repeated the clearance.

With aviator glasses in position and a huge smile on her face, Darby released the brakes and slowly advanced the power. Monitoring the engine instruments, she assured thrust increased evenly. She continued to advance the thrust levers forward while pressing the TOGA switches allowing the automation to take-over power control. She followed the thrust levers forward with her hand in place in the event an engine failed. The thrust automatically increased to max takeoff power.

"80 knots, power's good," the captain said.

Once at full takeoff thrust, Darby removed her hand and the captain placed his on the thrust levers.

"V1," the captain said, removing his hand from the thrust levers. They were now committed to fly and there would be no aborting.

"Rotate," he said.

Darby slowly pulled the plane into the sky, a smile plastered on her face. She was back. She was flying. Nobody could ever take this away from her again.

Chapter 6

Toulouse France
October 7, 2018

GOD WOULD FORGIVE him. Walter Croft walked out of St. Francis of Assisi Church and stood on the porch. He glanced to the sky and took a deep breath. God, too, broke the rules to accomplish the out of ordinary feats of biblical nature. Sometimes humans had to follow suit. He removed the sunglasses from his pocket and put them on. Stepping down the stairs, he glanced both ways and then headed across the street toward the car that waited.

The driver opened the door and Walt climbed in. They were minutes away and he could have walked the short distance. Instead, in no time the car pulled up to a massive building far superior to the church he'd just exited. This building was just a speck in the realm of the Airbus conglomerate that covered city blocks. He glanced at his watch—12 minutes. The driver remained seated. Another man appeared at the side of the car and opened the door. Walt climbed out.

"Good morning, Mr. Croft," the man said with a strong accent. "I trust your morning is going well."

"Very well," Croft said with a slow smile. A woman he never imagined having in his bed would be there waiting for his return. God had released him of all his sins, and he was about to confirm the deal of the century. How could his morning go any better?

Walt followed the man inside. He removed his glasses and returned them to his pocket as they walked across the lobby. This corporate office made his look like an encampment.

Despite being the CEO of Global Air Lines, one of the largest and most successful airlines in the world, Walt made sure that everything he did was understated, something he had learned from his predecessor. He glanced around the magnificence of the foyer, fully expected from Airbus. It was also empty on Sunday morning. They arrived at an elevator and the man pressed the up button.

Before long, they were riding in silence to the fourth floor. Croft was out of his element. But he had been advised that he would be the *only* person who could participate in this meeting. He was also required to come alone. The doors opened to an expansive lobby. The man extended a hand to the right and said, "Please, this way."

Walt followed the man across the lobby and through double doors into a boardroom. A 20-foot mahogany table filled the space. Jean-Pierre was sitting at the far end, diminished by the plush highback chair in which he sat. A cigarette dangled from his lips as he focused on the document he held.

The doors behind Walt closed firmly. Startled, he glanced back. The man who had escorted him into the room had remained outside. The audible click of the lock was unnerving. He returned his attention to the Jean-Pierre, who was now standing and smashing his cigarette into an overfilled ashtray. "Good morning."

Walt walked his way. "Jean-Pierre, it's great to see you again," he said with his hand extended.

Jean-Pierre approached him as well. They grasped hands and shook. "Good to see you, Walt. Thank you for making the trip." He then pulled out a chair for Walt and said, "Coffee?"

"Black, please," Walt said. He hadn't slept much the night prior, and the caffeine would be much appreciated. Between jetlag and Deborah, he realized he wasn't as young as he once was, and the very reason they made little blue pills.

"I am very sorry about your wife," Jean-Pierre said, setting a cup in front of him. "A lovely lady."

"That she is," Walt said, lifting his cup, wondering how much Jean-Pierre knew of Walt's situation. The coffee was rich and thick. European coffee was simply the best. "Delicious," he said. "Thank you."

Jean-Pierre poured himself a cup and said, "It's a crime the board forced that decision." He carried his cup to the table and set it on a coaster. Then pulled out a chair, sat and turned to face Walt. He then leaned back and crossed one leg over the other. The paperwork he had been working on was another six seats down the table. Jean-Pierre ignored it and sipped his coffee, staring at Walt over the brim. "You Americans are funny people," he finally said.

Walt shifted his chair to completely face Jean-Pierre. He crossed his leg mirroring him. Walt grinned broadly. "Perhaps. But things work out as they should. No?"

He was pleased that the story of the board's order was the version that had circulated. However, he doubted a tryst with a male flight attendant would have been looked down upon in France. In the U.S., that was another story. Unfortunately, Walt's wife held all the cards and wiped him out financially, of which would have given Airbus leverage had they known. He was thankful they did not.

Jean-Pierre unfolded his leg and waved a hand, as he said, "American's are prudes. To force a man to choose between his wife and his mistress. How do you say is… unconscionable." He reached into his pocket and removed a package of unfiltered cigarettes and extended the package to Walt.

Walt shook his head no, and Jean-Pierre tapped out a cigarette. He stood quickly and walked to the end of his table and grabbed a book of matches. He struck the match and lit his cigarette, then shook the flame out and dropped the match into the ashtray. He sucked a long draw and assessed Walt. Walt in turn sipped his coffee, his eyes not waving from his host's.

"You choose wisely?" Jean-Pierre finally asked.

Walt broke into a huge grin. "Yes, as a matter of fact I think I did," he said. "A flight attendant. Gorgeous, with a body I cannot get enough of. She knows how to do things that I never knew existed."

"I make my point," Jean-Pierre said, with a wave of his cigarette, ashes falling. "My girlfriends teach me things to make any wife happy." He took another drag and then slowly blew out the smoke, then smashed it into the ashtray with the others. "We shall talk business now. No?" he said moving toward Walt again.

Walt glanced at his watch. "I think we should talk business. Yes."

Jean-Pierre poured two fresh cups of coffee and handed one to Walt. There was a reason shot-sized coffee cups existed in Europe. They could have many and it was always hot.

Returning to the chair beside Walt, Jean-Pierre set his cup on the table without drinking it. He leaned forward, rested his arms on his legs and with hands clasped, he looked at Walt.

"Is the deal done?" Jean-Pierre asked.

"Yes. We've cancelled all Boeing orders at Global," Walt said.

"I understand. Merci," Jean-Pierre said. "My question is our competitor. We understand they have a plane with issues."

"Yes, they do," Walt said placing his cup on the table.

"But only one crash?" Jean-Pierre asked. "Not enough to ground a plane. No?"

"There has been more than one incident, but U.S. pilots have handled the situation, so they did not crash," Walt said. "We must be patient."

"Hmmm. Patience. Another American flaw," Jean-Pierre said, eyes narrowing. "When that patience pays off, you will ground the Boeing MAX. No?"

"We will have our boy in place when that time comes," Walt said. "Hundreds of Boeings will be grounded. That I can assure you."

"Triple seven too?"

"Yes."

"Fine. Fine." Jean-Pierre stood again. He headed back to his end of the table. "Come. Join me," he said, returning to the chair he had been sitting in when Walt first arrived. He reached for a folder and began thumbing through the pages.

Walt stood and followed Jean-Pierre to the far end of the table. He pulled back a chair to his right and sat. *Waiting patiently*, he thought. His great American flaw.

"Ah. Here we are," Jean-Pierre said. He handed two sheets of paper to Walt. Both the same document.

Walt read each page. This time Walt's smile entered his eyes, and he nodded. "Do you have a pen?"

Jean-Pierre handed him a black and gold Airbus pen, and Walt thanked him. He signed and dated the two duplicate papers. Jean-Pierre also signed the papers. He gave one sheet to Walt and tossed the other onto his stack of papers. Walt handed the pen to Jean-Pierre, but Jean-Pierre said, "Keep it. My gift."

Walt folded the paper and stuck it and the pen inside his suit pocket. Within seconds, the door at the far end of the room opened. Walt turned toward the noise.

The man who brought him in, entered and said, "Your car is waiting, sir."

Walt looked at Jean-Pierre, who shrugged with a smile and said, "How you American's say… honor among thieves?"

Walt replied, "Something like that."

What else would Walt have expected? He wondered if they were recording him as well as listening. Unfortunately, he knew that answer. He hoped his friends at Airbus were men of honor or this would be the beginning of his end.

Walt stood, as did Jean-Pierre. He thanked Jean-Pierre and they shook hands. Jean-Pierre, still holding Walt's hand, squeezing firmly, kissed him on one cheek and then the other. Something in Walt stirred. He hoped it was due to what was in his breast pocket, but he knew better.

"Enjoy your holiday," Jean-Pierre said. He returned to his seat, struck a match, and lit another cigarette. Instantly he was into a single-minded focus with the paperwork, the cigarette dangling from his lips, unaware that Walter Croft was still in the room.

Croft watched him for a moment and then turned toward the door, wondering who had actually made the deal with the devil.

Chapter 7

Narita, Tokyo International Airport
October 8, 2018

P LANES WERE LINED up in a long row on the taxiway, headed for the departure runway, and his was one of them. He had been flying as captain for little over a year, but his flight time was a little over seven thousand hours. His first officer was a cadet who had no more than three hundred flight hours. Quite the extreme difference in experience between the two, but this was his reality. Soon, this would be the reality of the rest of the world. That is, if he would be lucky enough to have a first officer in the future.

The boarding and rush to get an on-time departure always put the entire crew on edge, and today more so than most days. Even the most experienced pilots would have been flustered. *Hurry up and wait,* he thought. Pushing out of the gate was nothing short of what those American's called, a clusterfuck. Now they taxied in sequence for departure.

His airline had finally realized that putting kids into the right seat without experience could be problematic, thus they initiated a mentoring program. Hell, that program was nothing more than teaching the captains how to be babysitters. These planes were designed for two qualified crewmembers, not one. *Thank God Boeing aircraft were reliable,* he thought. *God help those on the Airbus with the same demands of non-experienced pilots.*

If the kid performed okay on this leg, he would give him the plane and monitor his performance on the next leg. If nothing went wrong, he could sign him off in a week. He grinned. Who was he kidding. He doubted he would be ready in a month.

"Global 93, cleared for takeoff 16 left," ATC said.

He glanced toward the triple seven as it moved into position. Then he cranked his head and watched the big bird lumber down the runway and rotate. He wondered what it would feel like flying a plane of that size. An experience he would never have in his lifetime. He was thankful, however, to be a captain at 29 years of age. He also had a job, and was honored to be flying the MAX 8, one of Boeing's newest 737 aircraft. She was a beauty that could fly 500 miles farther and carry 50 more passengers than her 737-700 sister, the plane that he'd been type-rated on. Today they were full, with 178 passengers.

"Everflight 203, cleared into position 16 left and hold."

He taxied onto the runway and glanced at his first officer, who was responding to ATC. The poor kid was nervous. But who wouldn't be with so few hours? He had hoped that the lengthy taxi would have calmed him, but the extended time only grew his nerves. The kid handled the radios okay, so he couldn't complain. He smiled at the term *kid*; he was not much older than the young man to his right.

They were cleared for takeoff. He advanced the power and pushed the TOGA switch. The thrust levers advanced to approximately 94% N1, the engine power setting for the low-pressure compressor section. But none of the new pilots knew that. He wasn't even sure if they would know what any of the performance numbers should be for takeoff because they were automatically set. Without a doubt, automation was dumbing down the pilot force.

In no time, they were racing down the runway. He glanced at the airspeed indicator and then pulled his attention back to the runway beyond the windscreen. The runway was wet, so he removed his hand from the thrust levers five knots earlier than he normally did and placed it on the control yoke.

"V1…Rotate," the first officer said.

The captain glanced at the speed and then pulled the control yoke back, and he began rotation.

"Positive rate," the first officer said.

The captain hesitated a moment as he glanced at the remaining runway and then at the radio altimeter and called, "Gear up."

The first officer raised the gear upon command.

They climbed for a few minutes and then the captain's eyes narrowed. He glanced outside and then back to his instruments. The angle of attack went from 11 degrees to 35 and then to 74. The stick shaker activated, sounding like a machine gun shaking the controls as it fired. He glanced at the first officer instruments, back to his, and then outside. His instruments had failed… or had they? He could not give a 300-hour pilot controls in this condition.

He stabbed the left autopilot button without a response. Then pressed the right autopilot button. With each press of a button the autopilot screamed a warning, telling him it would not engage.

"Contact ATC," the captain commanded.

"Tower, Everflight 203, climbing to flight level 320," the first officer said.

"Tell them we have an emergency," he yelled. He reached over and pressed an autopilot button again, and this time it engaged. Seconds later there was a small roll and the rudder shifted, changing their heading.

"Everflight 203, climb to 340, left turn direct to GULBO."

The captain yelled, "Flaps up," the stick shaker continued to fire.

The first officer raised the flaps from 5 to up and then responded to ATC, omitting the emergency part of the equation.

The captain had gone from a heading of 157 to 280 degrees. They would be impinging upon departures with the other runway. Then the autopilot disengaged, and the battle began. The airplane had a mind of its own.

"Tell ATC we have a control problem," the captain yelled. Seconds later the trim moved from 4.6 to 2.1 and the nose began falling as the stabilizer wheel spun forward. The wheel was spinning, and the plane was heading toward the ocean. The aircraft warning cried, "Don't Sink. Don't Sink."

About ten seconds later he regained control if only for a moment, and he pulled the control yoke back, stopping the descent. Slightly. Sweat dripped from his forehead.

"Ask for runway heading," The captain said, as trim went to .4 units. "Shit!"

"Don't sink." "Don't sink." "Don't sink." The airplane screamed.

"Help me trim," the captain yelled. They both attempted to move their electric trim switches, but they didn't work. "Cut off the stabilizer," the captain roared.

The first officer placed the stab trim switches down to deactivate the system. Their automatic trim was now inactive, and they would need to use the wheel. But suddenly and without warning the nose was pitching over again, this time without the wheel spinning.

"Pull up!" the captain yelled.

They both pulled back on the controls. Then the overspeed clacker began to howl. His eyes darted to the airspeed indicator. They were at 295 knots and increasing. "Is the trim functional?" the captain yelled over the ear shattering noise.

"It's not working," cried the first officer. "Do I try it with the trim wheel?"

"Yes! Do it!" the captain yelled.

"It doesn't work," he cried, trying to move the wheel.

"Get me radar vectors to return to the airport," the captain yelled. The overspeed clacker continued to wail. He couldn't hear himself think. He glanced at the speed which was now 435 knots. They were going so fast. Too fast. *What the hell is happening?*

"Everflight 203, turn left heading 330," air traffic control yelled. "Do you have a problem?"

"Pull with me," the captain yelled again, the overspeed screaming in the background.

"It's not enough!"

"Reengage the stabilizer switches," the captain commanded.

The first officer complied, which gave control back to the airplane, and both pilots pressed the electric trim switches on their control yokes. But without warning another un-commanded trim movement forced the nose forward, as the stabilizer spun wildly pushing the nose down.

They were headed for the ocean again, and the captain pulled back as hard as he could. But this time nothing happened. There was not a damn thing he could do. He fought the plane as it bellowed toward the ocean. Their speed was now 608 knots. Seconds from impact the captain glanced at the thrust levers and yelled, "Oh shit!" as he reached for them. But it was too late. That was the first time he had realized they had been in maximum takeoff power the entire time.

Chapter 8

SEATTLE WASHINGTON
OCTOBER 11, 2018

DRAGGING HER BAGS down the jetway Darby maintained a smile that contradicted her mood. She was anything but happy; she was tired beyond belief, and she could not shake the horror of the crash. She had also forgotten how exhausted she felt after an international trip. While her training was a quick six-days, it began with a sleepless night in Narita because another Boeing MAX had crashed. Darby had spent her first layover on the phone with Kathryn and John. The second night was more of the same listening to what they had learned.

Darby's flight had landed in Tokyo thirty minutes before the crash, and she first heard of the accident as they were clearing customs. During the second day, the check airman had asked her what had started all her trouble. She shared with him her safety concerns and told him about the internal report she had submitted to Clark and Wyatt. The remainder of her operational training led to discussions regarding Global's training department and how bad it was.

The check airman had disclosed to her what was happening behind the scenes at Global Air Lines. She had no idea that others knew of the problems, especially the instructors. Yet, nobody did anything.

Nobody said enough was enough. Training was being cut to shreds, which was significantly impacting operational performance, but management looked the other way and instructors remained silent in order to retain their jobs. But after what she had been through, could she blame them?

The check airman gave her a line check on their return to Los Angeles. She had passed and was free to fly. He had shaken her hand and wished her luck in the pending legal proceedings. He also told her that he was proud of her. A compliment that brought a tear to her eye. Once again, she'd been thankful her glasses were in place.

After securing the airplane, she rushed to customs. There she stood behind an Emirates crew long enough to miss her first commuter flight to Seattle. She headed out of terminal two and then power-walked to terminal six, hoping to catch an Alaska flight home. They had welcomed her aboard. *The joys of commuting,* she thought.

Now, stepping off the jetway and emerging into the Seattle terminal, she hesitated at the top of the jetway, looking both ways to orientate herself. She glanced at her watch—1605. She yawned. Inhaling a deep breath, she headed right. Only two escalators and one employee bus stood between she and her car. She would be home in twenty minutes tops.

It only took Darby a few minutes to remember where she had parked her car—another occupational hazard. Fueled with nothing but adrenaline, she threw her bags into the backseat, and climbed into the driver's seat. She closed her eyes and sucked another deep breath as she leaned her head back.

She could not imagine what could be worse than senseless deaths, simply because management refused to train pilots properly. Something was structurally wrong with the MAX, but there was more to it than that. Those pilots should have been able to manage that aircraft. It was always a blame game, and sadly this crash would be no different.

John's words echoed in her mind that they had known there would be another accident, and nothing would be done until that day arrived. She just never imagined it would be so soon. Now those people on that aircraft were dead, and the regulators who were paid to protect them suspected it was going to happen and they had done nothing to stop it.

She startled and sat upright, opening her eyes. "Do not sleep," she chided herself.

Her car started on the first try, and she patted the top of the dashboard and said, "Good girl." Darby shifted into reverse, and then backed out of her parking spot. Within minutes she was on the road, perplexed as to how management and even the FAA could be so corrupt.

The public would blame the foreign carriers due to poor training and a culture issue. But training was lacking in the United States as well. Not to mention Global had the culture of the Soviet Union. Thankfully the U.S. still had experienced pilots and was not putting cadets into the flight deck for on-the-job training. That, too, would only be a matter of time. When they did, the world would become balanced with airline accidents.

The FAA knew there was a problem after the first MAX crash, and they had done nothing. They were sure there would be a second, and they still did nothing. Then there was Global Air Lines' management who knew of serious safety issues, but attempted to bury her instead of looking into them. How the hell would she get management to understand that what they were doing was wrong? The FAA had no teeth and would be of no help.

Kathryn worked for the FAA and *wanted* to fix things, but even her hands were tied. Therefore, what hope did they have?

One thing she knew—it was difficult to get a anyone to understand something if his salary depended upon the lack of knowledge.

Turning onto her street, her house came within sight and she smiled. This time, all the way into her eyes. Then a siren screamed a quick shout. Startled, she placed a hand to her heart. She looked in her side mirror and saw flashing lights. Her attention then shifted to her rearview mirror to assess herself. Her eyes looked like she'd been in a 36-hour sleep deprivation marathon. Wearing a uniform for twenty hours and counting, was not the best look.

It is what it is, she thought.

She pulled into her driveway and the police car pulled in behind her. She reached into her purse, found a package of gum and popped a piece into her mouth, then rolled down her window as the officer approached.

"You were flying down that street pretty fast young lady," he said. "Unless you have a pilot's license, I'm going to have to take you in."

"Damn. Not my lucky day," Darby said with a slow smile. "I have one of those. Is there any other reason you could take me in?"

"I could think of a few," Tom said with a grin.

Darby opened the garage door and pulled her car forward. Once she parked, Tom gathered her bags, and together they went into the house. She tossed her gum into the trash and closed the door behind them. He set her bags to the side, then placed his hands onto her waist and lifted her onto the kitchen counter.

She wrapped her legs around his waist, and he leaned in. Their mouths became one. The kiss was unrushed, but with deep urgency. Passion that she had missed for a very long time was finally returning. Feeling the loss of lives of that crash tore at her soul, intensifying the feeling of life with Tom's kiss.

Taking a breath, she asked, "What time are you off work?"

He glanced at his watch, then his eyes returned to hers. "Fifteen minutes and thirty-two seconds."

With arms wrapped around him she placed her head on his chest. He pulled her in and held her tight. She could do anything for fifteen minutes, even wait for Tom. They had talked each day she was out, and he understood how hard the crash had impacted her.

Tom was the police officer who had arrived at her house when it had been broken into. A couple of homeless people had stolen her alcohol. She later deduced it was to steal the wine that had been sent her the day she received notice that she would never fly again. The same day that she was declared to be bipolar by Global's doctor.

It had been John's idea to test the wine, and that's when they found the wine contained drugs that would have ended her life. Someone, Rich Clark no doubt, had put this in motion. But the wine had been over at Kathryn's house the night of the robbery, so he was unable to destroy the evidence. Tom had been the investigator on duty. He convinced Darby to get an alarm.

She found it humorous at the time because nobody would have been able to do anything to her anyway. Everywhere she turned, he was there watching her or driving past her house. She loved having a personal bodyguard. Regardless, she complied and secured her home.

The night that the first MAX crashed, she and the ladies had had too much to drink. Darby found her way home, but she set off her alarm. She allowed the screaming to become white noise and ignored it. Reaching the toilet had been her priority. Tom had been the officer who arrived on that scene, and he'd taken care of her. She still reminded him that it was his fault by forcing the alarm issue.

Tom had held her hair during that prayer session over the toilet and had even placed a damp cloth to her forehead. He had gotten her to bed, and the next morning he was in her kitchen cooking bacon.

That was the morning she had remembered seeing the pill bottle on the floor. The same drug that had been in the wine.

Tom did not take that information to his department, but had told her to give it to John. He said that it was John's investigation. Darby suspected that had Tom reported it, in conjunction with the report from the theft, that would have accelerated his career. That was the day she realized that she liked him as a human. He was a good man and ethical. They had their first date, became good friends and incredible lovers.

"I have plans for you, tonight," he finally said. Then asked, "Are you hungry?"

"Not really," she said, having had a sandwich on the flight home. Hoping she could stay awake for whatever he had planned.

"Okay then," he said, stepping back and lifting her off the counter. "You're going to get out of this uniform and I'm going to take the lid off the hot tub. We'll have one beer in the tub. Then I'm tucking you into bed for a good night's sleep."

"Are you staying?" she asked.

"You don't need me keeping you awake all night," he said. "But I will be back for breakfast."

Darby smiled. There was nothing that she needed more than sleep. She was thankful that he understood without her having to tell him. She appreciated him more each day.

"Clothing optional?" she asked, unbuttoning her uniform shirt.

"No option. There is none," he said, not removing his eyes from her disrobing. When the bra and panties came off, he glanced at his watch. He could not officially get naked or have a beer until he was off duty. Murphy's law always turned to bite him. Something she understood so well.

Darby opened her suitcase, found a sweatshirt and smelled it.

Then she pulled it on. She dumped the rest of her laundry into the washer.

"I can't believe you don't sort," Tom said, handing her the bottle of detergent.

"I can't believe you're still dressed," Darby said smelling herself. She pulled the shirt over her head, placed it into the washer and closed the lid. She pressed the start button and headed outside and climbed into the tub.

Leaning back, she assessed the fall colors. The leaves were already changing to red, yellow, and orange. She breathed in the colors. Then glancing to the sky, she watched an Alaska 737 depart. More than likely, it was the plane she had been on not more than an hour earlier.

Closing her eyes, she flashed back to seeing the emergency equipment in the Pacific Ocean that had lingered during their departure out of Narita the following day. Death had filled the ocean, a sight she would never forget.

"Don't fall asleep," Tom said.

Darby startled and opened her eyes. She smiled at his nakedness. "Just resting them."

He handed her a beer, and then climbed into the tub. He extended his bottle and said, "Congratulations on the checkout."

Clinking her bottle to his, she said, "Thanks."

He sat across from her, and she put her feet in his lap. He rubbed a foot with one hand, while he held his beer with the other. They talked about his week of fighting crime. She laughed at his stories. Finding the humor in his job helped him to deal with life's challenges, too.

One thing she knew, she was one of the lucky ones. Despite what had been thrown at her, she was a survivor. There were some really screwed up people running around in the world, and Tom got to meet alot of them. Many of them did not survive. He continually reminded her she was not part of that group.

"Think this thing will go to court?" Tom asked.

"The most asked question," Darby said. "Unless they give me my attorney fees back and they hold all the bad guys accountable." She raised a finger and added, "And they write me a letter of apology."

"Do you know who's involved?"

"I know for sure Clark, the senior VP," Darby said, "and Abbott the pass travel lady. Maybe George Wyatt, the senior VP who was Clark's boss. And that dipshit psychiatrist, Wood."

"Quite a little conspiracy," Tom said. "Do you think that the CEO is involved?"

"We'll find out on Monday," Darby said removing her feet from his lap and replacing them with her body. Facing him she wiggled her legs around behind him. "Oh, I forgot to add Global's doctor, and the union."

"The whole union?" Tom asked pulling her close.

"All the way up to National," she said with a smile, feeling his body stir.

"You're really getting screwed," Tom said, and then took a long drink of his beer.

"Is that a promise?" Darby asked with a grin.

Chapter 9

Seattle Washington
October 12, 2018

Darby awoke to the smell of bacon, trying to remember the night before. Eyes closed, she smiled. She loved how her life had returned to normal. Notwithstanding one little distraction called litigation. There were far too many times throughout the previous two years of hell that she believed nothing would ever be normal again. There had been a high probability that she would never taste the sky again. Neal had broken up with her. She soon believed that she would never find a man that she could trust and who would love her. She had been wrong.

Trying to roll over she stopped short when her shoulder jerked in the socket.

"What the hell?" she said, and then began laughing. She thought she was going to pee her pants—if she had been wearing any. She glanced at her wrist and yelled, "Tom!"

Instead of hearing his footsteps run up the stairs she heard singing. *He is so dead,* she thought. She tried to pull her hand free, to no avail. She couldn't imagine how he had slipped in and handcuffed her to the bed, or when. Maybe he did it before he had left the night before, but that would have been too dangerous if there had been a fire. He had to have done it that morning, she was sure. Regardless, she would be in trouble if she wasn't released sooner than later.

She tried to pull her hand out by making it as small as possible, but the cuff was too tight. Glancing from one nightstand to the other, she looked for something to break herself free. And then she saw it. Beside the clock on the opposite side of the bed was the key to the cuffs. He had put it there, just out of reach.

Darby scooted as far toward that side of the bed as she could. Extending her free arm, she stretched it and extended her fingers as far as she could. She was still a foot away. "Shit," she whispered rolling to her back. She stared at the ceiling, then gave a sideways glance at the key again. Scooting her body sideways, she positioned herself horizontal across the bed, and extended a leg. A smile spread across her face. What her hand could not reach, her foot could.

Once upon a time a man had told her that they could teach a monkey to fly, but they couldn't teach it to think—just like a woman. Well, Darby was about to play like a monkey, because she in fact could think.

She pressed one big toe against the side of nightstand towards the top, making her leg a bridge. Then carefully she placed her other toe on top of the key. "Come on baby," she said pressing it firmly down. She slowly slid the key toward the edge of the nightstand toward her other toe. This would be her one and only chance.

With both toes pressed together, she held the key between them, then pulled her legs to her body and grabbed it.

Ten minutes later Darby walked into the kitchen. Her bed was dry, making it to the bathroom before it was too late, her teeth brushed, and she was starving.

Tom turned with a look of disappointment mixed with surprise, holding a platter of bacon. "We were supposed to have breakfast in bed."

"I had to pee."

"Guess I didn't think that one through," he said with a grin. "How the hell did you get out?"

"If I told you, I'd have to kill you," Darby said selecting a strip of bacon. "Let's just say that I have talents you can't begin to imagine."

"I should cancel my training," he said placing the platter of bacon on the table. "You could spend the week showing me all your secret talents."

He turned and grabbed the edges of her robe and pulled her close. Closing his eyes, he pulled her toward him for a good morning kiss and she stuck her slice of bacon into his parted lips.

His eyes opened. "I guess I deserve that," he said with a mouth full.

"Oh yeah, you'll pay," she said. *For at least five minutes,* she thought. Pulling away from him she said. "You should probably go to your training. I think you need it."

Tom chuckled. "Yeah, I need training alright. How to train your pilot," he said grabbing a coffee pod. He placed it into the Keurig and set a cup into place.

"Maybe they'll teach you the proper use of handcuffs," Darby said, pouring cream into a cup. She set the cup in the microwave and pressed the 30-second button. When done, she removed her hot cream from the microwave and poured it into her coffee that Tom held for her. Tom handed her the cup, and she stood on her tippy toes and kissed him gently and then said, "Thank you."

"For what?" Tom asked, "My exceptionally good coffee or the kiss?"

"Yes," Darby said with a wink, and sipped. "Yummy."

"Breakfast is getting cold. Sit."

"Yes master," Darby said with a little salute, and slid into a chair.

Tom set a plate in front of her, and then another for himself. He had made her a Spanish omelet with homemade salsa. "This looks delicious." She took a bite, closed her eyes, and said, "I think I've died and gone to heaven."

"I thought that's what happened last night." He kissed her on the cheek and sat beside her. "But how the hell did you sleep eleven hours?"

"Another one of my many talents," she said with a smirk, then stuffed a large bite of omelet into her mouth.

"Or one of mine," he said raising his mug toward her.

"I'll give you that one," she said, her mouth still full. She clinked her mug to his and then asked. "How long is training?"

"Two weeks for criminal psychology. Then the fun begins."

There was nothing that Darby wanted more than for Tom to get off the streets and become an investigator. He had a brilliant mind, and he was being wasted in his current position as a street cop. She often wondered how he fell into that position because he was so over qualified. She never pressed him because everyone has a reason for what they do. And he apparently loved it.

"I'll miss you," Darby said melting into his eyes. Even if he was sent away for a year, she would wait for him. "I've got a lot to keep me busy while you're gone."

"I wish you didn't have to go through this," Tom said, reaching for her hand. He was about to say something else but fell silent.

"You and me both," Darby said.

"If you go to trial, they're going to do everything they can to destroy you. They will dig into your past and find anything they could use against you. Their goal will be to destroy your reputation. To destroy you. When they get you on the stand, they will try to push you until you blow. Or try to break you emotionally to make you cry. What's worse is that you'll be sitting at the table, and these managers will go on the stand and lie to the judge. You'll want to yell the truth to defend yourself, but you can't. You must sit silent no matter what they say. You cannot show any weakness or any emotion."

"Shoot me now," Darby said, setting her fork on the plate. Her mouth had been hanging open at every word, but now Tom looked seriously scared, so she added, "Don't worry. You know me, the master of hiding emotions." She grinned with a wave of her hand then winked.

Tom gave her a half smile and squeezed her hand. Then she fought to keep the tears at bay. *How the hell will I survive this?* she wondered.

Darby was scared. Global had managed to buy a doctor to give a false diagnosis. They had ALPO, her pilot union, in their pocket. ALPO had not defended her, but more than that they conspired with the company to bury her. She prayed that the judge would allow them to depose the CEO, because then Global would settle before this ridiculousness went any farther. She did not want to go to trial. She did not want them to dissect her life in an open courtroom. She wanted her life back.

"What can I do to prepare?" Darby finally asked.

"For now, be involved. Learn the law from your attorney. Know the evidence better than anyone else. When you go through depositions, listen for inconstancies. Nobody remembers better than the person who lived through the experience." He hesitated a moment. "You lived through hell and that experience is in there," he said touching her temple. "When something comes to mind, write it down."

Think it, ink, Darby thought. She would heed his advice.

"That medical report still haunts me," Darby said. "Despite the many points that were just… stupid and inconsistent," she added, not able to find better words. But the simplicity explained so much. "If the judge has any common sense, he should see through the Global assassins."

"I hope he's a good guy," Tom said, squeezing her hand again. "You can do this."

"Thanks for the pep talk," Darby said. "I may need a few more before this is all over."

"You've got it," Tom said. "You'll have to count on your attorney to be smarter than theirs."

"He's brilliant," Darby said. "It's like he's got all these cases in his brain, and he truly is an AIR21 expert. He knows this law. He's also an honest man with a huge amount of integrity. I really dodged a bullet getting away from my first attorney."

AIR21 was the whistleblower law. Unfortunately, the more Darby learned of the law, she realized that it protected the airline more so than the employee. The law was essential, but the statute of limitations was the shortest for any law, at only three months. If the employee put their faith in the union, they would eat up those three months before lunch.

If the employee filed and won, they were only awarded reasonable attorney fees, not necessarily everything it cost them in litigation. Whereas the airline had the ability to throw any disgusting amount of money into their defense, unscrupulously spending their stockholder's profits at the employee's demise.

Thankfully, Darby got her job back on her own and did not have to wait for the resolution of a trial for that. Granted it took her two years, but without an income there would have been no way to pay for an attorney. Because this law also provided only compensatory damages with reasonable attorney fees, there was no way any attorney could afford to take such a case on contingency.

Darby was one of the lucky ones. How the hell could any pilot with a family to feed, and a mortgage to pay, survive litigation if they were unemployed? They couldn't.

She and Tom ate their breakfast in silence for a few minutes as Tom's words lingered. She thought about how lucky she had been to find Robert Allen. It wasn't until after she had already paid a small fortune to another law firm, but jumping ships was the best thing she could have done.

The other guy had not previously litigated an AIR21 case, despite his assertions otherwise. He also held the assumption that she would receive all attorney fees, so he proceeded to rack up the bills in the most unbelievable ways. Had she stayed with him and won, she would have been in the hole even if she were successful. But now she had Robert Allen.

"Robert has been teaching me the law," Darby said, reaching for her coffee cup. "I've got a lot to learn, but the more I do, the more I realize Global simply doesn't have a case. At least I don't think so."

"Sweetie, it's not always about the truth. It's about what you can prove in court."

Darby laughed. "I think I said something like that to Kat."

"Great minds," he said with a tilt of his cup before he sipped.

She adored Tom, and his honesty. How he had fallen into her life when she needed him most, was nothing short than a gift from God. They ate their breakfast and chatted about nothing important beyond what they planned on doing to each other when he returned. But as they talked, Darby could not shake his words. Global management would not give up in their effort to inflict pain. She knew two things to be true—he was going to make a great investigator, and she needed to avoid court.

"So," Darby said, "after training will you be able to work undercover?"

"Under the covers?" he queried, returning her grin. "Count on it."

Just as Darby was about to make a profound comment that they could rehearse that part, the doorbell rang, and she excused herself to answer it. When she returned to the kitchen, she was holding a large envelope and the rehearsal forgotten.

"What's that?" Tom asked.

"My weekend," Darby said tossing the package onto the table. "It's a damn good thing you're going to be out of town. I've got work to do."

Chapter 10

Seattle Washington
October 13, 2018

Cockroaches was the best she could do to describe what was laying on her desk.

The night before, Tom had kissed her goodbye and she grabbed a few hours of sleep. She had finally dumped the contents of the envelope onto her desk in the dark of morning. It was hard to believe the clattering of the plastic devices could very possibly be her salvation. She stood there for a moment staring at them. They seemed to grow legs as she stared, realizing this could go either way.

Inside the dozen flash drives were facts that would either help to build her case or hurt her. Either way, she was about to find out. She turned on her laptop and typed her password. Waiting for her computer to provide access she leaned back in her chair, held her coffee mug with both hands, and sipped. Morning was her favorite time to work. A time when nobody else was awake and she could focus on what was needed. No interruptions. After a large yawn, she took another sip of coffee and then set the cup on her desk.

The flash drives were from Dr. Wood. The day Robert had accepted her case, he had sent Dr. Wood a notice demanding that he preserve and protect all his electronically stored information by duplicate and triplicate. The ESI letter held a threatening tone, with many stipulations. It worked. Dr. Wood complied and readily provided the requested documents. Global was another story.

Darby lifted the first flash drive and stuck it into the slot and clicked on the blue folder, opening the files within. She selected the first document and began to read the contents. On a pad of paper, she wrote what was on the drive and in each folder. After an hour had lapsed, she had a list of documents from the first flash drive—her medical report, and internal emails between her and others within the company.

A couple of emails were those that Dr. Wood had referred to during her evaluation as he had questioned her why she had been polite. Wood had been confused as to how there could have been a problem between management and her if she had written such polite emails. Rolling her eyes, she remembered what an idiot he was during her evaluation and that opinion had not changed.

After swapping flash drives, she opened the first document on the next drive and her eyes narrowed. Then she opened the next document, and then another. Reading the contents made her angrier with each word she read. *Holy shit,* she thought. She jotted down the contents on her notepad.

"Those bastards," she finally said, pushing her chair back. Standing, she walked away from her computer and glanced at the time. It was still too early to call Kathryn. Folding her arms, she tapped a foot and drummed her fingers on her sleeve.

"Get a grip Darby," she said, chiding herself. She returned to her desk and began writing the discrepancies on her notepad. Darby's vision of cockroaches was not too far off. This disk was filled with nothing but garbage.

Tom had told her that they would lie on stand. They had started early with their emails. Global had provided Dr. Wood with documented recounts of all her meetings with the managers, but none of them were accurate. Nothing they said was correct. Things they wrote had never been spoken. Things she *had* said, were misquoted.

There was also no recount of her union's notes. Probably because her union never took notes during those meetings. ALPO had been useless through the entire process. Useless to her that is. They had served Global well.

After saving the contents to a file, she pulled out that flash drive and replaced it with another. Like Groundhog Day, she started at the first document and glanced at the contents within. Those also appeared to be emails. She opened the first email dated November 23, 2016, and read—*Dear Dr. Wood, we have a case we would like you to evaluate. I'm copying my colleague Martha Jones, as she has been part of this case. Joe.*

What case? Darby wondered, *and who is Martha Jones?*

Joe was Joe Wolfe, Global's labor relations attorney who was responsible to ensure the contract was enforced. Not only had he contacted the doctor outside the bounds of the contract, but he had been working on her case with someone before there was a case.

She had only met with the pass travel lady, Abbott, on November 22nd. *How the hell did they have a case the next day, with someone part of it?* Darby wondered.

Abbott had told the OSHA investigator that she had arrived in Oklahoma City about 11 pm on the 22nd, and that she had been so frightened that she couldn't sleep that night, so she took the next day off. That rolled into Thanksgiving. Abbot did not speak to the labor relations attorney until the following Monday, November 28th. Hell, Darby had not even been pulled from the line until December 19th.

Perplexed, Darby leaned back in her chair. This time she drummed her nails on the desk. The clicking sound was hypnotic. Then she had an idea. She typed Martha Jones into her company website. The results were immediate—a Global corporate attorney. *Why the hell was the pass travel lady contacting an attorney not even in her department?* she wondered.

Unsure if a word search only worked on an individual document, or if she could search all the files on a flash drive at once, there was only one way to find out. She opened the search box and typed Martha Jones. "Bingo!" Darby said.

She got lucky. The first name popped up on July 11, 2016, about fifteen documents in. This was over four months before she had met with Abbott. "What the hell," Darby said as she began to read.

"Holy shit!" Darby picked up her phone to call Robert, but it rang before she had a chance to dial. "I was just about to call you," she said, as she answered.

"I found a smoking gun," Robert said.

Chapter 11

THE SYNCHRONICITY OF their findings was more than coincidence. Robert had been working on the documents from Global while Darby was focusing on Dr. Wood. Her heart was racing with excitement with what she had learned, and now Robert had a smoking gun. She only hoped there were fingerprints.

"They sent a barrage of documents without Bates stamping them," Robert began. "I wasn't sure how to attack this. Most of it appeared to be nothing. Just filler. Then I decided to start at the end of the 18,000 pages and work backward. That's when I found it."

"What?" Darby asked. They needed something of substance to hang the rat bastards. Tom's words echoed in the room— *It's what you can prove in court.*

Weeks after Global's lawyers failed to meet their legal obligation to provide discovery, they had finally sent Robert 18,000 pages of documents that were not Bates stamped. Bates stamping was simply a form of indexing legal documents for digital reference points to identify and label each page. Global had sent them a hodgepodge of random documents that Robert was tasked to decipher.

"We have an email from Rich Clark to George Wyatt," Robert said, "in which he states his plans to place you into the Section 8 review process simply because you requested the meeting."

"Seriously?" Darby said dumbfound. "Holy cow."

"He writes," Robert said, "*here we go…just FYI I will brief HR and handle this with kid gloves, Darby could be candidate for Section 8 after this meeting goes through.*"

"What date was that written?" Darby asked looking at the email from Rich Clark on her computer.

"July 15, 2016," he said.

"Get ready for bullets for that gun," Darby said. "Wolfe had emailed Dr. Wood on November 23rd the day *after* I met with Abbott. But Abbott hadn't even met with him yet. In his email to Wood, Wolfe said that he was copying his colleague Martha Jones because she was part of the case. My thought was—what case? So, I word searched Martha Jones and it led me to an email dated July 11, 2016, when Clark emailed Oliver—"

"I'm lost. Who is Martha Jones?" Robert asked.

"I'm sorry. She's a Global corporate attorney."

"Who is Oliver?"

"Oliver Miller was a Director over the Regional Director Captain Robert Dodson." Darby said. "Dodson is the guy who gave me the Section 8 letter."

"Okay, go on," Robert said.

"Well, the email that Martha Jones was copied on, the one sent to Dr. Wood in which Wolfe is asking him to help with the Section 8, brought me to an email from Clark to Oliver written on July 11th, four days *before* Clark told Wyatt of his plan that you just read."

"What did he write?" Robert asked.

"Just a sec," Darby said as she scrolled to the top of the email. "Okay. He wrote—*Probably good to engage HR again at this point. We need to start tracking this phase. I think we should consider whether a Section 8 is appropriate. While I'm sure Darby would find issue with* that course action, if she cannot embrace and understand the reasons behind our actions, it stands to reason she might not be able to make appropriate decision for the safe operation of a flight as a crewmember."

"This is extraordinary," Robert said. "They planned this, but they waited over four months to create pretext."

"It gets better," Darby said. "Remember how they were arguing with me for three months because they didn't want to meet with me?"

"Yes," Robert said.

"Well, I found the reason why they changed their minds. Martha Jones had advised them I had *no* safety information so they could go ahead with the meeting."

"Nothing to report, so go ahead and have a meeting?" Robert chuckled.

"Clark wrote to Oliver and said—*after conferring with Mike, Jacob, and Martha, we have decided to give Darby Bradshaw her requested audience. I will ensure Wyatt is briefed up that we do not see any harassment substantiation in her correspondence, so we find no basis to start an investigation into her singular claim. We also do not find any identified safety threat (to the company or the operation), only her assertion there is a 'safety culture' concern.*"

"Good ol' Martha didn't understand that safety culture *is* an FAA requirement, did she?" Robert said. "Ignorance of aviation law and federal regulations while working for an airline does not make for the most competent attorney."

"Global's not getting their money's worth from her," Darby said. "It looks like they were denying the meeting with me while the legal department was determining if I had protected activity."

"They didn't believe you were protected by the AIR21 statute," Robert said. "So, they agreed to meet with you because all you had was safety culture and SMS concerns."

"Yep. And their HR investigation assertion doesn't hold water either," Darby said. "Clark clearly said he was *not* investigating any harassment issues. And yet, that was their excuse for my meeting with Abbott."

"This is just amazing," Robert said.

"I think we have them," Darby said.

"I hope so. In the meantime, do you think you'll have time to get through all of Wood's documents before we depose Wyatt and Clark?"

"Absolutely," Darby said. "I'll have them done this weekend."

Robert provided her the call-in number for their Monday meeting with the administrative law judge, at which time they would be arguing the merits of deposing the CEO, Walter Croft.

They ended their call and Darby headed downstairs. *How could I possibly not win this case?* she wondered. Then a chill wormed into her core. There was always a way for injustice to prevail in the legal system. But with this information, there would no way they would go to court. She had to believe that.

Once in the kitchen, she made another cup of coffee as she thought about what had transpired. Global management had said the only reason they put her into the Section 8 was because she became emotionally upset during her meeting with Abbott. They alleged the meeting with Abbott had nothing to do with her safety report, but everything to do with an HR/EO investigation. Yet, Clark said there was *no* harassment investigation. Why the HR investigation?

Clark then told Wyatt he was planning the Section 8 well before they did it based upon her request for the meeting. The icing on the cake was that Abbott had the safety report with her during the meeting. They clearly used that meeting with Abbott to set her up.

Darby knew beyond a reasonable doubt that Clark had planned this. But did a reasonable doubt stand up in an AIR 21 court? She had no idea. Regardless, Global would have no other choice but to end it based on all the evidence that Dr. Wood had provided them. Nobody would benefit going to trial. Especially not Global Air Lines.

She grabbed a banana and carried that and her coffee back up the stairs, smiling at her snack of choice.

Settling into her chair, she sipped her coffee and stared at the skies that had finally awoken. A new day always brought hope. She forced her attention back to her computer. If she was going to get this done by the end of the weekend, she needed to focus. She also needed to get organized and decided exactly how to do that.

She opened a new document, made a table with a header, and added the words *Date, To, From, Copied on*, and *Description* in the blocks across the top. Her plan was to chronologically add the information from the emails into the table in a date of occurrence sequence. She wanted to see what happened in the order that it had occurred and who all the players were.

Darby placed the first flash drive with the emails back into the slot and began to read and categorize each on the chart.

Three hours later her phoned dinged and she jumped.

A text from Robert—*emailed privileged log.*

Darby opened the email and downloaded the document. This was a list of communications that were company secrets that Global said they could not disclose because it was attorney-client privilege

How could there be company secrets that I'm involved in? she wondered. The list was three pages long. While she didn't know what was said, she did know who was communicating secretly about her and to whom, and what date those exchanges occurred. This was fascinating.

It took her the better part of an hour to copy and paste the data into the table, but it was well worth the effort. She inserted the dates of each item on the privilege log in sequence with the dates between the emails she had already documented. She also color coded the documents for ease of identification, and to determine what was confidential and what was not.

A picture was now forming as to what transpired. This was nothing short of a conspiracy. The names that she didn't recognize in the privilege log, she searched on the company website. As it turned out, before they ever stuck her down this rabbit hole of a mental health evaluation, they were discussing the matter with the Senior Vice President of the legal department *and* the Senior Vice President of marketing.

She glanced at the time. Having already put in the better part of nine hours on this project, she was not quite halfway through. She was, however, exhausted. With a huge yawn, she stood and stretched, then inserted one more flash drive while still standing.

"One more," she said, and then she would call it a day and go to the gym. She stood in front of her desk and opened the first document on the drive.

"What the hell?" Darby said quietly and slipped back into the chair. She wanted to walk away, but she couldn't. She could not stop reading with the realization of what she was looking at.

Darby downloaded the document to her computer and selected save. She saved it to the cloud, and then pressed print. She just sat there, staring at the pages emerging from her printer. It was bad enough that this had happened. But who in the hell at Global Air Lines was so stupid that they would give the proof to Dr. Wood? He apparently had no clue what he had in his possession, which was scarier than hell.

Chapter 12

ALCOHOL AND DISGUST might not be the best mixture in the shadow of death. Darby and Kathryn sat at the Mango Thai Cuisine and Bar, on International Boulevard. The atmosphere was thick. Kathryn held a glass of chardonnay and Darby sipped a scotch, neat. It had been six days since the 737 MAX crash, and four hours since Darby had learned how corrupt, unethical, and what soul-sucking bastards her airline management team really was. She glanced toward Kathryn and realized how negligent the FAA was, too.

Darby wasn't sure how to tell Kathryn what she'd learned that afternoon. They had always discussed everything in the past, but now she didn't know what to say. She sipped her drink and glanced over her rim at her friend. *Kat wasn't even in position when this happened,* Darby thought. Even now Kat's hands would be tied as much as John's were. But still.

"Have you learned anything more about the accident?" Darby asked, avoiding what she really wanted to discuss, dipping her lettuce wrap into the peanut sauce.

"It was the same as the first accident. A failed pitot static system with an MCAS system that took control of the plane," Kathryn said. "John had said this was going to happen. I just didn't want to believe it."

"You and me both." Darby lowered her voice. "Did they verify this accident was due to a knockoff part?"

Kathryn nodded and reached for her glass. Instead of sipping, she stared into the gold liquid, twisting the glass at the stem.

"But if you knew, if the FAA knew, why didn't you ground the MAX before the second accident?" Darby asked. "You had the warning."

"I tried," Kathryn said, her eyes leaving the glass to Darby's. They glistened with the pain that mirrored Darby's. "I couldn't defy John's confidence, but I did everything I could to ground that aircraft."

Darby locked her eyes onto Kathryn's. "I know you did. But nothing happens by chance. There are always signs, and if we don't heed the signs that are friggen neon billboards screaming to pay attention… then what?" Darby asked. "But this time, you knew. Everyone knew."

Kathryn lowered her glass to the table. She hesitated a moment, and then said, "These weren't the only two events."

"What the hell?" Darby said, a little louder than she should have. "There were more?"

Kathryn nodded, sticking her fork into her Pad Thai. "We've had a number of pitot static systems failing on the MAX with U.S. carriers. The MCAS kicked into operation, but the pilots immediately deactivated the stabilizer."

Darby could not believe any of this. The FAA knew there was more than one event, but they waited until a second plane crashed before grounding it. *How the hell could this be?*

"You had those ASAP reports," Darby said flatly.

"Yes," Kathryn said. "We received close to 100 of them."

"As in one zero zero?" Darby asked, dropping her wrap on the plate. Her appetite suddenly gone.

The Aviation Safety Action Program, or ASAP, was established in 1997 to encourage airline employees to voluntarily report safety lapses to help prevent future accidents. The program enabled pilots to self-report without the fear of disciplinary action from the FAA, for operational improvement. The pilots called it their get-out-of-jail-free card. The local FAA offices could see the problems and work with the airlines to solve them. But in this case, it was not the pilots' error they reported, but the plane's issue. Not unlike what she had learned earlier in the day.

"Why hasn't the FAA done anything?" Darby asked. "This is ridiculous. No…. it's actually criminal."

"Don't get me started," Kathryn said. "The ASAP program was supposed to improve safety, but the numbers of events are increasing at an alarming rate, and the fixes are not happening."

Darby was about to say something but stopped. Instead, she lifted her scotch and stared into the glass for a long moment, mulling over how to tell Kathryn what she had learned. There was no easy way, so she sipped her scotch instead.

"What's going on? Kathryn finally asked.

Chapter 13

LOATHING DID NOT even come close to the feelings he held of himself. Tom sat in a rental car at the DoubleTree hotel on International Boulevard across from the Mango Thai restaurant. He leaned back in the seat, the baseball hat pulled down low over his forehead, with the car shielded by the trees lining the sidewalk. He adjusted the earpiece and confirmed the recording was in progress when Kathryn said, *"The ASAP program was supposed to improve safety, but the numbers of events are increasing at an alarming rate, and the fixes are not happening."*

He raised his glasses and peered through the restaurant window. Darby was clearly upset. He sighed and dropped the glasses into his lap. She had every right to be upset. Then Kathryn asked that question, *"What's going on?"*

Tom rubbed his eyes with one hand and squeezed the bridge of his nose. He hated this assignment more than anything than he had done in his life, but what was he to do? He followed orders without question. Then he'd met Darby and began walking a tightrope.

Recordings were not necessary because Darby would tell him everything. But they wanted the documentation regardless. He also knew that he may not be the only one recording her. This was a love hate assignment from every angle no matter how he dissected it.

They'd developed a relationship that he'd never experienced. He'd never felt this way with anyone before. Perhaps because he never allowed anyone in before. He probably should have followed his own rules on this one, too, but now he was in too deep.

Did it really matter if a relationship was founded on lies and manipulations? Did it matter that he was destined to hurt her regardless of what happened? Most relationships ended badly anyway, didn't they? Did it matter that he was going to hurt the woman he loved?

They had ordered him to get close, and then he got closer despite his better judgement. He had also read the reports and knew of those who had been removed from her life unjustly. She had been broken many times over, but she always bounced back. He wasn't sure if this would be one of those times. But this was business, and those in charge ran the world. There was not a damn thing he could do even if he wanted to.

He closed his eyes as Darby told Kathryn what she had learned. *Those bastards,* he thought. With a sigh he raised his glasses again. He observed the women for a few moments, then shifted his attention down the sidewalk to the entrance of the airport and held it there for a couple minutes. He then turned his glasses to the Denny's parking lot across the street and focused them on Darby's car. He watched it for a moment, but there was nothing to see. He shifted his attention south down the street and nothing appeared out of the normal. Then he had a thought and began assessing the cars in the parking lot in which he sat.

He had been ordered to disappear for a week or two, and he complied. They wanted Darby to appear to be alone. They wanted her open. They were on a fishing expedition. All Tom wanted was for her to be safe. Instead, they put her in the center of something she did not deserve to be part of. Playing games with her life was not what he'd bargained for. Not that it was the first time placing a subject in danger, but he had never loved his subject before now.

There was no training to be an investigator, that was all a facade. His assignment at the police department, a ruse. His entire life was nothing but an illusion. One assignment after another. The only reality was that the woman sitting in the restaurant drinking a scotch knew nothing about him and never would.

Chapter 14

How do you tell someone you care about the truth, that will hurt them as much as it hurts you? Darby was not sure. She stared at Kathryn for a moment, and then set her glass on the table. To avoid saying what needed to be said, she told her the good news she had learned in discovery from Dr. Wood. She told Kathryn about the documents that proved Clark had premeditated the entire plan to get her, long before her meeting with the fake HR safety investigation.

"I'm so sorry Darby," Kathryn said, "but this is good news. It's the proof you need to win your case."

"It is," she said. "But there's more." Darby's eyes teared up. "Global sent Dr. Wood documents that identified that Global *and* the FAA knew of the pitot static problem that took down Air France 447 before it happened."

"What documents?" Kathryn asked. "What are you talking about?"

"There were pages of performance data and documentation with explanations of when and what happened on Global flights regarding the pitot static system. Global had *fourteen* of the exact same pitot static events that took down Air France 447," Darby said. She hesitated and then continued. "Global's events didn't end up in an accident because they were not in the same environmental conditions as Air France and the pilots had more experience, just like those MCAS events in the U.S., but they were the exact same failures as Air France."

"Seriously?" Kathryn said, setting her fork down and lowering her voice. "Are you sure?"

"I couldn't be surer," Darby said. "People died because Global management did nothing. Because the FAA did nothing. Wyatt, Clark, and the FAA ignored the ASAP reports with all those events and did not mandate to fix *anything* until *after* Air France crashed. How many more occurrences at other airlines? Many, I'm sure. The FAA knew and did not mandate the fix until after 228 people died."

"I don't know what to say," Kathryn said, placing a hand to her mouth. "This makes *me* sick."

"You and me both." Darby emptied her glass and then raised it to the waitress.

The waitress brought them each another drink. She also brought Darby a bowl of hot and sour soup. "For you my friend," she said, and patted Darby on the shoulder.

When the waitress was out of earshot, Darby said, "If Wyatt would have taken this serious, or the FAA forced an action, all those people would be alive today."

"It's bad enough that it occurred. But why would Global give anyone documents saying they knew about it?" Kathryn asked. "Hiding it is one thing, but why leak it out?"

"Because they wanted so badly to nail me, they would do anything," Darby said. "I think they told Wood that after Air France crashed that the FAA mandated training and issued an airworthy directive to prove they were taking my concerns seriously, to counteract my report. What they *didn't* tell Wood, was if they had mandated the training before the crash, 228 people would be alive today."

"Even so, how would those events have helped to support a negative evaluation?" Kathryn asked.

"That event was in my safety report," Darby said. "I was flying the A330 back then and concerned about the lack of training. I had written a blog about how to fly out of a stall because we hadn't received stall training at altitude. I guess they were using that against me to show that the company complied with the airworthiness directive, and trained their pilots, and I had to be crazy to think they did not train me. Part of my memory problems."

"But that was *after* the crash," Kathryn said. "It would have incriminated the company if he understood what he was looking at."

"Exactly. But Dr. Wood is a neophyte who thinks he knows more than he does. We actually debated whether or not manual flight was an emergency."

"I don't need to ask which side you took," Kathryn said with a grin.

"He was defending the Global pilot manager who declared an emergency because he lost his autopilot and autothrust," Darby said, and then she sighed. "Another concern in my report."

"I remember that," Kathryn said.

"This could explain why they were so reactive when I wrote about the Air France crash in my safety report," Darby said. "Rich Clark and George Wyatt killed those passengers by looking the other way. They wanted to silence me." She thought for a minute and then said, "No. They *had to* silence me."

"Can I have a copy of that report?" Kathryn asked.

"Of course. I can even legally give it to you. Anything we get from Dr. Wood isn't protected."

Kathryn pushed her noodles around the plate. "Do you find the irony that the pitot static system failure caused the Air France 447 crash, and it was also the trigger on the 737 MAX crashes, as well?"

Darby did not have to reply, her expression spoke volumes. She stirred her soup slowly, thinking about how easy it would have been to write the airworthiness directive before Air France crashed.

She took a bite of her soup. Despite the warmth she could not shake the chill. The FAA had the information. They could have stopped that accident. Global could have notified the FAA there was a problem with the pitot static system, but they simply did not want to spend the money on training. Exactly like the MAX.

At the end of the day, it cost them exactly as much as it would have in the beginning, but more than two hundred people would be alive if they had been proactive. The very reason for SMS. More than all this, the FAA ignored the ASAP reports that identified there was a problem, just as they had done for those ASAP reports on the MAX.

"How many more people have to die?" Darby finally asked. "This is the very reason we need a safety culture. The very reason SMS was established. What the hell is going on?"

"We're going to find out," Kathryn said.

Darby nodded, but she wasn't so sure. Then she asked, "Do you remember who the FAA administrator was when the Air France crash occurred?"

Chapter 15

Darby's mind was running full speed. Lying on her back she stared at the ceiling instead of sleeping. The vision of Air France falling like a leaf merged with the Boeing MAX crashes. Hundreds of deaths could have been avoided if the regulators would have acted on the ASAP reports for both events. What good was the system if nobody did anything? She rolled over and hugged her pillow.

Something that Kathryn had said bothered her, but she could not put her finger on it. Then there was Dr. Wood and his involvement. *Could he be involved more than just a hired gun?* Darby wondered.

Returning to her back she pondered who at Global was so incompetent to send Dr. Wood the information about the Air France accident. It was almost as ludicrous as giving Wood the transcript from the company's online training session that encouraged pilots to declare an emergency if they lost their autoflight system.

What Darby initially found humorous at the time, now bugged the hell out of her. Dr. Wood's feeble attempt to debate aviation safety as if he were an expert made no sense. He was supposed to be determining if she had a psychological problem. The company had been pushing safety information to him to use against her, but everything they had provided him, in contrast, supported her assertions. His attempt at challenging her was an oddity.

Giving up on sleep, she climbed out of bed and turned her desk lamp on, then reached for her computer. Her stuffed bear sat on the back corner of her desk with his head cocked sideways as if he were wondering what she was doing up at two in the morning.

While her computer came to life, she went to the kitchen and grabbed a bottle of water and a couple ibuprofen. Returning to her desk, she sat in front of the computer and placed another flash drive into the slot.

An hour later she found a document that was an index identifying a list of items Global had provided to Dr. Wood—A through I. Two of the items included the A330 systems failure, and the manual flight transcript. Other items listed included: company emails, CEO communications, social media concerns, Bradshaw books, A330 training manuals, safety report, and her safety presentation.

The sight of Bradshaw books made her smile. With a chuckle she looked at her bear and said, "All advertising is good advertising."

Darby printed the document and then proceeded to find each reference associated with the items listed. An hour later she discovered a FedEx receipt and another chain of emails. This time Darby laughed out loud. They had prepared a notebook for the doctor, four pounds as identified by the receipt, and FedEx had lost it.

She continued to read through the emails. There was sheer panic between the players, but their apparent concern wasn't so much that the book could get into the wrong hands, but that they wouldn't have it for their meeting the following day.

What meeting? Mine? she wondered, checking the date on the shipping label. She had not been scheduled to meet with Dr. Wood for another month. As she continued to read, her eyes narrowed and she whispered, "Those rat bastards."

Regional Director Robert Dodson and Joe Wolfe, the company

labor relations attorney, had traveled to Chicago to meet with Dr. Wood one month before her evaluation. Darby leaned back and folded her arms. She hadn't even received the results of her psych test yet.

Darby stood and walked to the window. She pulled back the curtain, and a movement across the street caught her eye. She stared for a moment but didn't see anything. She dropped the curtain back into place, and returned to her desk and stood there staring at her computer. Drumming her nails on her hips, she questioned what she was missing.

If Wood was meeting with the company assassins *before* he had met with Darby, there was no way this was an authentic evaluation. And the documents Wolfe had sent him to review had nothing to do with her mental health. They were all safety related and had everything to do with her safety report. That had to prove something.

She grabbed her bear and wandered to her bed and sat. Hugging him to her chest, she pulled her legs up close to her body. The bear had been with her for a lifetime and was a good listener. He was the only thing tying her to a past. She had kept him as a reminder that no matter what happened in life, your past did not predict your future. Unfortunately, she was now traveling into the past, back to those dark days of the abyss Global Air Lines had sucked her into. This time, however, she was willing to go into that darkness to uncover the truth.

"Why had they flown all the way to Chicago to meet with that doctor?" she asked. The answer was clear—to support his grandiose ideology assertion of which he attempted to convince her that her safety report was in error. Then she smiled broadly at that thought. The selection of Dodson to educate the doctor on anything aviation was nothing short of asking a rock for swimming lessons.

"You have to know the guy to appreciate the humor in that situation," she said tossing her bear to the side.

Before they had clipped her wings, Darby had asked Dodson who oversaw SMS. He had asked her if she meant social media. Where, in fact, SMS was the acronym for Safety Management Systems, a program that became federal law in January 2018. Global had an FAA-approved SMS system in place four years earlier, yet nobody followed it. She wondered if anyone in management really knew what SMS was.

Darby had intended to provide Dodson a book on the subject, but when she asked him what format he like to read, kindle or paper, he had replied that he didn't have time to read.

Perhaps the guy who had told Darby so many years earlier that you could teach a monkey to fly, but you couldn't teach it to think was in fact speaking of Global management. At the very least, Dodson. Curious as to what else was on the flash drives, Darby returned to her desk and stuck another into the slot. She opened email after email. Her eyelids became heavy, but the more she read the more unbelievable the story became.

She found language where Dr. Wood had told attorney Wolfe and Regional Director Dodson that he had a *strategy* and needed all the Seattle based pilot's flight hours. She found another series of emails that showed Dr. Wood had sent her medical report to Dodson for him to edit. Dodson had taken three cracks at it until he got it right. Right was an interesting term because there was nothing accurate about what he had done.

She continued to read document after document. Another two hours passed, and she was about to give up for the night when she found an invoice. Her heart skipped a beat. She scrolled to the next page and said, "Holy shit!"

Chapter 16

October 14, 2018

THE PHONE RANG, interfering with her dreams that had shifted from planes crashing to gold bars falling from the sky and burying her alive. Darby rolled over and looked at the clock. Sighing, she threw her covers back and dropped her feet to the floor. Having slept the better part of the day, she was glad for the wakeup call. She rubbed her eyes and yawned, then walked to the desk and glanced at the number. Smiling, she left the phone where it was and went to the bathroom to take care of business. Once she returned, she grabbed her phone and pressed dial as she headed downstairs.

"Sorry I missed your call," Darby said. "I was sleeping."

"At two in the afternoon?" Tom said. "Must have been one hell of a party."

"I wish," Darby said, sticking a coffee pod into the machine.

"Playing detective?" he asked, as Darby opened the fridge.

"You guessed it." She poured some cream into a cup and then placed it into the microwave. "I found out how much it costs to buy a fake medical diagnosis."

"More than the thirty-three hundred you paid the Mayo Clinic?"

"A little bit more," Darby said, removing her cup from the microwave and placing it into position on her Keurig. She pressed the start button. "Try seventy-three thousand, nine hundred and twenty-three dollars, and forty-five cents."

"Forty-five cents?" Tom said and then he broke out laughing.

His laughter made Darby laugh too. That was one of the things she loved about him, they were on the same wavelength finding humor in the same obscure thoughts. A bill of that substantiation, Dr. Wood had itemized it down to the cents. Forty-five of them, to be exact.

"Maybe he charges by the second," Darby said, retrieving her cup from the machine.

"This is more extreme than I thought," Tom replied.

"More extreme than sending me poisoned wine?" Darby asked, heading toward the living room with brew in hand.

"Good point," Tom said.

"I'm beginning to believe ignorance is bliss," Darby said. "But it gets better. If you remember… he sent me my diagnosis on December 24th. It turns out that he actually notified the company on October 28th."

"They waited two months to tell you on Christmas Eve?" Tom asked. "I'm really doing all I can to not impact bodily harm to that fucking doctor."

Darby chuckled. "You and me both. But remember, he was only doing what someone paid him to do." Clearly, they were attempting to push her over the edge. Thank God she hadn't drank that wine.

She sat on her couch and brought Tom up to speed on all she had learned throughout the night. The index, the documents, the strategy, and the meeting. When she was done, Tom was silent. Too silent.

"Are you still there?" she asked.

"I am," Tom said. "Just speechless. This will be to your benefit."

"True. But what I can't figure out is why *did* Dr. Wood give us all the incriminating evidence? Did the little parasite think he was above the law, and that it wouldn't impact him? He could have destroyed it."

"He may have thought Global would give it to you, then he'd have to explain why he didn't."

"He could have asked them," Darby said. "They're simply not that bright. None of them."

"The very reason you got your job back," Tom said.

There were a dozen ways they could have gotten away with this if Rich Clark had any brains. What worried her most was that she had no idea how far these guys would go, now that she learned how far they had gone.

"I keep trying to figure out why Clark did this," Darby said.

"The *why* probably doesn't matter," Tom said.

"Maybe not, but there has to be a reason greater than my report," Darby said. "Or maybe he simply has the psychosis of a rapist and gets off screwing people professionally."

"There could be more truth to that than you think," Tom said. "With a rapist, it's the control and power that excites them, more so than the act of sex. Without that feeling of power, the rapist becomes impotent. They can only get aroused by attacking and controlling."

"Hmmm. So, Clark might have to screw his employees, or he feels emasculated."

"Something like that," Tom said with chuckle.

"This makes complete sense," Darby said, slapping an open palm to her forehead. "The conclusion being… airline executives are screwing their employees because that's the only way they can get off."

"You could be onto a new executive profile," Tom said with a laugh.

"Technically Clark is not only a rapist, but he's also prostitute," Darby said with a grin.

"How's that?"

"He's screwing people without their permission, but he's also making a lot of money while doing it," Darby said. "I'm just curious who the heck his pimp is."

"Joking aside," Tom said, "the truth is most CEOs are sociopaths."

"Then Rich Clark could be a CEO," Darby said. "I only hope that Walter Croft defies that profile."

"You'll find out tomorrow," Tom said.

"How so?"

"If the judge gives you permission to depose him and they don't settle, then he could be the worst kind of sociopath."

"What kind is that?"

"The kind with connections in very high places."

Chapter 17

October 15, 2018

MONDAY MORNING WAS slow to arrive and Darby jumped on it before daybreak. Rubbing sleep from her eyes, she sent Robert a text to see if he had time to chat before their conference call. Her phone rang seconds later. Robert's excitement overflowed. He had found the golden ticket overnight that should make today's event a slam dunk. She feigned enthusiasm, despite not liking what it had to say.

"Can we use it?" Darby asked.

"I sent a copy to Judge Geraghty's paralegal this morning," Robert said. "It's on his desk, so we'll see."

Darby briefed Robert on everything she had learned over the weekend. What became most apparent was that Global had not provided any of the documentation in discovery that Dr. Wood had provided. Global was in contempt of court. Most, if not all, of the documents that had been sent to Dr. Wood originated from a Global employee. Those documents should have been duplicated in Global's discovery, but Robert had none of it in the files that he reviewed over the weekend.

Had Wood been as deceptive as Global management, they never would have known the details of how corrupt Global Air Lines' management really was, or how far they had gone in their efforts to permanently remove her. Dr. Wood was nothing short of a hit man and Global had employed him. He was also either incompetent or so arrogant that he believed he could not be touched, despite his turning over his gun with the bullets, and telling them who paid for the hit, and how much they paid.

"I still hope Croft is not part of this," Darby said. "Clark could have just lied to him about what was going on."

"There's one way to find out," Robert said. "You ready to go?"

"Yep." She breathed deep. "Ready as I'll ever be."

They said their goodbyes and Darby found a seat on the edge of her fireplace and waited. She wondered what kind of person the judge was. *Would he be fair? Would he favor the corporation? Would he talk more or listen?* Her alarm rang on her phone, startling her. She silenced it and then dialed in.

There were already two callers on the line when she connected. As Robert had advised her, everyone stated their names. She texted Robert and told him she was on. Robert then said, "Attorney Robert Allen here for the Complainant, Darby Bradshaw, who is also on the line listening."

The other attorneys came on board. Once everyone had checked in, a woman said, "Residing is honorable Judge Patrick G. Geraghty."

"Who do we have on the call?" Geraghty asked.

All parties introduced themselves, but Darby remained silent as Robert introduced her.

"Mr. Kowalski, you asked for this conference call prior to my ruling, therefore, I think it only befitting that you begin," Geraghty said, his voice authoritative and all business.

"Thank you, your honor," Wendel Kowalski began. "As I wrote in my motion, the Complainant cannot show that Mr. Croft has the type of unique, personal, and non-cumulative knowledge required for an apex witness deposition. Indeed, she has not presented any basis for suggesting that Mr. Croft had any involvement in the decision to refer Ms. Bradshaw for a Section 8 evaluation—the sole issue before this Tribunal.

"Mr. Croft was not present during any meetings during which the possible referral of Complainant to the Section 8 process was discussed. Mr. Croft *did not* communicate with Dr. Marsh, Dr. Wood, or any other medical examiners. Not only did Mr. Croft never communicate with Ms. Abbott, whose report triggered the Section 8 process, but he never personally met or spoke in-person with the Complainant or communicated substantively in writing with Complainant regarding her safety concerns or her Section 8 referral. While certainly not required here, Mr. Croft can provide an affidavit attesting to these facts and others that could conceivably demonstrate his lack of unique, personal, and relevant knowledge."

"Is that all?" Judge Geraghty asked. His voice was deep and firm, but with a pleasantness about it that Darby liked.

"Well, uh… I would also like to add that Mr. Croft is the CEO. He is responsible for Global operations and 86,000 employees ensuring safe passage for passengers worldwide. Requiring Mr. Croft to participate in a deposition or hearing is completely unnecessary, unduly burdensome, and would adversely divert his extremely limited and valuable time away from managing the Respondent's operation. More so, the Complainant's sole basis for seeking to depose Mr. Croft stems from her unsolicited emails to him. You would never expect to bring Lee Iacocca into a deposition for an issue with one of their thousands of employees."

"He's so full of shit," Darby said, and then froze. She looked at her phone. Her heart skipped a few beats before she realized she had in fact muted it. *Thank God,* she thought.

"Your points are taken sir," Judge Geraghty said. "Mr. Allen, what do you have to add?"

"Thank you, your honor. This situation is not remotely comparable to seeking to depose Lee Iacocca because Chrysler failed to competently design a car. In that case, you would beeline to the engineer. That's not the case here. Ms. Bradshaw submitted a Safety Report exceeding 40 pages and Mr. Croft received that report and thanked her for it. Mr. Croft requested that his subordinates George Wyatt and Rich Clark brief him with respect to that report."

Where Wendel's voice was pleading with an element of whine, Robert's was assertive and professional. Wendel reminded Darby of an ankle biter who barked because he could, but whimpered if you looked at him wrong. Robert also had a natural kindness to his voice as well.

"A primary focus of Ms. Bradshaw's safety report," Robert said, "was Global's failure to comply with its SMS obligations and Mr. Croft was the person responsible for SMS compliance. Ms. Bradshaw and Mr. Croft exchanged correspondence, which he concluded by stating—*Good to hear from you. Looking forward to many great chapters for us to write.*

"My client and Mr. Croft exchanged correspondence regarding her safety report, which he concluded by stating—*I would appreciate seeing the report and will be sure to follow up. Walt.* Then on November 23rd Mr. Croft had a meeting with Mr. Clark regarding Ms. Bradshaw, the day *after* she had met with Ms. Abbott. Your honor, this was eight days *prior to* the meeting in which Mr. Clark allegedly heard the facts and made his decision."

"I object your honor!" Wendel snapped, and Darby jumped.

"You object to the CEO having a meeting with Mr. Clark?"

Judge Geraghty asked, and Darby smiled. She really liked this judge.

"No Sir. I object to Mr. Allen withholding the document identifying the meeting, and then blindsiding us with it. It's not fair," Wendel said.

"Your honor," this is Mr. Allen. "I am a one man show here. Mr. Kowalski delayed getting us the discovery items for three weeks. Furthermore, they were not Bates stamped. I am doing the best I can under these unbelievable circumstances."

Robert took a breath before he added, "And your honor, I would like to remind the tribunal that this memo was delivered by and originated from Global. We could hardly blindside them with a document that they provided us."

"Three points for the good guys," Darby said, staring at the memo that Robert had found while he was going through Global's discovery. The very document that broke her heart because it screamed that Croft was part of this. And yet, Rich Clark could have lied to him during that meeting. She prayed that was the case.

Apparently Global did not sanitized their documents as well as they thought they had prior to producing them in discovery. Robert had found the proverbial needle in a haystack, where the CEO requested a meeting with Rich Clark and an SVP corporate attorney. Subject matter—Darby Bradshaw.

All parties concurred they would be available. A meeting that occurred the day after Darby had met with Abbott, but well before Abbott had reported Darby's alleged behavior to her management team.

"I will accept this document," Judge Geraghty said. "Please continue Mr. Allen."

"We have a Section 8 letter in draft and dated on December 15th, but the delivery of that letter was delayed until December 19th. The purported reason was to allow Mr. Dodson, the Regional Director to deliver that letter personally. However, he claimed to Ms. Bradshaw that he had no knowledge of why the decision had been made. Yet, the day *before* the Section 8 letter was delivered, Mr. Croft was having correspondence with Global's attorneys designated as—Privileged communication between client and counsel containing legal advice regarding Global's response to Complainant's communications with Flight Operations."

"Anything else Mr. Allen?" Judge Geraghty asked.

"Yes, your honor," Robert said. "It's perfectly clear that Mr. Croft had knowledge in that he asked to be briefed. That memo indicates that he was briefed. He was also part of an adverse diagnosis. A personal card that Ms. Bradshaw had sent to Mr. Croft with the safety report that *he* requested, was used against her. Dr. Wood used Ms. Bradshaw's and Mr. Croft's correspondence as a part of the foundation for mis-diagnosis, when he stated she had 'undue familiarity' in addressing Mr. Croft as Walt, even though this was how Mr. Croft ended his emails to her."

"Very well," Judge Geraghty said.

"Your honor, this is Kowalski, again. Depending on your decision, we would like to request an opportunity to write another motion based on the new information received today."

"Mr. Kowalski, we are here to provide *you* the courtesy to have your voice heard," Judge Geraghty said. "The only new information I have heard today is the existence of this memo, and communications between Ms. Bradshaw and the CEO as part of her medical diagnosis. I will not grant you the ability to file another motion if in fact *you* do not like my ruling based on your display here today."

"Of course, your honor," Kowalski said, softening his tone. "But I simply have to emphasize that Mr. Croft is a busy man, and this targeting him by the Complainant is nothing short of harassment. As I stated he has 86,000 employees he must deal with daily, and as the CEO he is far too busy."

"Sir," Judge Geraghty barked. "You've made your point. However. I would like to know why a man with 86,000 employees spent thirty minutes regarding one of them. I rule in favor of the Complainant and will grant a deposition of CEO, Walter Croft. However, this will be limited to three hours, and will occur in Oklahoma City. Mr. Kowalski, he will make himself available in a reasonable amount of time."

Chapter 18

Paris France
October 20, 2018

If anything could go wrong, it did. Despite arriving two hours late into Paris, with an extended 90-minute drive to their hotel, their rooms hadn't been ready. Yet, an hour later the challenges were all but forgotten.

"Thanks for giving me the landing," Darby said, toasting her mug to captain Bob, and then toward Roger the other first officer. She had forgotten how much she missed layovers with a good crew.

"The company owes you a lot of landings," Bob said, dipping a fry into the mayonnaise. "It's hard to believe they went as far as they did."

"Rich Clark's a fucking asshole," Roger said. "I'm glad you stood up to him. It's about time somebody busted his balls."

"I'd kind of like to put his little girl balls under a pair of my stilettos, and add full weight," Darby said. "Maybe do a little happy dance."

Bob cringed, and then he laughed. "Remind me not to get you pissed off at me."

They were across the street from the crew hotel at the Canadian Embassy. The bar reminded her of college days when everyone hung out at a bar named *The Library*. There was one major difference—this group was older and flew airplanes for a living. The bar was loud with about a dozen guests filling the not-so-large room. By the look of it, all flight crew.

She and her crew were tired, and an early dinner and to bed sounded like heaven to Darby. But in Paris it was difficult to find a restaurant serving before 7 p.m. Their very excuse for stopping for a beer or two before a proper dinner.

"I'm confused," Roger said. "Why didn't they agree to settle?"

Darby dipped her fry into the mayo and shrugged. "The hell if I know. Maybe Croft knew nothing about this, and he wants to prove it."

"Don't count on it," Bob said. "If he met with Clark, he knows exactly what went down. More than that, he was probably part of it."

"Clark could have lied to him," Darby said, and stuck the fry into her mouth, still hoping that Croft was a good guy. "When we depose him, we'll be able to show him that Clark premeditated this, that the company paid that doctor seventy-four grand, *and* that Dodson and Global's labor relations attorney, Wolfe, met with the doctor for the purpose of nailing me."

"If he didn't know before, he will after," Roger said.

Darby nodded. "Once he learns the truth, he'll end it."

"Don't count on that," Roger said. "With marketing involved anything could happen."

Then Bob said, "I think you have an admirer."

Darby glanced sideways. There were several guys standing at the bar talking loudly. A couple were seated eating burgers. There was one guy sitting at the far end, alone. "The one at the end?" Darby asked. "Drinking what appears to be a coke?"

"Yeah. He's looked your way a dozen times," Bob said.

"Good taste," Roger said, and winked at Darby.

"He might be checking you out." Darby waggled her eyebrows toward him.

"Like I said, good taste," Roger said, raising his beer.

"Is he one of ours?" Bob asked. "I don't recognize him."

"Me neither," Darby said.

Roger turned and looked over his shoulder. Then waved a hand at the guy and returned his attention to his beer. "That's Stan Branson. An ALPO guy. He's the chairman of the HIMS program."

"Finding drunk pilots for his program?" Darby said.

"ALPO should've helped you," Bob said. He emptied his glass and raised three fingers to the bartender.

"It wasn't only that they didn't help," Darby said. "ALPO filled the straight jacket with bricks, then watched Clark push me into the river."

"Global owns this union," Roger said. "They always have."

"Been here for thirty years and nothing's changed," Bob said. "Nobody notices because they take care of the little disputes. Anything big, it's whatever the company wants."

"Why?" Darby asked, as the bartender arrived with the second round. She tossed back her first beer and handed him the empty mug. She thanked the waiter and Bob, and then asked, "What do they hope to gain by forming an alliance with management versus helping the pilots?"

"Don't you know?" Roger said sarcastically. "They're working with the company for the greater good of the overall membership." He raised his beer and said, "They forgot one point." And then lifted his beer to his lips and drank.

"What point's that?" Darby finally asked, when she thought Roger lost his train of thought.

"They're required to represent each pilot not just the group."

"You're giving them too much credit," Bob said. "Most of those guys are vying for management positions. Play nice with management as a union guy and get recycled into a Global manager for three times the pay."

Darby grinned, as her crew discussed the fornication of management with the pilots while the union representatives rolled around in bed with them. She realized that maybe Tom's and her conversation, the other morning, might not have been too far off.

They drank their beer and shifted the conversation to the pending contract. All the time Darby kept a watchful eye on the guy at the bar. She glanced his way, and they exchanged a smile. He *was* watching her.

"You guys ready to go eat?" Bob asked.

"Why don't you go ahead. I'm going to see if I can get my admirer to rat out the union."

If Global wanted to push forward with depositions, then she could use all the information she could find. Besides, the fact that the union could be part of this haunted her. Darby figured an admirer with insider knowledge would be easy to crack.

"Be careful with that," Roger said.

"I will. But would you mind poking your head in here on your way back to the hotel to see if I'm still here?"

"Of course," Bob said. "Better yet, why don't you just wait for us. We'll be back in an hour or so and walk you to the hotel."

"Thanks, I'd like that," Darby said. "I'll grab something here."

The guys walked out the door, and Darby headed over to the bar and stood by Stan. "Mind if I join you?"

"It's my pleasure," he said extending a hand toward the stool to his right.

The bartender slid down the bar and asked, "What can I get for you?"

"How about two cheeseburgers with frites," Darby said.

"How do you keep your figure eating like that?" Stan asked.

Darby laughed. "One of them is for you. I hate to eat alone."

"Then I'm buying you a drink. What do you like?" he asked.

"What are you drinking?"

"Diet coke."

"Perfect." Darby turned toward the bartender and waved. When he returned, she ordered the sodas. Then returned her attention to Stan. Extending her hand, she said, "Darby Bradshaw, it's nice to meet you, Stan."

He shook her hand and said, "How did you know my name?"

"Roger, one of the guys I'm flying with said you were one of the good ones at ALPO. It's nice to see and very nice to meet you."

"I'm not fucking one of the good ones," he said. "I'm a gutless, spineless…."

"Dickless?" Darby added interrupting him.

He placed his hand into his crotch. "Nope, don't qualify on that one," he said with a huge laugh. Then he said, solemnly "I'm sorry for what they did to you."

"Who? The company or our union?" Darby asked turning toward him. She placed her right elbow on the bar and her put face in her hand. She tilted her head slightly and gave him a slow smile.

He stared into her eyes and then quietly said, "Both."

The bartender brought their Cokes, and Darby up-righted, and lifted her glass. "Cheers."

They toasted and he asked her how this had all started. She told him the Reader's Digest version—she'd given a safety report to Wyatt and Clark, and they retaliated by giving her a mental health evaluation and paid a doctor a very large sum of money for a negative diagnosis.

Stan told her that the stories he'd heard were sketchy and none of it made sense. She was answering his questions as their burgers arrived.

"This is great. Thank you," he said after taking the first bite. "I am *really* sorry the union screwed you over."

Darby almost choked on her burger. She wanted to record him, but the room was too loud and there was no way she could do it without his knowing. She also had to tread lightly. But the lack of sleep and a double beer might have impacted the light steps.

"Why didn't they help?" she asked.

He took another bite of his burger and assessed her a moment. "Clark gave Joey P. the thumbs down."

"Thumbs down?"

"Yeah. Kind of like a wink, wink, we're here to help," he said, "while you bend over and we stick it up your ass."

Joseph Patolee, or Joey P. as he was called, was the National President of ALPO, and a Global pilot. He was also friends with Clark. Good friends.

"Did they ever say why the thumbs down?" Darby asked.

"No. I knew they were giving you the screw job. I feel like a shit for not doing anything. I kept telling myself that if they got away with it, I would speak out. But when you got your job back, then thought it didn't matter."

"It does matter," Darby said. "Doesn't it?"

He pulled his attention from his glass, and looked into her eyes. "Yes. It does."

"You can do something about it now," Darby said. "You could testify for me in court."

"Court?" he said. "That would be the end of my career."

"It wouldn't," Darby said. "If you testify in an AIR21 case, that's protected activity. If they do anything to you, then you're also protected under federal law. If we subpoena you, the company even has to buy your trip. But you would be completely protected."

Darby hoped she sounded convincing. The truth was, Global did not follow the law and neither did ALPO. Unfortunately, she also knew that the AIR21 statute did not extend to the union. At least she didn't think so. They made laws of their own.

"There's so much more you need to know," Stan said under his breath. He stared into his drink and then added, "Count me in."

"Count you in for what?"

Darby and Stan both turned their heads toward the voice. Stan stiffened ever so slightly, but enough for Darby to notice. He returned his attention to his hamburger. Darby looked from Stan to the man.

"Hey, I'm Darby Bradshaw," she said extending her hand to the man. "Do you want to join us?"

"Joe Patolee," he said, not accepting her hand. "No, thank you." He glanced at Stan's glass on the bar, and then turned toward Darby. "Nice to meet you, sweetheart." He smiled an unsettling grin. She watched him walk out of the bar and returned her attention to Stan.

"That was our national union president?" Darby said. "What a putz. Not to mention, he's a rude condescending ass."

"A powerful putz," Stan said with a chuckle.

"Being the chairman of the HIMS program doesn't prevent you from being at the bar, does it?" Darby said. "We'll just copy the bar tab and show that you were drinking coke."

"That's not it," he said with a slow smile. "Timing is everything."

"Would you just talk to my attorney?" Darby asked. "He's really a good guy and you can trust him. We probably won't even go to trial. I'm just trying to gather all the information possible so this doesn't happen to anyone again, and to fix our union in the process."

Stan sighed and made no response. Instead, he ate his hamburger in silence. Darby did the same. She'd said all she could, and now it would be up to him. She only hoped he would do the right thing.

He finished his burger and then asked the waiter for the bill.

When Darby reached for it, he grabbed it.

"I've got this." He gave the bartender his credit card, and turned toward her and said, "I'd love to meet your attorney and tell him all that I know. I'm sure he'll be pleasantly surprised. Besides, the toothpaste is out of the tube, and we can't put it back in."

Chapter 19

Oklahoma City
October 23, 2018

GOD HELP ME if this is to be my new reality for the next four months, Darby thought. Her phone alarm was blaring from across the room, while she thought about where the heck she was. Then her eyes popped open, and she squinted at the clock. Thank God she had not overslept. Only two hours until she would meet Robert for a 7 a.m. breakfast before their first deposition.

Oh God. I need more sleep, she thought, rolling out of bed, and dropping to the floor. She crawled to the desk and reached up and grabbed her phone, then silenced the alarm. Turning, she sat on the floor and leaned against the dresser with her hands covering her face.

"You can do this," she told herself, and sucked a deep breath and pushed to her feet. She walked across the room and dug through her suitcase for her exercise clothes.

Two days earlier she sat in the jumpseat as the third pilot during their landing into Los Angeles, then rushed out of the flight deck as fast as possible. She cleared customs quickly and ran to her Seattle flight. She was lucky and got a seat. Arriving late, she dumped her laundry into the washer and then fell into bed. The day had been 22 hours, followed by sleep that wasn't even a legal domestic crew rest.

Waking early the next morning, she had put the laundry in the dryer and grabbed a quick workout. Then she rushed to pack her suitcase, this time with business attire. She drove to the airport, but her first flight cancelled. The next flight was oversold, and she ended up sitting in the jumpseat to Oklahoma City. She'd arrived late and fell into bed. Five hours later, her alarm had gone off.

Darby finished tying her tennis shoes, grabbed her stack of papers, and headed out the door. Two hours later she walked into the hotel restaurant in a pair of black pants, white shirt, black blazer, and a cute pair of heels. Robert was at a far table. His glasses were low on his nose, and he was writing on the legal pad in front of him. She headed his way.

She pulled out a chair and sat. After ordering an egg-white spinach omelet with salsa, Darby lifted her recently-filled coffee mug to her lips. *Heaven*, she thought, waiting for Robert to finish whatever it was he was working on.

"How are you feeling?" Robert asked, finally assessing her.

"Better now," she said raising her coffee cup ever so slightly. "If I purchased a revenue ticket to fly to these depositions, would they reimburse me when we win?"

"Absolutely," Robert said. "I have to say I'm surprised the ALPO representative is going to talk. Depending on what he says, you'll have a DFR prospect."

"A DFR?"

"Duty of fair representation," Robert said. "I never take those cases. They are difficult to prove because the crime isn't poor representation, it's lack of representation. I'm not recommending that route… but their behavior is appalling."

Darby sipped her coffee and then said, "He's joining us for dinner tonight so you can talk to him."

"Wonderful," Robert said. "Did you have a chance to read the final questions?"

"I did," Darby said as the waitress arrived with their breakfast. "I finished this morning at the gym. I think you've covered it all."

Darby and Robert had spent endless-hours preparing deposition questions based on discovery. She appreciated that he allowed her to be part of the process, more than he could have known.

Robert prepared a litany of questions he would have in front of him. He'd told her that by the end of the day they would both be exhausted, and he did not want to leave anything out. She was excited to witness her first deposition. Experiencing this process as an observer would also make it much easier when she was in the hot seat, something she was not looking forward to.

George Wyatt was first on the list. Darby wondered if he knew that Global had inadvertently given them Clark's email notifying him of their Section 8 plans. The legal team had been unaware of the CEO's memo pushed her direction, perhaps this would be the same. Either way, it would be fun to watch him squirm.

"If they'd Bates stamped that first set of documents, I don't think they would have given us Clark's email to Wyatt," Darby said, sticking a fork into her omelet. "They would have seen it and removed it."

"I agree," Robert said. "Or the memo that gave us Croft on a platter. I'm beginning to think their legal team is sloppy."

"Corrupt *and* sloppy," Darby said. "Global should have given us the same documents that Dr. Wood provided since everything originated from Global. "That has to be illegal."

Darby had gone through hell scanning and locating documents to ensure she gave them everything she had. But Global had given them next to nothing, other than company manuals.

"They are in violation of the court order," Robert said.

"Then why can't we get them for that?" Darby asked.

"Our focus is on your case. It wouldn't be worth the time because there is nothing to be gained. They know that."

What a screwed-up system, Darby thought. "Makes it difficult for anyone to get justice."

"Perhaps," Robert said. "Regardless, Dr. Wood gave us enough ammunition to take them out."

"Then let's go fire some of it," Darby said with a grin.

Chapter 20

Oklahoma City
SVP George Wyatt Retired
Deposition
October 23, 2018

Darby wondered if there was a legal defense termed justifiable assault. She wanted to walk over and smack Wyatt in the face, and then ask him why the hell they did this to her. Instead, she took the high road and said, "How's retirement treating you?"

"Great," Wyatt said. "We just had our first grandchild. Six months old and so much fun. My daughter and son-in-law are living with us while they remodel their home, so we get to spend a lot of time with him."

"I bet your wife is in heaven," Darby said.

"She is."

They took their seats. Darby sat to the right of Robert on one side of the table. The court reporter was to his left at the end of the table. To the left of the reporter, on the opposite side of the table from Darby and Robert, sat George Wyatt. Next to Wyatt sat one of their attorneys, Johnson Von Dietrich. If Darby didn't know any better, Johnson literally had a stick up his ass holding him upright, in which he was feeling the pain and afraid to move. He was more tense than anyone she'd ever met. He was also a very angry young man with a permanent scowl etched into his forehead.

To his left was Wendel Kowalski. Leaning back in his chair in a loose-fitting suit, he looked like a little boy dressing up in Daddy's clothes. Darby grinned. He was exactly as she'd pictured him when he told the judge he wasn't being fair. Sitting beside Wendel was a Global corporate attorney, Martha Jones. *The wicked bitch of the West,* Darby thought. Emails didn't lie and Martha had worked closely with Clark to set her up from the get-go. If there was justice, her broom would burn with her on it.

The court reporter gathered everyone's business cards to obtain the correct spelling of their names. Stacks of exhibits were piled a foot high, in triplicate, on the table in front of Robert. A legal pad was situated in front of Darby. Armed with a pen, she was ready to take notes and write follow-up questions as needed.

The reporter swore Wyatt in. He was officially under oath.

Robert said, "Good morning. My name is Robert Allen. I represent Darby Bradshaw in this matter. Today I'm going to ask you questions which you will be responding to under oath concerning her AIR21 action against Global Air Lines. Do you understand that?"

"Yes," Wyatt said, looking far too relaxed.

"Do you understand that the deposition today is going to be transcribed by the court reporter and that everything you say here today will be recorded?"

"Yes."

Robert advised him to speak slowly and clearly. Told him all responses were to be verbal. Explained that if there was anything he didn't understand, he should ask for clarification. Robert asked him if he understood that his testimony would be under oath, as if he were in a court of law. Wyatt did.

"If you subsequently testify in a different manner before the court or tribunal, we will use this deposition to impeach your testimony. Do you understand that?"

"Yes."

"Objection," Von Dietrich said, then spoke directly to Wyatt. "And wait just a moment before answering just in case I have an objection. You can answer if I object. If I state do not answer, then don't."

As if Von Dietrich hadn't said a word, Robert continued unfazed by the interruption. He questioned Wyatt on his participation in the company arbitration process.

"Do you recall if there have been any credibility assessments of your testimony by arbitrators that were negative?"

"Objection," Von Dietrich said. "Vague. Calls for a legal conclusion."

"I have no knowledge of that," Wyatt said. "I don't read the arbitration decisions at issue after I've participated in the arbitration process."

"Have you ever lost your temper at work?" Robert asked

"Objection," Von Dietrich said.

Von Dietrich was not going to make it through the day if he didn't relax. His eyes were bulging. He stared at the table, intently listening to every word. With each objection he didn't even remove his eyes from the spot on the table. He just spat the words.

"No," Wyatt answered. Darby eyes widened. She doubted that statement.

"Have you ever addressed a co-worker with profanity?"

"On occasion," Wyatt said.

"Can you recall any of those instances?"

"No. Not specifically," Wyatt said.

A slow smile spread across her face. He'd never lost his temper, but he had used profanity.

"Have you ever cried at work?" Robert asked.

"No. Well, I will rephrase that. I was emotional when I announced my retirement."

Darby thought Wyatt was going to cry just mentioning it. She was sure Robert assumed as much, too. He glanced down looking away from Wyatt to his list of questions, more than likely giving Wyatt a moment to compose himself.

Von Dietrich's eyes didn't waiver from the spot on the table. The urge to reach in front of him and pretend to wipe away the imaginary spot that he was glued to was overwhelming. She glanced to Wendel who theatrically looked at his watch and rolled his eyes at Robert's delay. Martha texted. Robert paid no attention to any of their antics.

"Are you familiar, or have you heard of the AIR21 statute?" Robert finally asked.

"Yes."

"What do you understand the AIR21 statute to provide?"

"Objection. Calls for legal testimony."

"I'm not intimately familiar with the statute. I know that it is, in general, it protects anyone who is raising concerns from a whistleblower standpoint."

Darby glanced at Wendel. He and Martha were both texting as if sitting casually on a bus. Neither appeared to be paying attention. She wondered if they were texting each other. Robert then asked Wyatt if he was taking drugs or was suffering from any illness that might affect his ability to testify. He wasn't.

"Did you review any documents to prepare for your deposition today?"

"Yes. With counsel."

"What documents did you review?"

"Ms. Bradshaw's initial complaint."

"When you say Ms. Bradshaw's initial complaint, are you referring to her AIR21 complaint?"

"Yes."

"Can you recall any of the other documents."

"Let me think. There was Global's response to the initial complaint. There was the OSHA ruling. And then there had been some additional… I think, as part of this proceeding, some additional protected activity that had been outlined. I also went back to the report that Darby went over with Captain Clark and myself."

"The written safety report?" Robert asked, while Darby wrote on her pad—additional protected activity.

"Yes. Yes. Again, not in great detail but… just sort of. I looked at the outline and other documents to refresh my memory in terms of timeline of how things occurred."

Robert continued to ask questions. Von Dietrich stared and objected over and over again. If his objections had been sneezes, he was having one hell of an allergic reaction to this process. The interesting thing was that each objection was all but ignored. They were simply being recorded on the transcript so the judge would decide at a later date what could be allowed.

"What was the position you held prior to your retirement?" Robert asked.

"Senior vice president, director of flight operation," Wyatt said.

Wyatt proceeded to give his experience from the military and the positions he held at Global. He specified his type ratings and flight experience. He didn't have much flight time, which Darby noted. But he held a few high-ranking positions in the military. At least on paper he sounded impressive. Darby had heard far too many stories, and they would soon learn if some were real. Robert had leaned back and removed his glasses as he listened.

Replacing his glasses, Robert asked, "While you were holding any of the commander positions, were you familiar with the phrase and usage, quote, I can't make it longer, but I can make it harder?"

"Objection."

"That was not... I'm familiar with that phrase. Yes. But it was not associated with any of those positions."

"What does that phrase mean to you?" Robert asked.

"That was a... I was in the last all male class at the Air Force academy. And there was a group of cadets my senior year. There was a controversy associated with our class ring on what was... uh what was going to be on our class ring. And there was a group that was upset by the decision of the commandant to mandate a change in the design. And they put essentially a poster up on the academy grounds, and they were disciplined for that."

Darby grinned at his account of the details. She wished she had a copy of that *poster* to submit into evidence. It was a drawing on a bedsheet that hung over a railing with a sketch of the commanding officer with a nose, a rather large nose in the shape of penis with glasses on top. The boys had displayed it over the courtyard.

"What does that saying refer to?" Robert asked.

"That refers to... that was a dig at the commandant of cadets that, uh... the graduation date was coming up, and it was already set. And, you know, essentially, I can make your experience more difficult. But the timeline is what it is. We are all going to graduate and go on after that. It was in very poor taste, but that was what the message was about."

"How would a position, or a person in that position make it harder?" Robert asked.

"I don't recall."

Like hell you don't recall, Darby thought.

"During your service, were you familiar with the acronym LCWB?"

"Yes," Wyatt said, a tinge of red working around his neck.

"What did that mean?"

"That means… well, that was the design that had been on our class ring. And again, not in the best taste. But it stands for last class with balls."

Not in the best taste was an understatement, Darby thought, but it was kind of funny. Then she looked at Von Dietrich waiting for an objection that did not come. *Interesting*, she thought. Maybe he didn't want that flagged for the judge. She jotted a note on her pad.

Robert's attention returned to the list of questions in front of him. He lined through a couple, flipped the page, and then looked up.

"Would you agree that your total number of flight hours are substantially less than the average Global pilot of 10 years tenure with the airline?" Robert asked.

"Objection. Asked and answered."

When the hell was that asked and answered? Darby wondered.

"My hours are certainly less than if I had flown the line for my entire career. Yes."

"Would you agree that that makes you less qualified to render opinions on flight operational issues than pilots who have more hours than you?"

"No."

Dr. Wood had used a strategy to diminish her ability to write a safety report since she had fewer flight hours than the other captains in the Seattle base, because she had been on reserve. Everyone knew that time in the seat did not give you a greater amount of knowledge. Robert's goal was to have the Senior VP at the airline affirm that.

"Can you explain why the answer is no?"

"Experience is important," Wyatt spoke with more assertion than when he began. "But, you know, beyond a certain point, you know, I have always maintained my qualifications and currency throughout my tenure and have the benefit of benchmarking flight operations and safety programs not only within the U.S. but around the world. So, I think I offer a perspective that more than compensates for the fact that I wasn't flying a regular schedule."

Interesting, Darby thought. She had not expected him to be defensive of his limited experience. He was either proud or very insecure.

"Did you ever have direct communications with the CEOs, Walter Croft or Lawrence Patrick?" Robert asked.

Von Dietrich interrupted. "I will just say we have been going about an hour. If you are going to switch to a whole new topic, it might be a good time for a break."

"Are we going to take a break every hour?" Robert asked, incredulously.

Wendel shifted in his seat, and Martha's fingers tapped her phone like little birds picking at seed. Von Dietrich's glare shifted from the table directly to Robert for the first time that morning. Darby found his death glare amusing.

"Okay. Maybe just two questions," Robert said, and then looked directly at Wyatt. "Did you know that Ms. Bradshaw, during her psychiatric examination, was kept in a locked room for six hours without a break?"

"Objection. Foundation," Von Dietrich snapped.

"No," Wyatt said, looking at Darby. "I did not."

"You need a break?" Robert asked. "How long do you need?"

Chapter 21

They returned to the room after a short break, and everyone took their seats. Darby grabbed a Diet Pepsi from the mini fridge and handed Robert a bottle of water. Once everyone was in position the court reporter put them back on the record.

"Did you ever have direct communications with the CEOs, Walter Croft or Lawrence Patrick?"

"Yes. Lawrence Patrick, before he was… uh before he passed. And Walter Croft and I would have, on occasion direct contact."

"In general, what would you communicate with the CEOs about?"

"Objection. Overbroad."

"Anything that they wanted to communicate about or anything that I felt I needed," Wyatt said, shifting in his seat. "Now, when I was doing that, I *always* made sure that, you know, my boss knew what I was communicating about."

"Can you describe the types of communications that you would take directly to either CEO?"

"Objection. Assumes facts not in evidence. Overbroad."

Oh my God. Darby thought. She wished Von Dietrich would just shut the hell up.

"Well, certainly when I decided to retire, I spent some time with Walt. He was the first one that I talked to about that decision and the considerations for, you know, what I thought the roadmap should look like going forward," Wyatt said.

The roadmap? Darby thought. *Why would the CEO be involved with Wyatt's retirement planning?*

"Anything else?" Robert asked.

"There were, as I recall, there were one or two occasions that came up where Mr. Croft had just referred issues back to me. I believe, or as I recall, these were emails from Darby to Walt. And… so he just wanted to make sure that we had, that we were handling everything appropriately." Wyatt glanced at Darby, and then said, "And it was not that, uh… anytime I would ever hear from a line pilot I would talk directly to the CEO, you know, he would make sure that I was aware and that we were handling whatever the issue was."

"Did Mr. Croft ever communicate to you or Mr. Clark, a request that he be briefed about issues that Ms. Bradshaw was raising?"

"Yes."

"Did you brief him on the issues related to Ms. Bradshaw?"

"In a very general way, yes."

"What did you say to him about the Section 8 process?"

"Objection. Foundation," Von Dietrich snapped.

"I didn't say anything specifically about the Section 8 process to him. I just told him that we had… we were working through an issue with one of our pilots and that we were handling it in accordance with the processes that we had in the pilot contract and also, you know, making sure that the operation was going to be… to be safe and that we were, uh… we were handling the situation. It was not… I don't normally talk about individual employee issues with the CEO."

"But in this case, you did?" Robert said.

"Just in response to his question."

If they didn't have him before, they had them now.

Robert continued to ask more questions regarding what Wyatt spoke about with the CEO. They had been talking about her, but Wyatt would not share specifics. There was no reason the CEO of an airline should be discussing her with Wyatt regarding anything.

"What were your responsibilities in your position?" Robert asked.

"I was responsible for, most importantly, the safety of our daily operations, particularly as they pertain to the flight deck but also the interfaces with the other operating departments. I was responsible for the training and standardization of our pilots and the planning and resources and scheduling of the flight crews to execute the network schedule," Wyatt said. He sat upright as he discussed his many responsibilities.

Robert listened intently and nodded as Wyatt spoke, silently encouraging him to continue. Wyatt complied.

"And then I was also the chief labor negotiator with the Airline Pilots Organization," Wyatt continued. "So, I worked very closely with the labor relations department to work with the pilots' union on a whole range of issues."

"In that position, did you interface with the FAA?" Robert asked.

"Yes," Wyatt said lowering his voice. He glanced to Von Dietrich, whose eyes remained glued to the table.

"With respect to what issues?" Robert asked.

"A couple of… several different ways. In Washington, I interfaced with the FAA, at times, all the way up to the administrator level on issues about, you know, how Global is doing with respect to our daily operations in the air traffic control system and the, you know, any regulatory or compliance matters that we had. But on a day-to-day basis, I generally worked with the Global certificate management office here in Oklahoma City. And we will refer to that as the GCO."

"What did you interface with the GCO about?"

"We would have monthly meetings with the GCO as a group to go over, you know, training initiatives, and safety metrics performance. There were a whole host of issues that we were talking about. Also, as we were seeking approval for curriculum modifications or bringing new tools, new technologies into play, we would make sure that they had visibility and all of that."

"When you talk about curriculum modifications, are you talking about pilot training curriculum?"

"Yes."

"Do these modifications to Global's training program for pilots need to be approved by the FAA?"

"In general, yes. You know, we are a culture of continuous improvement. So as there are new training vehicles, new technologies, new ways of thinking about training, we would certainly, you know, make sure that the FAA was informed. It didn't always require a formal approval. It kind of, uh… it sort of depended upon how that interfaced with the rest of the training program."

"And these discussions that you listed in terms of discussions with the FAA in Washington and with GCO office in Oklahoma City, did they frequently concern compliance with federal aviation standards?"

"Objection. Overbroad. Foundation." Von Dietrich said eyes still glued to the table. Hell, his body didn't move. He was a statue. Darby wanted to stick a pin in him and see if he would pop.

"Yes. Absolutely," Wyatt answered, pulling Darby's attention back to him.

"Now, as senior vice president of flight operations, did you have responsibilities with respect to pilot performance issues?"

"Yes."

"Could you describe what those responsibilities were?"

"Well, more broadly, certainly from a people perspective, we also were making sure that, you know, pilots were following the company's, you know, our policies for performance, and our, you know, executing our core values and also that the company was complying with the pilot contract, and that the pilots were also living up to their obligations in the pilot contract as well."

"Is there any obligation of cockpit crew members if they have determined that a fellow pilot is compromising inflight safety that they have an obligation to report that to management?"

"They should. Yes," Wyatt said.

"You say they should. Is that codified anywhere? Is that a written policy?"

"Yes. I can't tell you exactly where it is written, but we want to get feedback about performance issues from our flight crews. Absolutely."

"So, if a pilot determined that a fellow pilot was compromising safety during a flight, to whom is he expected to report that occurrence?"

"A couple of different ways, one of which is an ASAP," Wyatt said.

Wyatt proceeded to explain how many ways notification would have occurred if a pilot was unsafe. None of which occurred in response to her alleged behavior.

Darby had found a letter in her medical report that had been written a year and a half before her mental health evaluation, in which a check airman had said she had been a threat to the safety of the aircraft. He falsely asserted that the captain had forced her to sit in the jumpseat for the safety of the flight, yet he failed to mention that both the he and the captain had gone on break together and left her in the captain's seat on the operational side of a locked door.

They should have diverted if what he wrote was true. At the very least the check airman and the captain should have written an ASAP report. Nothing was ever spoken. There had been no reports or actions taken internally either. Wyatt's testimony now supports that it was not an authentic report.

"But you would expect in that ASAP report that the person submitting it would specifically identify the individual who is compromising safety?" Robert asked pressing that issue.

"Yes. I mean, we, the event review committee would know which flight it pertained to, and they could follow up with that individual."

Proof that ASAPs are not confidential, Darby thought. The biggest ruse to the pilot population that ASAPs were anonymous.

"And ASAP reports are not brought to your attention?"

"No. I mean, I have them available to me. But I'm not, uh… I think we are going to have something like 27,000 ASAP reports this year. So, I'm not reviewing every one of those. We are mainly looking at my level, for trends and elevated areas of risk that we need to mitigate."

Mitigate risk my ass, Darby thought. She drummed her fingers on her legs under the table. Kathryn had been spot-on—Global's events were increasing and they were doing nothing about it.

The next hour was spent discussing Wyatt's knowledge of the Section 8 process. He affirmed that he allowed Rich Clark to manage the process, and he agreed that sending Darby to a psychiatric review had been the correct course of action.

Darby's thoughts shifted to why he had allowed Clark to send her down the rabbit hole when Von Dietrich objected and said, "Don't answer that."

The *don't answer that* caught Darby's attention. But Wyatt was so used to hearing objection, he answered anyway.

Von Dietrich turned and yelled, "I told you not to answer that."

He couldn't leave it at that. He then told Wyatt how to answer the question. Robert objected and Von Dietrich spat back, and the legal procedural protocol verbal battle began.

After ten minutes of getting nowhere, Robert finally said, "I have stated my position. You are taking up my time. Direct him not to answer my questions as you will. Please do not coach him because that is a violation of Rule 30."

"Answer the question," Von Dietrich finally said.

The argument had gone on for so long, nobody remembered what they were arguing over, and the court reporter had to go back and find it. A huge nothing, but a mere distraction by Von Dietrich.

Robert went through the exhibits one at a time as they applied to the questions he asked regarding facts. Everything Wyatt knew was second hand from Rich Clark. Von Dietrich continued to object often.

"What were those concerns as identified by Captain Clark?" Robert asked.

"They were concerns about whether she should be flying a Global airplane at that particular point in time because of various things that came up in her interview with Ms. Abbott."

"Did Captain Clark give you any particulars about what Ms. Bradshaw had reportedly said to Ms. Abbott?"

"He gave some detail. I don't recall specifically what it was."

"You can't recall any of the references that Captain Clark made to Abbott's report in terms of Ms. Bradshaw's statements?" Robert asked incredulously.

"The one thing that I do remember was there was a concern expressed by Ms. Abbott that her interview was kind of uncharted territory for her. And she felt that some of the concerns that Darby had expressed about Global… that there was a statement made to the effect of, you know, she, Darby, feels like someone is out to get her. And I think Ms. Abbott… well, I will leave it at that."

Chapter 22

**Oklahoma City
Corporate Office
October 23, 2018**

JOE WOLFE SAT across the desk from Walter Croft listening to his side of a conversation. Wolfe's anger and embarrassment slowly diffused as the minutes ticked by. The call began on speaker phone including Wolfe, as it should have. But the caller, far too abruptly, ordered to be taken off speaker when Croft said he was present.

Wolfe worked to convince himself that the caller's order would have been the same regardless of who was in the room. He had no idea who Croft was speaking with, albeit there was something very familiar about the voice. He also wasn't sure if the shade of embarrassment highlighting Croft's face was due to getting snapped at, or having Wolfe hear the tone of disrespect to the almighty leader.

Croft sat behind his desk listening more than talking. Wolfe finally stood to leave, and Croft shook his head and raised a finger. That was a good sign, but whomever he was talking to obviously didn't trust him. Hell, he was in the thick of this with the rest of them. Yet he was being kept in the dark. *From what?* he wondered.

"You can count on that," Croft said, glancing at Wolfe for a moment before looking away.

Wolfe knew there was more to this story than everyone let on. He had been paid a nice stipend to remove Bradshaw and had done everything he could to accomplish that. Hell, he even violated the contract. But there became a point that there was not a damn thing he *could* do to keep her off property. He glanced at his phone and read the most recent text messages, feigning disinterest to Croft's call, but listened intently.

"There is not a problem sir," Croft said, loosening his tie. "We have everything under control." Looking at Wolfe, Croft rolled his eyes and gave him a half smile. "We're monitoring that now sir."

Bradshaw had become a formidable opponent, nothing like Wolfe had ever dealt with before. He'd removed many pilots from property in the day. Yet, none of them fought like Bradshaw. They had always trusted the union, to their demise. For some reason Bradshaw knew better. He had to give her that. Now their only hope was breaking her financially through the legal process, then step in at the end, and give her a stipend to go away forever. Everyone has a price.

Global took that process to an outside firm, as they often did. His personal goal would be to mitigate his involvement and hide behind attorney-client privilege when he was deposed. He loved the fight and the challenge, and he was very well rewarded. But at the end of the day, his alliance was to himself and his bank account.

"Everything is on schedule sir," Croft said. "Uh huh. Exactly. Thank you." He pulled the phone from his ear and set it into the cradle. "Sorry about that," he said to Wolfe, leaning back in his chair. Then he sighed.

"Nothing to be sorry for, sir," Wolfe said. "Is there a problem?"

"Nothing I can't take care of," Croft said. "But we've got another issue and I need your help."

Chapter 23

George Wyatt Deposition
October 23, 2018

ROBERT CONTINUED TO query Wyatt about the Global/ALPO mental health process, and Darby listened for inconsistencies, writing each contradiction on her legal pad as they occurred. Robert then doubled back to an earlier line of questioning.

"Aside from the reference to, *she feels like someone is out to get her,* did Captain Clark make any further reference to statements by Ms. Bradshaw as reported by Abbott?"

"Objection. Asked and answered."

"I don't recall."

"And what did you say in response to Mr. Clark's communication to you?"

"I told him that I was, uh that I certainly shared his concern based on this feedback and that we needed to make sure that we were getting the necessary support from the subject matter experts outside of flight operations in the company such as HR so that, uh… and we also needed to make sure that we follow the process. And that was my guidance to him, was just make sure that we are fair and we follow the process."

"What process?" Robert asked.

"In terms of reviewing what the next steps might be."

"Well, did he raise the prospect of a Section 8 referral?"

"That prospect was raised," Wyatt said. "I don't know if it was in this initial conversation or not."

This process was nothing but a tennis match. The ball was being lobbed back and forth from one side of the court to the other. Von Dietrich's objections were nothing but a net that didn't impact their play. She hoped Robert would make game, set, match. He was clearly heading in that direction.

"You did discuss the Section 8 referral with Captain Clark sometime before the letter? Well, let me pause here. I would like to introduce Exhibit 2."

He handed Wyatt the letter dated December 15, 2016, which Darby received from Regional Director Dodson on December 19, 2016. He confirmed that he was familiar with it.

"So, any time prior to December 19th, did you have any discussions with Captain Clark about the possibility of Ms. Bradshaw being referred to a Section 8 process?"

"Yes."

Darby raised an eyebrow.

"Okay. So, when did that discussion take place?"

"It would have been a day or two prior to this communication," Wyatt said, and Darby slowly shook her head.

"What did he say to you?" Robert asked. "Well, let me actually back up. Why was he talking to you about it?"

"Because he wanted to make sure that I was aware of the steps that he, uh… that he and the team were taking to follow up on Ms. Abbott's interview."

"Why would he want to make sure that you knew what the steps being taken were?" Robert asked looking up from the document and over the top of his glasses.

"Objection. Calls for speculation."

"Well, I am ultimately responsible for everything that happens in flight operations," Wyatt said. "And he knew that I wanted to make sure that the process was a fair process from an individual perspective, but also that we ensured the safety of our flight deck operations."

"So, what did he say to you?"

"He said that he had consulted with the stakeholders from HR, labor relations, and legal and that, although ultimately it was going to be a flight operations decision, it was going to be based on the input and advice from those areas."

Darby glanced toward Martha Jones, whose attention found a new focus beyond her phone. She was now listening intently. She was the "legal" that Wyatt spoke of.

"But had he told you that he had already made a decision?" Robert asked.

"No. I want to make sure I have got the timing correct. So, in the earlier, uh… you know, before he had consulted, he had not made any decision. It was a potential outcome, but it was not a decision. After he had the consultations, he made the decision, and he informed me of that decision."

"But you made a determination at that point when you spoke to Mr. Clark, that it was appropriate for the Section 8 referral to proceed. Correct?"

"Objection. Foundation. Misstates his prior testimony," Von Dietrich said.

"Yes. I made the decision that it was a sound course of action based on the diligence that had been performed."

"What diligence are you referring to?"

"The internal consultations that I spoke about earlier with EEO,

HR, and labor relations."

"Was it your understanding at that time that EEO, HR, and labor relations were recommending a Section 8 referral?"

"Objection."

"I don't know," Wyatt said with a shrug. "I assume that was one of the items that was discussed. I think that was my understanding from Captain Clark at the time."

"Okay. Do you know upon what facts EEO, HR, and labor relations were basing their recommendation?"

"Not specifically."

"So, when you refer to *diligence* on the part of Mr. Clark, you are just referring to the fact that he was being… he was doing what he was told to do by EEO, HR, and labor relations. Correct?"

"Objection. Foundation. Calls for speculation."

"No," Wyatt said.

"Well, what other diligence on the part of Mr. Clark were you aware of other than seeking advice from those three departments?"

"He was also concerned about if we have a pilot who is not in a state where, either through distraction or whatever other physical or mental situation, was able to safely execute flight deck operations. The safety of the operation had to be a primary consideration in his mind."

"Did he give you any facts upon which he based his concern about flight operations safety?"

"Objection. Asked and answered," Von Dietrich said.

"Only the general context of the interview that had led to the consultations," Wyatt said.

"So, do I understand correctly that you had two separate discussions with Captain Clark about the Section 8 referral? Is that correct? Prior to December 15th, and in the second conversation he advised you that subject to your approval that he was going forward with the referral? Correct?"

"Objection. Foundation. Misstates prior testimony."

Darby rolled her eyes.

"Correct."

"Did you have any email communications with him concerning his decisional process prior to the issuance of the December 15 letter?" Robert asked.

He was pressing Wyatt to admit to the email communications between he and Clark. It wouldn't matter if he did, they had the email. But it did matter if he perjured himself in his testimony.

"I don't recall an email exchange. There probably was one. But during this timeframe, I don't believe so." He hesitated and reflected for a moment then asserted, "Between the December 15 and 19 dates I don't recall any email exchange during that timeframe."

Robert pressed Wyatt regarding discussions with Clark prior to the decision. He gave Wyatt every opportunity to admit what they already had in evidence. Von Dietrich objected throughout. What Darby could not figure out is why they didn't tell Wyatt they had the email. Robert had received it in discovery from Global.

Finally, Wyatt said, "I did not have any discussion with him via email. He may have raised it in an interview, but I don't recall specifically."

"That is not something you would remember?" Robert said. "Strike that. What was Captain Clark's position?

"At the time, he was the vice president of flying operations and the chief pilot."

"And if he had, prior to December 15, 2016, raised the possibility of referring Ms. Bradshaw to a Section 8 process, that is not something you would remember?"

"Objection. Asked and answered. You are badgering the witness," Von Dietrich snapped.

Darby watched Wyatt closely during this line of questioning. When Von Dietrich objected to his being "badgered," something shifted in Wyatt's eyes. He had finally become aware, just after his last assertion denying the email. His expression shifted ever so slightly, and Darby knew exactly the moment when the thought crossed his mind that they might have access to that email.

Wyatt opened his mouth to answer the question. But he paused and thought for moment before he spoke. Then he said, "No. It was so long ago I just don't, uh… I don't remember what the exact sequence of events was."

Robert set down his pen and turned his attention to Von Dietrich. "I would like to note, that I think you are creating an incorrect record there. I want the record to note that my tone of voice is very moderate. And at worst, there was an asked and answered issue. I reject and frankly resent the characterization of badgering."

"For the sake of the record," Von Dietrich countered. "I agree that your tone was modest. It was the substance of your question that I considered to be badgering."

While Robert and Von Dietrich argued the merits of badgering a witness, Darby leaned back and folded her arms, staring at Wyatt. She wondered if his final admission of, *I don't remember what the exact sequence of events was* would be equal to, *I can't recall* where he could change his testimony in court and base it on his memory returning.

Chapter 24

ROBERT SHIFTED THE questioning to Wyatt's knowledge of the Director of Health services, Dr. Marsh, and Regional Director, Robert Dodson. Wyatt spoke as if he were having a chat at a backyard picnic, discussing those who lived on their block to the new guy who had just moved in. Wyatt knew the players well and expressed as much.

"What is the initial role of Dr. Marsh in the Section 8 process as you understand it?"

"In general, Dr. Marsh is responsible for providing advice to the decision maker. Uh… in this case, Captain Clark, about, you know, any relevant medical information that might be germane to making the decision. And once the process kicks off, then Dr. Marsh needs to select the company medical examiner."

"Could you describe your overall understanding of the Section 8 process?" Robert asked.

"It has been a long time since I have referred to the specific contractual provisions. But it essentially provides for a medical review of a pilot to ensure that they are able to hold a first-class medical certificate. In the contract, there is a provision for a company medical examiner to be appointed, and then a pilot medical examiner, and then a neutral if it gets to that point."

"And you refer to the fact that this is a flight department decision?"

"The decision to conduct the Section 8 ultimately lies with flight operations."

"And in terms of mental health issues, have you been involved in any prior decisions prior to that of Ms. Bradshaw to refer to a Section 8?" Robert asked.

"It is, uh… I mean, there have been other cases. Yes."

"Can you give me an estimate of how many cases?"

"Objection," Von Dietrich said. Calls for speculation."

"I don't remember. It is, again, probably a handful."

"Can you, without naming names, describe the circumstances relating to any of these Section 8 referrals?"

"I don't remember any other particulars."

Seriously? Darby thought. Mr. Calm, cool, collected was not disclosing the full extent of his knowledge. A pilot with a mental health condition is an unusual circumstance and would be remembered. Furthermore, Kathryn and Darby had located a case where Global did the same thing to a pilot after he exposed pension fund fraud that forced Global to pay $640 million in federal penalties.

There was no way in hell that Wyatt did not remember that. Not to mention that the doctor involved in that case was prevented from ever working with Global, but he subsequently became the head of the FAA medical department. Wyatt had to know the FAA's Deputy Flight Surgeon, Michael Banks. Banks had worked directly for Global.

"Can you identify any person at the company who might have better knowledge of prior Section 8 cases?"

"Objection. Calls for speculation," Von Dietrich said.

"I mean, certainly Captain Clark and Joe Wolfe potentially," Wyatt said.

Darby wanted to raise her hand and say, 'ask me, I know.' Robert looked at his notes and began silently reading through his questions. He lined through those that he already asked, or that were no longer pertinent.

Wendel shifted in his seat and sighed loudly. Then, he looked at his watch and rolled his eyes again. It appeared he may have taken behavioral lessons from Kathryn's twin daughters when they were thirteen. She doubted Robert was even aware of Wendel's theatrics.

Robert removed his glasses and asked, "Are there any limitations, in the mental health context, on what the company medical examiner can investigate?"

"Not that I'm aware of. If it is germane to… if the company medical examiner says that he or she needs it to complete a full evaluation, then I believe that we would provide that."

"Okay I want to make sure I got a complete answer to a prior question. I had asked you, were you aware of anything in terms of Ms. Bradshaw's conduct at work that warranted a Section 8 referral in your mind?"

"No," Wyatt answered.

"Objection. Overbroad. Asked and answered," Von Dietrich said, after Wyatt had already responded. Darby grinned. He was getting slow, but his intensity never wavered.

"Then the reason I wanted to bring that up again is to be more specific. You were at a meeting with her face to face concerning some safety issues that Darby raised. Correct?"

"Yes."

"Was there anything in her comportment during that meeting that in your determination warranted a Section 8 referral?"

"No."

That meeting had occurred just weeks before Darby was removed from duty. *It's a short path from sane to crazy,* Darby mused.

"Are you familiar with the aviation rulemaking committee on mental health?" Robert asked.

"No. I'm not familiar with that particular ARC," Wyatt said.

Darby could not contain her expression of surprise. How the hell could he not be familiar with the mental health ARC?

That rulemaking committee was headed by the Federal Aviation Administrator, Mike Hackman, a man Wyatt testified that he had worked closely with. It was Hackman who had made a ruling that the neuropsychological testing would not be useful to determine mental health of airline pilots.

That determinate was also two weeks *before* they had sent Darby in for the exact testing, that at the time was no longer valid. That testing would have cost the airline millions and perhaps thousands of job losses in the process. *He is familiar with that,* Darby thought folding her arms, an eyebrow involuntarily raising. He had to be.

Robert directed Wyatt to refer to document one, interrogatory number 20. Identify all persons involved in Respondent's decision to have Ann Abbott interview the complainant. Answer—*The decision to refer Complainant's equal opportunity concerns to Global's human resources department was made by Captain Rich Clark, in consultation with Joe Wolfe. Ms. Abbott was selected as the individual to interview Complainant by her supervisor.*

"Is it your understanding, that the purpose of Ms. Abbott's interview of Ms. Bradshaw was to investigate equal opportunity concerns?"

"Yes," Wyatt said.

"But isn't it true that Ms. Bradshaw never requested an equal opportunity investigation?"

"Objection. Lacks foundation. Calls for speculation."

"Not to my knowledge," Wyatt said.

"Can you explain, if Ms. Bradshaw did not request an EEO

investigation, why would the company have initiated one?"

"Because we could not ignore her report and the discussion in my office with respect to some events that she described in training. And so we had to, we had a line of follow-up activity that was associated with investigating those allegations. And so that is why we had to bring in the HR experts."

Experts my ass, Darby thought. She had been told that Abbot was an HR safety investigator. Instead, she was the manager of the pass travel complaint department. The woman was also aviation illiterate. Then Darby remembered what Tom had told her. Her greatest challenge would be to maintain her composure during their untruths. She sighed, knowing no matter what they said, Robert knew what he was doing.

"So, were you part of that determination process, that equal opportunity should be involved?" Robert asked.

"I had delegated the follow up from the meeting to Captain Clark, and we came back... uh, he came back with a proposal to divide the follow-up activity into the safety issues that Darby had raised and then the matters that we just discussed with respect to harassment and unequal treatment. And then there was a third line of activity that was associated with Global policies and procedures."

"Okay. What were the issues that she raised with respect to harassment and unequal treatment?"

"The one I remember specifically related to an instructor and his, the way that he had conducted some training and then his... you know, his interactions with her in the training environment."

What Wyatt did not state was that the simulator event had occurred six years earlier, with her and a male captain who was a year from retirement. Nobody had investigated anything when the event occurred, despite her reporting his behavior. That was not a gender or age discrimination event. The event consisted of a shitty instructor who was sitting in the back of the simulator texting instead of paying attention to two pilots new to the aircraft.

There was no discrimination, he was just a lazy ass going for a ride texting his girlfriend. She drummed her nails on her leg. Yet, they waited for six years to investigate. He was also the check airman who had fabricated the report about Darby being a threat to the safety of the flight.

Darby was not quite sure how anyone in the company thought they could turn a lazy instructor into an equal opportunity issue to create context six years after the fact. But they certainly were trying. Meaning—they were digging deep.

"And what were the other harassment or unequal treatment issues that you recall?"

"I don't recall."

"But your feeling at the time was that they were significant enough that they warranted investigation?"

"Absolutely. She brought them forward, and we took them very seriously."

Chapter 25

San Francisco
San Quentin State Prison
October 23, 2018

GROUNDHOG DAY BEST described prison life, and it had driven Bill Jacobs crazy. Until the move, that is. The monotony factor had shifted the moment they transferred him to San Quentin to serve his sentence with Drake, the former President of the United States. Drake held the notion that Bill could somehow help him crash planes from inside a prison, and Drake wanted him close. Bill had advised him that those days were long gone. Primarily because anyone who would have helped him was dead.

That ship had most definitely sailed... or crashed, he thought.

He appreciated his alliances more than they could have known, and now they were dead. Prior to their demise he had stayed connected to the boys that he'd saved in Vietnam. He had also convinced them to become airline pilots. Then he systematically broke their lives without them knowing he'd been their guide to the bottom.

Bill blamed the industry and convinced them of as much. When a person hits their bottom, they will do anything for respect or redemption. Especially if it was a noble cause and it would redeem their abysmal existence. They were gone, and he was in prison. Not exactly the outcome he'd planned. He holds his ex-wife, Kathryn, and Darby Bradshaw responsible.

His life of hell had shifted abruptly when they pulled him to San Quentin. He'd initially fought the intrusion to what he'd learned to accept as his daily routine and reality. But now he wasn't quite sure why he'd ever objected. He had no choice but to assist Drake with whatever game he was playing. *Hell, everyone had a choice in life,* Bill thought. Free will was a universal liberty. Something he'd learned a long time ago. The truth was, he quite liked the President and they had built a solid friendship. A friendship that he hoped would provide him the key to freedom.

It wasn't long into their association that Drake had asked him what the most difficult failure for a pilot to handle was, and then shortly thereafter a crash occurred with that exact failure. How the hell he pulled that off, Bill had no idea.

The MAX had malfunctioned, which created a runaway stabilizer, and Drake grinned as they watched the news together after the first plane had gone down. He had said there would be more crashes, and he had been correct. The second had just fulfilled that prophecy in Tokyo.

Bill now watched the news from the back of the game room. The reporter was discussing the malfunction on the B737 MAX.

The President was in no uncertain terms bordering on being a sociopath. Bill smiled at that thought. There were some circles, perhaps many, who felt the exact same way about him. He had to admit that it was nice to have someone to talk to who had ambitions beyond the godforsaken prison walls. Walls that were a barrier, without hope of a future... *Unless there **was** one,* Bill thought.

Hanging with Drake gave him that hope. Hell, hanging with Drake even got him laid on occasion. Bill rubbed his chin and smiled.

The man had connections.

Bill had no idea what Drake was up to, but he respected him immensely. He also knew that if he were useful to Drake, he could be his ticket out of this hellhole, despite a life sentence. The fact that they had both been convicted of murder and were in a state prison spoke volumes of what Drake could do. And Drake wanted Bill. Drake needed Bill.

Folding his arms, he leaned back in his chair and assessed the room. He was untouchable because of Drake. Nobody as much looked his way or stepped in his space. Just the way he liked it.

Drake had power unlike anyone he'd ever seen. Bill had the brains. Together they could accomplish anything. Bill just wasn't sure if he could trust Drake. He grinned, wondering if Drake could trust him. *But then, who the hell can you trust?* Bill wondered

He glanced around the room, again, at the bottom feeders of society and knew trust was all that he could do. He also understood that lives had to be sacrificed for the success of long-range plans. That's one truth they held in common. Then he grinned at the thought of Darby. He had underestimated her. They all had.

Chapter 26

Wyatt Deposition
October 23, 2018

ANYONE CAN TEAR down a building, but it took a craftsman to build one of quality. Robert had been building his case brick by brick throughout the day. There were four criteria necessary to win and AIR21 case. One of the elements was to bringing forth safety information, another was to do so in good faith. This was the path Darby prayed the afternoon would take.

Interrogatories, a set of written questions were required to be answered by both parties to clarify matters of fact. The more undisputed facts that could be determined in advance, the more efficient court would be. Unfortunately, Global refused to admit that Darby reported anything that qualified as protected activity, or even that she brought forth her report in good faith—both requirements of the AIR21 statute.

Global would also not admit that forcing her to a psychiatric evaluation was retaliation. If Robert could draw out these admissions from Wyatt, they would be one step closer to the ending these proceedings.

"Okay, and what were the safety issues that she raised?" Robert asked.

"There was… it was difficult to, uh… we had to spend some time unpacking what all the safety issues were," Wyatt began. "One of the most important issues that I do remember, was around reporting culture and being able to bring safety issues forward. And there were other concerns about how Global was developing its safety management system."

"Was it your understanding at the time of your meeting with Darby Bradshaw that having a reporting culture was a requirement under federal aviation standards?" Robert asked.

"Yes."

Darby glanced at Martha Jones and their eyes met. She then gave Martha the *I guess you were wrong* look. Whatever that looked like, the message was sent and received. Martha flushed ever so slightly and then she looked away.

"So, you recall reporting culture issues and SMS system issues," Robert affirmed. "And as you sit here right now, can you recall any of the other safety issues that she raised?"

"There were issues with respect to flight scheduling concerns that were raised and whether we were compliant with federal aviation regulations. I'm sure there were some other issues raised, but those are the ones that I remember."

Oh my God! Darby thought. This is exactly what they needed. She wanted to jump up and kiss the man who threw her into a pit filled with snakes. She was experiencing the Stockholm Syndrome.

Wyatt had just provided testimony that she brought federally-mandated safety concerns forward. There was no way Global could not deny this any longer. She wanted to do a happy dance. But the truth was, she would never respect the man who had looked the other way and sent her through hell.

"And did those flight scheduling issues also concern whether

Global was complying with federal aviation regulations?"

"Yes."

"Who was charged with following up on the safety issues that Darby raised?"

"Well, again, I charged Rich Clark with following up with Darby directly to make sure that we understood the issues because we weren't able to get into all of them in a tremendous amount of detail in a 90-meeting in my office. So, he was charged with following up and basically categorizing the issues for follow up, also, subsequently, on the safety issues to consult with our corporate safety and compliance department, which has overall responsibility for SMS at Global."

"Do you recall whether there were any final determinations by Global as to the validity of the concerns that Ms. Bradshaw had raised?" Robert asked.

"Objection. Overbroad," Von Dietrich said.

"Yes. Yes," Wyatt said.

"What was the determination?"

"Well, the determination was that, you know, we have a culture of continuous improvement. But there are always opportunities to improve your performance. And so, we eventually, we sought the assistance of an outside auditor. We felt that would be a healthy process for us to go through at that point in time. And the catalyst for that frankly, I think we would have done it anyway. But certainly, a catalyst for it was the meeting with Darby."

I was a catalyst for safety, and they still threw me into a mental health evaluation a month later? What the hell? Darby thought.

She shifted from excited to perplexed. Perhaps Wyatt and Clark should be evaluated for being Bipolar. She then glanced at Martha Jones again, curious if she realized the incongruity with his statement and the entire process.

Martha's face showed no expression, but the speed of her fingers over her cell phone told another story.

"Did you at any time reach a determination that any of the compliance issues that she had raised during her meeting with you or in her safety report had been raised by her in bad faith?"

"No."

"Did you make a determination at any time that any of the compliance concerns that she raised during her meeting with you were without any validity?"

"No."

"She also gave you a written safety report. Correct?"

"Yes."

"All right. And did you throw that out, or did you read it?"

"No. I read it."

"Assuming as a factual premise that Global pilots are, in fact, not engaging in hand flying because they lack understanding and confidence, would you agree with me that that would reflect a failure in Global's training program?"

"If that is a fact, that is an area particularly with newer, more automated aircraft where we would want to make sure they had that confidence. Absolutely," Wyatt said.

"Okay. But if they come out of training and they don't have the understanding and confidence to engage in hand flying, would you agree with me that that is a problem?" Robert asked.

"I would say it is an opportunity for improvement."

"That is not my question. Are you saying that would be acceptable in—"

"No."

"Okay. So, then you would agree with me that would reflect noncompliance with FAA approved training programs, that pilots don't have the confidence to engage in hand flying."

"It is a higher level than compliance. It is an undesirable outcome," Wyatt said. "So, we hold ourselves… we are talking about managing safety risk as a higher bar than simple compliance."

"Would you agree with me that, under your training programs that are approved by the FAA, Global has an obligation to train their pilots on how to operate the aircraft via—"

"To have basic proficiency of the airplane," Wyatt said. "Absolutely."

"And would you agree with me that Ms. Bradshaw, in this report, is communicating to you that Global pilots are not adequately trained?"

"Yes. I think she is alluding to the fact that we can improve our processes for making sure that our pilots are informed about emerging safety risks in the operation and actually events that are going on in the line."

Alluding? Darby thought. What part of her placing her concerns in writing and giving them directly to he and Clark had been anything but a direct statement. Or a slap in the face, as they saw it. Regardless of his word choice he was giving them everything they needed.

"Let's look at bullet points that follow. The first bullet point reads, quote, *at 300 degrees ILS 16L, thrust went to idle at 300 degrees. A/S 7 knots below ref*," Robert said. "Can you explain the reference to A/S 7 knots below ref?"

"Airspeed seven knots below your normal final approach speed."

"What is TOGA?" Robert asked referencing the pilot pressing the TOGA button.

"That is takeoff/go-around mode. It is essentially maximum throttle position."

"And why would a pilot engage TOGA momentarily?"

"Usually if they were going to abandon the approach and take the airplane around."

"Now, the pilot states, quote, *landed in T/D zone with full aft stick to achieve normal T/D attitude.* Closed quote. Is that a source of concern for you as described?"

"Yes."

"Why would that be a source of concern?"

"Well, it indicates that the airplane was below the final approach airspeed that in order to arrest the descent for the landing, that they were at maximum control authority."

"The pilot concludes, quote, *We didn't know and lucked out. Any idea?* Closed quote. Would you agree that that communication conveys a degree of helplessness?"

"Yes, I mean, I don't know what was in the author's mind exactly, but I can surmise that."

"It conveys a sense of a lack of operational control. Correct?"

"Yes."

"And are you comfortable with a pilot expressing these sentiments about his own flight competency?" Robert asked.

"I would want to know if we had an event like this happen. I would hope that the pilot would have reported it and that we would have followed up on it with our normal process."

"Okay. Did you ask Ms. Bradshaw to identify the pilot involved?"

"No."

"Did you follow up in any way in terms of investigating?"

"No. I did not personally follow up."

"Did anyone else follow up in terms of investigating the facts of that bullet point?"

"Objection. Foundation."

Darby startled. Von Dietrich had been so quiet during Wyatt's admissions, she all but forgot his presence.

"I don't know," Wyatt said.

Robert read another two examples of flight concerns. Wyatt agreed they, too, were concerning and confirmed nobody ever investigated either, and that Darby had brought them forward in good faith.

"The last bullet point reads, *During OE, the wheels fell off when, on my first leg, and my instructor told me to go vertical speed on the descent into DTW. I was high and fast, and that just made it worse. WTF.*"

"Would OE be operating experience?"

"Yes."

"And DTW would be Detroit?"

"Yes."

"And WTF, based on your life experience which I share, would you understand that to mean *what the fuck*?"

"Yes."

"And OE is a training event. Correct?"

"Yes."

"And OEs are typically conducted on live revenue flights?"

"Correct."

"So more likely than not there were passengers onboard the flight that is referenced here?"

"Yes."

Darby surmised it was a good thing that Linda was not listening to this testimony. Robert, however, continued to read the report that identified a training instructor having reviewed the test so all pilots would be assured to pass it electronically.

"Is that consistent with Global's FAA approved training manual?" he asked.

"I would object to that as being vague," Von Dietrich said. "It may be my lack of understanding. I am not sure what that is referring to, review a test so that it would be assured to pass it electronically."

"That was a violation of Rule 30," Robert said. "You have to be more concise, raise the objection that it is vague but not coach this witness, which is what you just did."

"I'm in no way coaching the witness. I'm stating a valid objection to the use of a document, Counsel."

Darby assessed Wyatt while Robert and Von Dietrich argued the elements of Rule 30. He could not have been a better witness for her. If all the depositions went this way, she would have this thing locked up. *They could close the record with his testimony alone,* Darby thought. There would no waiting for Global to offer a settlement; she could win a motion for summary judgement and end this. The legal process, as slow as it was, might be more expeditious that waiting for Global management to acquire an iota of common sense.

Chapter 27

SHE COULD NOT hear what they were saying, but they certainly had done it animatedly. During lunch, Darby had watched Global's legal team chew on Wyatt from across the restaurant. He had sat quietly and ate a sandwich as they each gave him a piece of their minds. The legal team appeared to be chastising him. He had taken it in stride. However, after lunch, Wyatt's demeanor had changed. Either he was tired, or they had told him to stop being *her* witness and to help protect Global.

"The two paragraphs beginning with the subtitle *Captain emergency,*" Robert said, "which reads, *Captain emergency. Shortly after departure, a flight lost their auto flight system. The captain continued to fly to Oklahoma City. He requested a block altitude and flew in RVSM airspace. Then upon arrival, not when the issue began, he declared an emergency because ATC would not provide a block altitude for the arrival phase.*

"The training department used this as an example of workload management and created a video. The problems with this video were many, and the author can only suspect the lack of SMEs involved, did not understand the ramifications of what happened, and how the video created a liability to Global.

"An FAA advisory, FAA 2013, and Global have encouraged hand

flying due to loss of hand flying skills. However, this training video stated that hand flying is an emergency procedure. Secondly, the pilot flew in RVSM airspace without required equipment, thinking that requesting a block altitude would alter that requirement. Legally, it did not. So did I read that much correctly?" Robert asked.

"Yes."

"As read to you, and assuming the facts are accurate, are these facts a source of concern?"

"Yes. They would be."

"Why would they be a source of concern?"

"Well, because an airplane flying in RVSM airspace would need to maintain a very precise altitude. So, again, it gives the impression that we are going to place operational requirements above safety requirements. It probably would have been a better decision to turn the airplane around and get it repaired."

But that's how Global rolls, Darby thought. *Money over safety every decision they make.* The captain on that flight had been a management pilot tasked to write operational procedures. He had emailed Darby because she queried him about what he had done in response to the training video. He then told her that the loss of the autoflight system was a personal wakeup call to him because he had lost his flying skills. He had stated that *most of the pilots could not fly level four—fully automated, or level zero—no automation, so said ASAP.*

Darby had included this in her report and Wyatt had taken no action. Dr. Wood had also argued against the very points that Wyatt now confirmed in support of her assertions.

Wyatt didn't need to ask Darby who it was. He already knew and had approved of the ensuing training program that encouraged pilots to declare an emergency versus train them. However, declaring an emergency did not necessarily provide the operational support that the pilot might need to safely land.

"Isn't it true that the Complainant advised you during your meeting that Global was failing to treat deadheading time as duty time for the purposes of computing daily and weekly flight time limits?"

"Yes. That was something that we would have investigated."

"Do you know what the result of that investigation was?"

"I don't remember."

"Regarding the safety report, with whom did you have any communications? I'm not asking about content. Just persons relating to Ms. Bradshaw and the safety issues she raised."

"The safety issues would have been Captain Clark. He was the only one that I talked to during that time period."

"But Mr. Croft also made inquiries about Ms. Bradshaw and the safety issues she was raising during this period. Correct?"

"Objection. Lacks foundation. Misstates prior testimony."

"I don't remember."

Bullshit, Darby thought. Wyatt had testified earlier that he had talked to Croft about her and the safety report in a general manner.

"In the aftermath of receiving Ms. Bradshaw's safety report, did Global make any changes in its policies or training materials?"

"Yes."

"What changes were made?"

"We put a number of process improvements in place, invested in new analytic technology. We were able to hire resources within our flight safety department with some expertise that we were lacking in-house to help with analyzing and being even more proactive about transfers, all in the interest of continuous improvement. But those were outcomes that came out of that external safety audit. We also, I don't remember exactly what the timeframe was… We made upgrades to our ASAP reporting platform to make it more user friendly as well."

"So were the ASAP improvements furtherance of SMS compliance?" Robert asked.

"SMS and, yes. Certainly. Among other things."

"Were those changes, in part, promoted by Ms. Bradshaw's report of SMS issues?"

"Yes."

Wyatt continued for the better part of fifteen minutes explaining all the changes to operations, training, and on all the fleets. Robert asked the questions and Wyatt was open to sharing all that he had implemented. Darby was more surprised than ever by his testimony and the outcome.

"And to some extent, were these new resources dedicated to improving training?"

"Of course," Wyatt said. "Yes."

"And was that the impetus in that direction, was that contributed to by Ms. Bradshaw's reports related to training issues?"

"It certainly didn't hurt," Wyatt said.

Darby was dumbfounded as to how many changes they had made because of her report. None of this made sense. Why the hell did they do this to her, if everything she said was accurate and that they had taken her report seriously? It was somewhat ironic that Global had invested such a great deal of time and treasure based on the report of a woman they deemed mentally unstable.

"Since the time of Ms. Bradshaw's safety report, are you aware of any changes in Global's policy related to the treatment of deadheading under FAR117?"

"No."

"Do you have any recollection of the company coming to a conclusion as to whether deadheads were not, were improperly, not being credited towards FAR 117 calculations?"

"Objection."

"I don't remember a specific finding to that effect. But certainly, we are always looking at our systems and how we are capturing that information."

"Do you recall any determinations by the FAA with respect to whether Global had violated FAR117 with respect to its treatment of deadheading?"

"I don't recall."

How could it be possible the senior vice president didn't know that Global received a violation regarding FAR 117? Darby wondered.

"Do you recall saying to Ms. Bradshaw at the outset of your meeting with her that some people like to sit in the back of the room and throw spit wads?"

"I don't recall that, but that is something I have said before."

"Are you aware that several weeks after Ms. Bradshaw received the Section 8 letter that she was asked to give a safety presentation to divisional leaders?"

"She was asked to give a presentation. Yes."

"Who asked her to give that presentation?"

"Captain Clark."

"Were you consulted with respect to that decision?"

"Yes."

"And why was that decision made?"

"Because we were taking the report seriously. We wanted to follow up on all of the issues that had been raised."

"Who were the divisional leaders to whom she was assigned to talk?"

"I can't say. Well, let's see. It would be certainly the managing director of flight training, the managing director of flight standards, and the managing director of… more than likely the managing director of line operations. There may have been, I don't know how large the meeting was. There may have been fleet representatives as well."

"Given that she had already been referred for a Section 8 evaluation based on mental health concerns, did you have any reluctance to authorize her meeting with the divisional leaders?"

"I did not."

"Why did you not?"

"I felt that in that... in that environment, she was perfectly capable of making the points that needed to be made. And in any case, you know, we didn't know what the... we didn't want to wait for the whole process to run its course. We felt that she could play a valuable role in continuing to help us improve the performance of the division. But I would say that about any pilot who had raised concerns."

"Did you attend the meeting with the divisional leaders?"

"No."

"And the SMS manager did not attend that meeting with the divisional leaders. Correct?"

"I don't know if he was there or not. I don't remember. I believe flight safety was there, but I... again, I don't know for sure."

"As you sit here today, do you have any concerns with respect to Ms. Bradshaw's continued flight operations for Global?"

"No."

"Do you know if anyone in the company ever apologized to her for charting her through this process, the Section 8 process?"

"I don't know."

"Let's take a quick break," Robert said. "I'm about ready to wrap this up, but I need a few minutes."

Chapter 28

WITHIN TEN MINUTES they were ready to go at it again. Wendel and Martha were still texting when Robert and Darby returned, and neither looked up from their phones as they entered the room. Darby lifted her phone as if she were going to join the texting crowd and took a couple photos of the legal team. Robert turned to the final page of his questions.

"So up until your retirement, you worked fairly frequently with the FAA's Oklahoma FAA office?"

"Yes."

"Are there any former Global employees employed there?"

"Yes. I don't pretend to know all their names. But, yes, there are some."

"Rough estimate of how many?"

"Objection," Von Dietrich, said.

Darby marked his objection on her pad. Wendel watched her, and his expression of a lightbulb moment told her that he finally figured out she had been tracking them.

"No idea," Wyatt said. "I can tell you among the *principal inspectors* that we deal with on, you know, each fleet there are probably, you know, a handful or so. Maybe five."

"Are you going to be returning to flight operations for some other airline, or do you have plans to—"

"No! I will not," Wyatt said, not waiting for Robert to finish the question.

He had intended to ask Wyatt if he had plans to go to work anywhere else. Darby wanted to laugh. Apparently, Wyatt had enough of working and retirement fit him well. That was the fastest question he had answered all day.

Robert assessed him for a minute and then said, "I have no other questions other than I want to thank you, because I got a real education from you today. So, I appreciate it." Robert looked directly to Von Dietrich and said, "Unless you have questions."

"No redirect," Von Dietrich said. "We are going to mark the transcript confidential pursuant to the protective order. I will just note that the protective order states that confidential information, quote, shall be used solely for purposes directly related to the prosecution or defense of this proceeding and shall not be used for any other purpose whatsoever and shall not be used in any manner in connection with any other claim, demand, suit, action, or proceeding. I just want to have the record clear on that. Otherwise, the witness will read and sign."

"Then I would like to make a comment," Robert said. "I think the order is directed towards designating appropriate portions of the deposition. I think we just used a couple of documents that related to confidential issues. We would take that as noncompliant with the tribunal's order if, as with the documents we received, there is an indiscriminate classification of this entire deposition as confidential."

"And we disagree," Von Dietrich snapped, red growing up his neck, his eyes bulging more than they had all day. The difference being he was no longer looking at the spot he had burned into the table, he was scorching his stare into Robert.

"We believe the entirety of the deposition will be confidential. If there is a challenge to the confidential designation, there is a procedure in the order itself. And no sort of publication or otherwise bringing to public any of the information from the deposition can be done unless that procedure is followed."

"I understand what you have told us you are going to do," Robert said calmly. "Our request is that, in order to avoid an undue burden on the tribunal, that the respondent identify those portions of the deposition which are properly classified as confidential and provide its rationale. That is our request. We think conforming to that request is required by the tribunal's order. I understand that, and it appears to be the intent of the respondent not to honor that request and to classify the whole deposition as—"

"For right now—" Von Dietrich said.

"I wish you wouldn't interrupt me," Robert replied.

"I thought you were done. I apologize," Von Dietrich said with a tone of arrogance. He stood and added without waiting for Robert to finish, "For right now, we are designating the entire transcript as confidential. We have not refused to heed your request. But in the interim, any disclosure of testimony from this designation we believe would be a violation of the protective order, and we would seek remedies consistent with that. I think there is nothing more on our end for right now."

They went off the record.

Von Dietrich was stacking his papers and then he turned to Darby. "If you provide this to *anyone*, you will be in violation of the court order." He stabbed his finger in the air at her, "I mean nobody! This is *all* confidential."

"What's confidential?" Darby asked, feigning confusion. But before he exploded, she winked with a grin. *You want this confidential?* Darby thought, *you'd better best advise your client to end it.*

Chapter 29

THERE WAS NOTHING like a good argument at the end of deposition to get your blood boiling. Von Dietrich had been a timebomb ready to explode from the moment they had started, and Darby was not surprised at the final outburst. Now, their primary short-term goal was to get to the hotel and find an adult beverage.

Thankfully, they were able to leave all their boxes in a secured storage area, so they walked the few blocks back to their hotel. Robert talked the entire way. He was excited and charged after the Von Dietrich exchange, and all they had learned from Wyatt. After they arrived at the hotel, Darby scooted up to her room and changed her clothes. She left a message for Tom, texted Stan again, and headed out the door to meet Robert for dinner.

Walking into the restaurant she looked around. Robert was sitting at a table in the corner drinking a beer. He waved, and she strode his way grinning.

Darby sat across the table from him, exhausted. She waived to a waitress who arrived quickly. "May I have a Glenmorangie neat?"

"Of course, sweetheart," the waitress said. "Would you like a double?"

She snickered. "Is it that obvious? Why the heck not? I think we deserve the right to celebrate."

"That we do," Robert said, raising his glass. "I'd like another, too."

"Are we going to put a little food in the celebration tonight?" the waitress asked.

"Yes. But may we have a few minutes?" Darby asked. "We're expecting one more guest."

"Of course," the waitress said. She quickly told them the specials, and set three menus on the table, and left to get their beverages.

"You earned your money today," Darby said. Not that he didn't earn it every day he had to deal with Global's legal team.

"My Dad always said that ever since Eve tempted Adam with the apple, man has been condemned to earn his bread by the sweat of his brow."

"How appropriate," Darby said, "says the man who has the patience of Job. I'm not sure I could have held my temper with that attorney. He's an ass."

Robert grinned. "I think they should want to settle now. With what Wyatt testified today, and if Stan has what I think he does, we'll have them cold. It would be nice to hold ALPO accountable, too."

"You mean nail them?" Darby said looking at her phone. Stan still had not responded to her text messages.

Darby had texted him first thing that morning, again when they had finished the deposition, and then sent a message with the hotel address to confirm the location. She also texted him that she was heading to the restaurant.

"I think I'll call Stan," Darby said, dialing his number. The phone went directly to voicemail. "Hey Stan, this is Darby. It's six fifteen and we're at the hotel restaurant. We'll see you soon or call if something came up. Thanks."

Darby set her phone on the table just as the waitress arrived with a relish tray and their drinks. Robert gave her his empty glass and accepted his beer. She set Darby's drink in front of her and stepped away.

Lifting their glasses, they clinked them together. Darby sipped her scotch, and then said, "Yummy. This is exactly what I needed. That was insane today."

"Wyatt's a likeable guy," Robert said.

"What's not to like? He made me the angel of safety."

"That he did," Robert said. "He appeared genuine. The guy even cried when he announced his retirement. I kind of felt sorry for him."

"Good thing he didn't do it in front of Abbott or he, too, would be crazy," Darby said. "He did tell a few… uh…" Darby stopped herself from saying the word lies and said, "untruths."

"How's that?" Robert asked, leaning back in his chair, clearly relishing in the success of the day as he nursed his beer.

"Well, he clearly wasn't going to tell you he had received that email."

"Maybe he forgot?"

"Hardly," Darby said. "But it was more than that. At one point he had said that Walter Croft had asked him specifically about my case. Later he said that during their discussions that he had communicated to him very generally about a pilot." Darby reached for a carrot stick and added, "First, it was specifically me, later I was just some pilot. Then, later it was he could not remember ever talking to him."

Robert nodded, taking in what she was saying.

"Wyatt also said he didn't recall any other Section 8 actions, but what about Captain Hill? Not only did he go to the same doctor they sent me to, but he's suing them as we speak. How could he not know? Then there was that case that went to court involving the FAA aeromedical doctor in which Global was fined for pension fraud. No way in hell would he forget that either. That guy is the current Deputy

Federal Air Surgeon, and he had worked for Global."

"Selective memory," Robert finally said with a grin. "But none of that matters. He helped us tremendously."

"I don't think Global's legal team liked it," Darby said. "After they chewed on him during lunch, he wasn't quite as forthcoming with the compliments."

"The damage was done," Robert said. "He admitted exactly what we needed him to."

"All this should have been undisputed anyway," Darby said. "I provided them a written safety report with their non-compliance of federal aviation standards. What more did they need?"

"Yes, it should have been undisputed," Robert said, and he took a long drink of his beer and then smiled. He, too, was elated by the outcome of the day. Darby wasn't sure if this was normal, but so far depositions appeared effective.

"Wyatt agreed that *all* your statements in the report regarding the safety issues were not in compliance with Global's SMS program or FAA approved training protocol," Robert said. "More than that, he couldn't recall whether you were ever asked for the identity of the persons who made those statements. Most compelling was his contention that you brought everything forth in good faith. Absolutely *everything*. He described you as being a catalyst for an SMS compliance review."

"A catalyst for change," Darby repeated. "Then why did he agree to send me to a psychiatric evaluation?"

"The *why* we may never know," Robert said gently. "But Judge Geraghty has already acknowledged that a forced psychiatric evaluation is an adverse action."

"Then all we have to do is prove that my safety report was the reason they did this to me." Darby said, she stared into her drink for a moment and then reality hit. "That will be their word against mine."

"Don't worry about that. Administrative law judges often rely on circumstantial evidence in terms of satisfying the contributing factor test because direct evidence of a retaliatory motive is rare due to the safety imperative underlying AIR21 claims. The contributing factor standard is often satisfied by evidence of *any factor* which, alone or in connection with other factors, tends to affect the outcome of the decision."

"Okay…" Darby said, not sure if she fully understood. "What worries me is their assertion that they were investigating an EO complaint, not safety." Then she added, "But all Abbott had with her was my safety report when we talked."

"None of that matters," Robert said. "The Administrative Review Board has repeatedly held that protected activity and employment actions are inextricably intertwined where the protected activity directly leads to the unfavorable employment action in question, or if the employment action cannot be explained without discussing the protected activity."

"What does that mean in English?" Darby asked, with a chuckle.

"Global's contention that the Section 8 referral was triggered by the results of an equal opportunity interview of you," Robert said. "That was prompted by and based on your safety report that led to an investigation. The causal chain of protected activity—your report—to a subsequent investigation, even if it were an *alleged* EO investigation, led to the adverse action. That dispositively establishes the AIR21 prima facie causal requirement. Your protected activity contributed to the adverse action."

"Is there case law supporting that?" Darby asked.

"Absolutely. I'm familiar with a case where an employee was injured. The contributing factor requirement was satisfied because the report of workplace injury led to an investigation as they were looking into the root cause for the injury, which in turn resulted in the employee's suspension."

"Then we have them," Darby said, raising her glass and air toasting Robert.

"That we do," Robert said. "I will finish the motion for summary decision by next week. But tomorrow we'll focus on preparations for both Dodson and Clark's depositions."

The waitress arrived with a basket of bread, and asked, "Are you still waiting for your guest?"

Darby sighed and looked at her phone again. "I think we can go ahead and order."

They both ordered the salmon special with sautéed spinach and a glass of wine.

When the waitress left to place their orders Darby said, "You drove Wendel nuts today. He was sighing, rolling his eyes, and looking at his watch when you read your notes. The rest of the time he just texted."

"He wasn't paying attention?" Robert asked surprised.

"No. Neither was Miss Martha Jones," Darby said. "But how the heck is Martha even able to be one of the attorneys? She was involved in this. Wolfe had written to Dr. Wood and said that she was part of the case from the beginning. Technically, she's one of the bad guys."

Chapter 30

Fully embracing a very good buzz, Darby went to her room. The rush from the deposition, followed by a celebratory dinner with her attorney was a nice end to the day. A perfect ending would have been to have Tom there. Once off the elevator, she removed her cell phone from her purse and dialed his number.

"Hey babe, how was dinner?" Tom asked.

"Delicious and informative." Darby stuck the plastic card into the slot in the door. "How's class going?"

"Good," he said. "I've been waiting all day to hear how you enjoyed your first deposition."

"It was awesome," she said opening the door. "I thought one attorney was going to have a heart attack, and another might have fallen asleep if he didn't have his phone to play with. The Global attorney… well, she was just an empty skirt that risked chipping a nail while she texted."

Tom laughed. "Empty skirt?"

"Kind of like an empty suit but with heels," Darby said, sitting on her bed.

"Were they cute?" Tom asked.

"Are you feeling your feminine side tonight?" Darby asked, kicking off her heels. "Or have you've spent too much time with me?"

"I'll blame you," Tom said. "But I'd really like to be feeling *your* feminine side."

"If you play your cards right, I think that can be arranged," Darby said stacking her pillows. She leaned against them and said, "By the way, they were butt ugly shoes. I wanted to tell her what Erin Brockovich had said to that lady attorney when she said they got off on the wrong foot."

"What was that?"

"That's all you've got lady…two wrong feet and fucking ugly shoes."

Tom laughed. "Promise me, you'll refrain when you see her again."

"I'll do my best," Darby said, closing her eyes, wishing she were lying beside him. "But I think Robert is getting her kicked out of the depositions."

"He appears to be a miracle worker, but how exactly is he going to pull that off?"

"She's the same attorney who told Clark that I had no safety information and advised him to meet with me."

"She could be a witness," Tom said.

"Exactly. You're pretty smart with all this legal stuff, for a cop."

"I'm even smarter when plugged into the smartest woman I know."

"Oh God. And such a tease too," Darby said with a groan. She relayed the highlights of the deposition and included the fireworks at the end. "The show was so good, all I was missing was the popcorn."

"Did you get anything from your dinner guest tonight?"

"He never showed," Darby said. "It's really weird too. I sent him multiple text messages. Then called and it went to voicemail on the first ring."

"Maybe he decided to get some sleep," Tom said. "Still reeling from when you drank him under the table in Paris, perhaps?"

"A great interrogation technique," Darby said. "But I think

somethings up because we were drinking Diet Coke."

"I'm sure everything's fine," Tom said. "He probably got cold feet."

"Maybe it's women's intuition, but I don't think so." Darby reached for her laptop. "I just have a feeling that he's the kind of guy who wouldn't no show. He would have at least let me know he wouldn't be there."

"Maybe he got called out on a trip," Tom suggested.

"Great minds. I'm checking now," Darby said as she logged into the company website. "Oh shit. Houston, we have a problem."

"He's on a trip?"

"No. He's on reserve," Darby said.

"Why's reserve a problem?"

"He would never have his phone turned off." Darby set her computer aside. A hollow feeling came over her as she thought of her friend Don. Flashbacks of blood splatter against the windshield came rushing back. He had been murdered shortly after he confided in her and had agreed to come forward to meet with Kathryn.

She proceeded to tell Tom about Don's murder. That they'd had dinner while she was in Oklahoma City during her 757 captain checkout, shortly before Global had removed her. Don Erickson had shared the details of what happened on a flight where he had pulled a gun on the captain to take the plane from him. He'd said the captain was planning to fly it into the ground.

The company tried to brush it under the rug. Darby had convinced him to talk to Kathryn. They had a meeting scheduled for lunch, and Don had planned to tell her everything. But he no showed. They found him dead that same day.

"He was murdered in his car, and someone made it look like a suicide," Darby said. "It wasn't."

"Sweetheart, I'm sure this guy is okay."

"Is there any way you could make a call to the local police and have someone stop by his house?" Darby asked.

"I don't think that's necessary," Tom said.

"You're right. I'll just take a cab over to his house tomorrow and check on him."

"No. You stay put," Tom said. "You've got work to do with Robert. I will make that call and get someone to swing by first thing in the morning. I'm sure everything's okay."

"You'd do that for me?" Darby asked demurely, already knowing the answer.

"I'd do anything for you," Tom said, "but you'll owe me."

Darby grinned. "More than you'll ever know."

Chapter 31

Oklahoma City
October 24, 2018

When you wake up, get up; when you get up, do something. Darby laid in bed with her eyes closed trying to determine how to start her day. She wondered if getting a cup of coffee counted for *doing something*. The only debate now was whether she should hit the lobby for a Starbucks or make a pot of coffee in her room.

Ten minutes later Darby was in the hotel lobby at Starbucks, without her phone. And therein lays the problem of going out for coffee before you've had your coffee. She ordered a Venti Raspberry Mocha with whipped cream, and once in hand she headed upstairs.

She and Robert had planned their day off to prepare for the next two days of depositions. She took a sip, then stuck her key in the slot and opened her door to a ringing phone. She ran across the room and grabbed it.

"Are you okay?" Tom asked.

"Yeah," Darby said, breathless. "My coffee low-level light was on. I forgot to take my phone."

"Turn the TV on," Tom said, strained. "Find the local news, then call me back."

Darby reached for the remote and clicked on the television. She flipped through channels until she found the local news and sat on her bed. Sipping her coffee, she watched the events unfold before her. Her eyes narrowed. Something about a pilot's death last night.

"Oh shit," she said, and dialed Tom. "That's Stan Branson's house, isn't it?"

"Yes. They found him just after four this morning," Tom said. "You did not hear this from me, but he had a bullet to the left temple. They believe it to be self-inflicted. Out of privacy for the family, they are not disclosing the manner of death."

"His kids?" Darby asked.

"Out of town with his wife," Tom said. "But the dog took a bullet."

"I'll call you back," Darby said, fighting tears.

"Of course. But… stay in the hotel today, okay?"

"Okay," Darby said distractedly, and disconnected the call.

She lifted the hotel phone and pressed 7 and then dialed 402. Robert answered on the first ring. "I know why Stan didn't join us for dinner last night," Darby said. "Turn on the television, channel four."

A few moments later Robert said, "What the hell?"

"Stan," Darby said. She felt a wave of nausea grow. A sinking feeling that his death was because of her. He wouldn't kill himself. She had put him in harm's way, and someone had killed him, and they were keeping it quiet.

"Can we talk at breakfast?" Robert asked.

"Of course," Darby said. "I'll call you in a few." She set the phone in the cradle and sat cross-legged on her bed glued to the television.

They were removing the body. She glanced at her watch. It was just after 7 a.m. *Why did it take them three hours to get him out of there?* she wondered. The camera zoomed in on the stretcher. Stan Branson lay beneath the sheet. Fresh tears filled her eyes.

The reporter interviewed neighbors that were now filling the street. Nobody knew the cause of death, but many had watched the police arrive around four or five in the morning.

A couple had witnessed a black SUV on the street around midnight, but they were returning from a party and really weren't paying that much attention. Another guy said it looked like someone was taking something out the front door before the police got there. One lady said that he was one of those union pilots who made a lot of money and didn't work much. Darby smiled at that comment and swiped a tear from her cheek.

The few things they all agreed to was—*he had great family. Everyone in the community loved him. They had no idea that he had been sick. Most assumed the cars were family coming to visit.* The reporter was filling space because this was a huge unknown. Simply theatrics because there was a body.

The reporter turned to the camera and said, "On behalf of Channel Four news, we send our prayers to Captain Branson's family."

Why was the media there? Darby wondered. People died of natural causes daily and that was not newsworthy. Perhaps it was nothing more than Tom asking the police to check on the house that had brought the media in tow.

Darby clicked off the television. Empty. Scared. Sick. Despite being unsure of the exact feeling that encompassed her, she knew that he did not kill himself. Startled by the ringing hotel phone, she answered.

"Can we meet me for breakfast now?" Robert asked.

Chapter 32

ROBERT WAS SITTING in the same table they held the night before, drinking a cup of coffee when Darby walked in. She'd forgotten her Starbucks coffee in her room. Sighing heavily, she reached for a cup and turned it over hoping that it would be filled soon.

"This is incredible," Robert said. "I wonder how the police found him so early with his family out of town?"

"I asked my friend, Tom, to call the local authorities to check on him." Darby sighed, "I'm not sure why they went so early this morning."

"I wonder how he died," Robert said.

"Tom said he killed himself," Darby said, "but I don't believe it."

Robert sipped his coffee without a response.

"He was going to come forward, and rat out the union," Darby said. "Why would he kill himself if he was coming forward? He wouldn't. He may have lost his job with the union, but he wasn't losing his career, and everyone said how much he adored his family." Darby tapped a fingernail on the table. "This stinks like the Philip Marshall case."

"Who?"

"Marshall was a Boeing 767 captain for United airlines whose good friend died in the September 11 attack. He had become obsessed with learning the truth. He had also been a special activities contract pilot in the military before joining the airlines," Darby said. "He had written a conspiracy book called *The Big Bamboozle*."

"That's why I recognized the name. I read his earlier work about running drugs during the Iran-contra scandal," Robert said. "I believe his associate was murdered in the mid-eighties. But what does that have to do with Stan?"

"The way Marshall was murdered," Darby said. "They also claimed it was a suicide."

"You don't believe so?"

"No. Marshall thought our government was involved in the September 11 attack," Darby said. "He was writing assertions, researching, and apparently had proof. He wrote about most of it in his book. But he was also working on some other controversial topics."

"I've heard those theories about the government and September 11, but I'm not so sure I believe them."

"He investigated the 911 attacks for ten years," Darby said. "He explained that there was no way a novice could have done what they did in those planes. What I found most interesting was that he had tried to hit the building in the simulator and missed it on the first go. He had thousands of flight hours and a ton of experience, but he couldn't hit the building."

"How's that possible?"

"He did not anticipate the excessive nose-down trim that was necessary for the last-minute excess power as he shoved the thrust levers forward. The airplane pitched up and climbed on the first go because he added thrust to increase his speed." Robert made no comment.

"Think about this. They delayed sending our military out after the first plane hit. The others were supposed to crash immediately after, but they had been unexpectedly vectored. It was as if the government knew there was going to be more hits, and they were waiting for the other two. Not until after the third crash did they scramble the jets. Why not scramble them after the first hit? Why wait?"

"Something I had wondered at the time," Robert said. "I have no answer."

"I initially thought it was due to the startle effect and they simply didn't react. That may have been a good excuse for the first, but not after the second. Not until I read the reports on how Marshall died, did I believe it might all be true." Darby stared into her empty cup. "The report said Marshal shot his two kids. Both teenagers and their dog, too. Then he shot himself."

"You don't believe that?"

"No. And for the same reason I don't believe Stan killed himself," Darby said. "Just like Marshall, they were both shot in the left temple."

Robert gave her a questioning look.

"Stan was right-handed. He would have shot himself in the right temple.

"Are you sure?"

"Absolutely." Having spent the better part of the evening with him, sitting on his right he used his right hand. "And they killed the dog. The only reason someone would shoot the dog is if he were barking. Why would the dog be barking at his owner?" Darby asked. "He wouldn't."

"You know that this makes you sound crazy," Robert said with a grin. "The very thing we are trying to disprove."

"I'm not worried about that." Darby gave him a slow smile. "Technically, I'm now the only certified sane pilot at Global."

The waitress arrived with menus and took their orders. She also filled their coffee cups. When she was out of earshot, Darby said, "The black SUV, that one of the neighbors saw reminded me of what was identified in front of the Marshall house."

"So you think the government did this?" Robert asked.

"No. Nobody mentioned antennas like they did with Marshall," Darby said, tucking a strand of hair behind an ear. "I think it was the union. They're a billion-dollar business and might have had a hell of a lot to lose."

"I would agree ALPO had motive to silence him," Robert said. "But murder?"

Darby shrugged. "Did I tell you they had tried to kill me?"

"Who?" Robert said. "The union?"

Darby shook her head no. "It was Christmas Eve, the day Dr. Wood sent me my letter saying I was bipolar. I also received a bottle of wine the same night." Darby sipped her coffee thinking back to that day. "There was a note saying it was from my ex-boyfriend. Turns out it would have put me to sleep for a very long time, as in *forever*."

"Nobody was charged?" Robert asked.

"Nope. John McCallister, the department of transportation secretary was investigating. They knew it came from this lovely town," Darby said, spreading her hands. "But no proof as to who sent it."

"Any ideas?"

"Oh yeah. I think Rich Clark had his name all over it," Darby said. "Do you think it would be funny if I brought the same bottle to his deposition and offered him a glass?"

"Now that *would* be funny," Robert said, as the waitress arrived with their omelets.

Darby dumped salsa on her eggs, then lifted her fork. She looked up at Robert. "Tom told me not to leave the hotel."

"Was he warning you?" Robert asked and Darby nodded. Then he asked, "Are you scared?"

"I don't know," Darby said. "Maybe a little. Why would Tom

warn me to not to leave the hotel because a pilot committed suicide? He wouldn't." She pushed the hash browns around her plate. "I think Stan's dead because of me."

"Probably not," Robert said.

Darby shrugged. "One day I'll have to tell you how many men in my life have seen untimely deaths because of me."

"As long as *you're* not killing them, I'm good."

Chapter 33

Sun Tzu had said—*if you know the enemy and know yourself, you need not fear the results of a hundred battles.* Darby wasn't so sure anymore. Stan's death was surreal. He had worked for the union and was supposed to support and protect others. While he had looked the other way to protect himself, when he had finally decided to step forward to help her fight the battle, he lost his life. She sighed knowing what would have happened if a guy in the HIMS program came forward. Granted the program did a lot of good for those in need, but God forbid those who became a byproduct. What they were doing was criminal.

It would be more than the end of Stan's ALPO job, it would be the end of his career. He had integrity and finally found his courage. He was going to do the right thing, and someone took his life because of that. Stan knew the enemy, he knew himself, and yet he died in that first battle. Something was horribly wrong with that.

Darby's phone rang and she startled. Opening her eyes, she reached out of the tub and grabbed a towel. After drying a hand, she stuck her headset into position and answered.

"How are you doing?" Kathryn asked. "I'm sorry it's so late." They had talked earlier that morning, but Kathryn had meetings all day. She'd promised to call back as soon as she could. It was now 8 p.m.

"No worries," Darby said. "Tom already kissed me goodnight and Robert and I are ready for tomorrow's deposition. Now… I'm just having a little soak and thinking about stuff."

"Stan's death was not your fault."

"If I had gone to dinner with my crew he'd still be alive."

"You don't know that to be true."

"The union did this," Darby said. "I can't get that exchange out of my mind from the bar. The coldness in the President's eyes and the fear in Stan's. He said he didn't care if they knew, and he was going to come forward anyway. He probably never imagined he would end up dead."

"Darby, you need to realize that people die before their time. Be it murder, or suicide, or a tragic illness. Unless you pulled the gun or convinced him to do it, it was not your fault."

"I guess," Darby said. "But I was just imagining the Philip Marshall events and visualized that car as the same black car the witnesses saw."

"Are you positive it couldn't have been a suicide?" Kathryn finally asked with a plea, that Darby rarely heard. "Nobody ever knows what's going on in someone else's life."

"I know. But I think someone killed him, they had to," Darby said closing her eyes, sinking a little lower into the water. "I'm just thankful his kids weren't home."

"Me too." Kathryn sighed heavily. "But I think you're right."

"About the murder?"

"Yes, but not who did it."

"Who then?" Darby asked.

"This was more than your fucking union trying to cover up that they had supported Global to throw you away, and their fear of getting out of a DFR."

"What then?" Darby asked.

"I also know why Global reacted to your safety report the way they did and why they *had* to bury you no matter what," Kathryn said ignoring her question. "Why they *had* to destroy your reputation. Why they tried to kill you making it look like a suicide, and now fighting this inane lawsuit in which they have no case."

"You're scaring me," Darby said.

"I'm scared," Kathryn said. "I'm scared at how far this corruption goes. I'm mad that we pride ourselves on freedom in the United States, and justice for all. And there is none. No fucking justice. Nobody is safe. Those with power and money make the rules and can do any damn thing they want."

It was the very rare occasion that Kathryn ever spewed a swear word. That was Darby's job. "Have you been drinking?" Darby asked.

"Guilty as charged," Kathryn said. "I'm sorry. I was calling to comfort you and I failed miserably." She laughed a bit. "I'm just so… incensed."

"What happened today?" Darby asked pulling her legs close and wrapping her arms around them.

"Other than the ultimate betrayal of the traveling public and corruption on every level? And… the fact that I'm feeling a little homicidal?"

"Yeah. Other than all that," Darby said.

"I think you should probably get out of the tub before I tell you."

Chapter 34

Regional Director Dodson Deposition
Oklahoma City
October 25, 2019

Darby hadn't slept well and the application of concealer did not adequately hide her racoon eyes. The thought of wearing her aviator sunglasses to Dodson's deposition was overruled by her need to look him in the eye. Her looking forward to his deposition had shifted to dread because of what she might say or do that would not be to her benefit. *Snap out of Darby,* she thought.

Something was up bigger than herself, but she could not place her finger on it. Stan's death, and now if Kathryn was correct… the death of aviation safety as the world knew it was underway. To say Robert was surprised was an understatement, but Wyatt lying to him had been unsettling. Technically he didn't lie, he just cut Robert off at midsentence.

Darby's attention was immediately drawn to the new face on the opposing team. A slight smile crossed her lips as she thought, *Robert does in fact work miracles.*

She walked directly to the woman and extended her hand. "I'm Darby. Are you replacing Martha Jones?"

The woman did not shake her hand. "No… uh… this has *always* been my case. Martha was just filling in for me the other day," she said with a condescending look.

Yeah right, Darby thought with a smirk. They both knew that Robert had Martha removed because of her involvement in the case.

Darby's eyes then dropped to the woman's shoes. She grinned with her lips sealed so nothing would escape, heeding Tom's words—*don't do it,* she thought. The woman, who had been staring condescendingly at her, now glanced down to her feet and then back up with a questioning look.

"Welcome to the fun." Darby walked around the table and found her seat, feeling much better about the day. This was nothing more than a chess game, and they were moving pieces around the board. While Robert was positioning himself for checkmate, they were losing pieces daily.

Everyone provided their contact information to the court reporter. Today's line up was Johnson Von Dietrich, Wendel Kowalski, Betty Dickson, Global's new in-house counsel, and the Regional Director, Chief Pilot Dodson. She didn't care the size of their team. Robert Allen had more brains and talent than all of them together.

After the preliminaries were done and Dodson was sworn in, Robert asked the typical questions regarding the understanding of truthful testimony. He also asked Dodson if he was on drugs, then explained the requirements to verbally speak his answers. Dodson grinned as Robert spoke, as if he found this situation humorous. It could be a diffusion of his emotions. Regardless, he remined Darby of the Pillsbury dough boy, and for some reason made Darby want to beat him with a wooden spoon.

"Who did you talk to about your deposition today?"

"I'm going to object to the extent that that calls for disclosure of attorney-client privileged information," Von Dietrich said.

Here we go again, Darby thought.

"I don't think he's asking you to do that, but I just want it to be very clear," Von Dietrich explained to Dodson as if he were two-year old. He might have the two-year old part right, but *Jesus,* Darby thought. *Can we just get on with this?*

"You can answer who you spoke with, just don't reveal the substance of the communication if it was with an attorney. So, for example, if you talked to me, you can say, *I spoke with Mr. Von Dietrich* or *I spoke with Mr. Kowalski.* You *can't* disclose what it is we talked about," Von Dietrich explained.

Darby closed her eyes in disbelief. She sighed and tilted her head back. *Shoot me now,* she thought. This was going to be a very, long, fucking day. They all knew Von Dietrich had already briefed Dodson on what he could say, and this was simply a ploy to waste time and then bill Global for as many hours as possible.

She righted her head and opened her eyes. Von Dietrich was staring at her, so she rolled her eyes and gave him a slight headshake with another sigh, sending the message that he was being a dick and she knew it. His face reddened ever so slightly, and he returned his attention to the spot on the table. A sign that he was done talking.

"At this point, all I'm asking you is the identity of the persons that you spoke to about the deposition in anticipation of the deposition," Robert said calmly.

"And that's what I understood the question to be," Von Dietrich said looking up at Robert. "I was just making sure that he didn't misinterpret it and then start saying more stuff and have privilege issues, that's all."

Darby grinned. Maybe this wasn't a game with Von Dietrich, maybe he had spent enough time with Dodson to realize that Dodson was, in fact, an idiot and might just say something he shouldn't. She gave a couple points to Von Dietrich for that one.

"I spoke with Johnson… uh, Mr. Von Dietrich," Dodson said, glancing at him. Von Dietrich's eyes were once again nailed to the desk.

"Anybody else?" Robert asked.

"No."

Now Darby wondered what the hell Dodson and Von Dietrich had spoken about that Von Dietrich had to make certain would not be conveyed.

"Was anyone else in the room when you spoke to Mr. Von Dietrich?" Robert asked.

"No."

"You know that Ms. Bradshaw was given a letter referring her to a Section 8 evaluation, correct?"

"Yes."

"What was your title at the time of the issuance of that letter?" Robert asked with a friendly tone.

"I was the Regional Director and Chief Pilot of the West Region for Global Air Lines," Dodson said proudly.

"How long were you in that position?"

"From March 1st of 2013 until September 1st of 2017."

Robert jotted something on his paper and then asked, "And were you asked to leave your position?"

"No. It was a normal rotation out of that position," Dodson said.

"You're back flying the line currently?"

"Yes."

"You say it was a normal rotation," Robert began. "Is there a standard term of duty for a Regional Director at Global?"

"Typically, it's about three years. I was in four and a half."

"Is that published anywhere that that's the standard duration of service for Regional Director?"

"I don't know," Dodson said with a shrug.

"Have you ever testified in court before?"

"Yes."

"Can you tell me how many times?"

"I'll object to the term court as being vague," Von Dietrich said.

"I think only once."

"Can you describe the action for me?"

"Yes. It was an AIR21 Action."

"Whose action, was it?" Robert asked.

"Mr. Smith."

"First name Keith?

"Yes."

"On what day did you testify?" Robert asked.

"I think that it was the 28th of November 2016."

Darby copied the date on her pad of paper and wrote, *excellent memory. How the hell did he remember that?* She glanced up and caught Wendel looking at what she had just written. She placed her hand over the words and slowly extended her middle finger with a perfectly manicured red nail and wagged it back and forth. Wendel's eyes widened and then he looked up, their eyes locking. She responded with a wink.

You're such a dweeb, Darby thought, but might be fun to play with.

Darby had watched that entire trial and Global had set Keith up for a fall. As it turned out, his case did not meet the elements of an AIR21 statute, yet Global went to court without as much as a request for a summary judgement, in which they could have won. They also did not claim collateral estoppel considering that Keith adjudicated his case and lost in the grievance process. Management and the union had agreed to the same arbitrator for Keith that they tried to force on Darby after ex parte communications. He was set up from the beginning, and his attorneys took him for a ride.

Global had retaliated against him for his calling out the company for placing an unairworthy plane into the sky. The problems were many. He had acted in the capacity of fuel tank expert when he identified the issue, for his personal business. The plane was also on contract from a foreign carrier, not a Global plane. Then there was a certification issue. Regardless, he did the right thing and lost his job in the process.

Darby had learned while sitting in Smith's trial that Dodson had spent months collecting data for the company to legally terminate him. The proverbial "look back."

"And have you ever testified in an arbitration before?"

"Yes."

"How many times?"

"Three."

"What were those arbitrations about?" Robert asked.

"Mr. Smith, Mr. Jones, and Mr. Hill."

"Were those pilot termination cases?"

"Yes."

It was Captain Jones' case that Darby wanted to smack Dodson for setting him up. Jones needed help to get his life together. Instead, they terminated him because he abused the pass travel privileges and flew positive space from his mother's deathbed to work. Poor guy had so many life stressors, he just needed to regroup and settle them.

Dodson had known of Jones' first transgression when it had occurred, but instead of counseling him, he proceeded to allow the behavior to continue over the next three months so they could gather more infractions to have enough reason to terminate him.

Those who needed help didn't get it unless they were in the club. In Captain Jones' case, he was just trying to make life work. Yet, Clark had sent him to see a corporate-purchased doctor and then they got rid of him. Opposite to Darby's case, they paid the doctor to claim Jones did not have a medical problem so they could terminate him for the violations. All the while, another doctor had diagnosed him with a stress-related disorder.

ALPO should have helped, but Global owned the union at the highest level. Rich Clark had selected the doctor and Jones met him at a yacht club. Due to the informal setting, Jones had thought they were trying to help him. It was just the opposite.

"Were any a Section 8 referral?" Robert asked.

"Yes."

"Which cases?"

"Captain Hill."

"Was Captain Hill fired in part due to his refusal to comply with a Section 8 directive?" Robert asked.

"I believe the answer is, well, it was for not cooperating with the process," Dodson said folding his arms. He leaned back and said, "Yes."

"Was there a psychiatrist appointed by the company as the Company Medical Examiner in that case?"

"Yes."

"That would've been Dr. Kenneth Wood, correct?"

"Yes."

"And did Dr. Wood actually reach any determination with respect to the mental health of Mr. Hill?"

"Objection. Foundation," Von Dietrich snapped.

"I don't know," Dodson said with a shrug as he glanced toward Von Dietrich and then to Wendel.

"But isn't it true that Dr. Wood took the position that Mr. Hill's resistance to a Section 8 evaluation was indicative of a mental-health issue?"

"Objection. Foundation. Asked and answered," Von Dietrich said.

"I don't know," Dodson said.

"During the proceedings for Mr. Hill, did there come to your knowledge any objections from Mr. Hill to the manner in which Dr. Wood conducted himself?"

"Objection. Vague," Von Dietrich said.

"Yes, I think Mr. Hill did object."

"Okay. What were Captain Hill's objections?"

"Objection. Foundation. Calls for speculation."

"I don't know what his specific objection was."

"Did you attend the entirety of the Hill arbitration hearing?"

"Yes."

"So, you heard all of Mr. Hill's testimony in that case?"

"Yes."

"And you recall his expressing some objections to Dr. Wood's conduct, correct?"

"Objection. Asked and answered."

"I recall that he referenced filing some criminal charges against Dr. Wood, but I don't recall him stating what the charges were. I don't know the specifics."

Darby knew exactly what had happened. Global sent Hill to Dr. Wood to get rid of him like they had with her. The difference being, Captain Hill had walked out of the evaluation after spending not more than an hour with him, unwilling to play the game. Whereas Darby had stuck it out, with Robert's concurrence that she had to complete the process outlined in the contract.

Shortly after Captain Hill walked out on Dr. Wood, Wood had sent him a letter that stated if Hill reported Wood to anyone, filed a claim with the medical board or hired an attorney, he would be found mentally unfit. Wood had written if he came back there would be a *chance* he might be found okay. Hill had also filed a complaint against Dr. Wood with the Illinois Medical Board.

Another major difference was that ALPO stood by Hill and wrote a letter to attorney Wolfe advising him that Global should not use Dr. Wood and they had a deep concern for his ethical behavior. Hill then went out on medical leave for the next couple years to get a paycheck from another source and wait until the dust settled to return. When he decided to return to Global after learning of Darby's return, Global reasserted the mental health issue. They immediately dropped it and terminated him days later for allegedly falsifying a medical record from years earlier, despite that being a false assertion.

As it turned out, Global had the power to make any claim fact whether it was or was not, simply because they said so. Ironically, it was Dodson who terminated Hill, despite his not being the regional director at the time, but back out on the flight line.

"Are you a line check airman?"

"I'm in the process of checking out as a line check airman now."

"Are you currently a member of ALPO?"

"Yes."

"But today you're represented by Mr. Johnson Von Dietrich?"

"Yes," Dodson said glancing at Von Dietrich, who was still focused on the desk, but listening intently. Dodson shifted his attention back to Robert.

"Do you know the conduct that was the basis for the issuance of the Section 8 letter to Captain Hill?

"I'm going to object to this line of questioning," Von Dietrich snapped, flailing a hand, and yelling directly at Robert. His eyes were blazing. "He indicated he was not involved in the decision at all in these issues and I would like a proffer, on the record as to the relevance of this testimony! It's my understanding Mr. Hill has a separate lawsuit where currently you are listed as counsel, and it would be improper to use this deposition as a way to conduct your discovery in that case. Now, if there's a reason why it's relevant to this case, I'm happy for you to make a proffer on the record but we're not going to conduct discovery in any unrelated litigations in this proceeding, and Judge Geraghty wouldn't want that to happen. So articulate for the record the relevance of these questions."

Darby folded her arms. *Game on,* she thought, her eyebrow involuntarily raised. Robert had hit a nerve with Captain Hill's case, and he was also not representing him. It was interesting that Von Dietrich thought so, or he was simply distorting the record.

"Let me state," Robert said, "and you don't really have to raise your voice to communicate your position, but—"

"I'm not raising my voice and I object to you saying that on the record!" Von Dietrich yelled.

Darby's eyes widened and she glanced at the court reporter whose face held the same expression. This was the very reason Darby could not be a court reporter. She would have typed—*Hell yes he is yelling!*

"Rule 30 prohibits speaking objections," Robert said.

"I'm not making a speaking objection. I'm asking for a proffer on the record of the relevance of this testimony. The Rules of Civil Procedure and the Office of Administrative Rules and Regulations governing this deposition do not allow you to conduct totally irrelevant discovery. I don't see any relevance to this case and I'm giving you an opportunity to articulate the relevance. If you choose not to articulate it, that's fine but I may shut down this line of questions."

"Well, that's always your option," Robert said. "It's not an option to have a prolonged speaking objection. It is your option to take the risk of directing him not to answer. What I would tell you is AIR21 is a discrimination statute and what is always going to be relevant is how individuals in similar or somewhat similar situations have been treated. What's always going to be relevant is the histories of a pattern and practice of similar abuses. That's all the explanation I'm going to offer and it's not an explanation frankly to which you're entitled, however—"

"I—" Von Dietrich began.

"Sir, please don't interrupt me. At this point, you can either direct him not to answer or permit me to continue, but I really don't want to have more of this angry exchange."

"There's been no angry exchange at all and I wish this were video-taped so that would be demonstrated," Von Dietrich said.

"So do I," Robert replied.

"I take strong offense and objection to your mischaracterization of anything in this deposition," Von Dietrich said, his voice lowered sightly, but every bit aggressive. "I asked you not to. I've asked you repeatedly in this case to be professional! I'm going to ask you that again right now. Irrespective of that, this witness has testified that he was not involved in the decisions involving Mr. Hill, and I have allowed you to ask those questions for the very reason you stated.

"What you're now asking the witness is if he has knowledge about a third party's decision making, a third party who is not involved in this case and has nothing to do with this litigation. I'm going to allow you to ask your questions for now but I'm telling you, as far as I can tell, there's no relevance here and I'm getting very close to instructing him not to answer. I appreciate your proffer on the record. Please continue with your questions."

"Could you clarify the question please?" Dodson asked.

"I think now is a good time for a break," Robert said.

Chapter 35

ROBERT NEEDED A few minutes alone, and he walked out of the deposition room and into a briefing room. He closed the door to be alone. Darby took care of business and when she returned, she peeked through the briefing room window and Robert was on the phone. She returned to the deposition room and found a Diet Pepsi in the fridge. Walking to the window she opened her soda and stared out at the buildings across the street as she sipped, not really seeing them.

Both Darby and Robert were on edge and exhausted. That was not a good combination with Von Dietrich being an ass. Hill's case was relevant. Global had sent Darby to the same psychiatrist as Hill, and ALPO voiced their concerns about that very doctor being unethical, directly to Wolfe. The ALPO attorney voiced no concern when Global sent Darby to Dr. Wood. Instead, they played dumb as to having any knowledge of the man.

There were many psychiatrists on the West Coast that could have been used. The fact that Wolfe was writing the play book for Darby's demise and used Wood, who had been voiced to be off limits with another pilot, made this testimony extremely relevant. Now they were trying to hide their actions by purchasing what they thought to be the best legal team in the country. She grinned at that thought.

Robert outshined the opposing counsel.

Then she thought of Stan. Darby opened her phone and sent a text to Neal—*Did you hear that Stan's death was a suicide? Anything you can tell me? I don't think he killed himself. He was going to testify.* Despite their breakup, Neal was still a good friend and would help anyway he could. Darby turned toward the commotion.

The other team shuffled into the room and seconds later Robert joined them. He grinned at Darby with a nod and took his seat.

Robert asked Dodson a few more questions regarding Captain Hill with Von Dietrich's objections. Then he took a moment to read through his list of written questions, lining through some and jotting notes on one page, then flipped to the next and read for a few more minutes. This time Robert took long enough to break Von Dietrich's stare.

Von Dietrich looked up at Robert and then turned his head and scowled at Wendel. Wendel in turn rolled his eyes and shrugged. Then Wendel made a show of looking at his watch for his well-rehearsed theatrics. Global's inhouse attorney simply ate chocolate covered raisins.

The games they played with frivolous objections and the unnecessary arguments took more time than Robert's few minutes of reading notes. The theatrics had to be an attempt to rattle him. However, they'd yet to figure out that Robert Allen was in a zone, not unlike that of an athlete who tuned out the crowds to focus on the challenge before him.

"Is the FOM an FAA approved document?" Robert finally asked Dodson, regarding the company's flight operations manual.

"Objection. Foundation," Von Dietrich said.

"I'm not really sure what the legal approval of the FOM is, and whether or not it is an official FAA document."

Darby's eyes widened and her mouth opened. Dodson glanced

her way. If he could read her mind, he would have known she was thinking, *are you an effing idiot or what?*

"I'm asking if the company Flight Operations Manual is reviewed and approved by the FAA?"

"Objection. Foundation. Calls for speculation," Von Dietrich said.

"I honestly am not sure, sir," Dodson said, looking perplexed.

"Okay. Does the FAA require an air carrier to comply with its FOM?"

"Same objections and it calls for a legal conclusion," Von Dietrich said.

A legal conclusion? To determine if the airline is required to follow the FAA approved manuals... are they frigging kidding? Darby thought.

She was experiencing an episode in the twilight zone. Did any of these attorneys think about who was being questioned and the level of knowledge expected? Based upon Dodson's position he was legally required to know that answer.

"Kind of my same answer," Dodson said. "I know some of our regulations or procedures do fall into that category. I'm not sure about the FOM."

He was the regional director and a chief pilot *and* about to be a check airman, but he didn't know that the FOM was an FAA approved document. Darby could not believe what she was hearing. Robert sighed, and then took a few moments to read through his questions clearly upsetting Wendel once again. He circled a couple words, gathering his thoughts, and then set his pencil down and looked directly at Dodson.

"Was part of your job responsibilities to familiarize yourself with the Collective Bargaining Agreement between ALPO and Global Air Lines?"

"Yes."

"You're familiar with the Section 8 process contained within the ALPO collective bargaining agreement with Global Airlines?"

"I'm familiar with it, yes," Dodson said.

"Can you explain your understanding as to the purpose of the Section 8?"

"Objection," Von Dietrich said.

"Yes, I can," Dodson said. He folded his arms with a smirk and said nothing more.

Darby mirrored him and folded her arms, but the smirk was returned with a glare. She was funding this party and now he was wasting their time and her money by playing games.

"Would you please do that?" Robert asked, and then added, "you've been well prepared as a witness."

"Thank you," Dodson said, leaning back with a grin that Darby wanted to slap off his face.

Robert said. "Would you go ahead. Can you explain your understanding?"

"Section 8 is a process available when the Company has reason to believe that perhaps an individual pilot does not meet the standards for a first-class medical or is not fit to exercise the rights of a First-class Medical."

"And who is authorized to initiate a Section 8 process?'

"I don't know, sir, if there is a specific list of who's authorized to do that," Dodson said.

"Can you answer the question in terms of a department within the company?" Robert asked dumbing down the question to Dodson's level.

At the very least, he must know it's flight operations, Darby thought.

"To my knowledge, it would be a decision… uh, to my knowledge it would be a collaborative decision between the Director of Health

Services, DHS, and probably Captain Clark."

Darby was impressed at how Robert kept his cool to Dodson's method of responding. First, he didn't know who, but when asked what department, then he answered the who. Dodson was simply being evasive, and it took Robert three questions to pull a simple answer out of him. Dodson was not the brightest crayon in the box, but now she wondered if he was mentally slow. She shifted her attention to the Global legal team.

Von Dietrich was obnoxious, Wendel irritating, and Ms. Dickson couldn't get the candy in fast enough. Quite the team they were fighting. They were definitely from another Universe.

Robert handed Dodson another exhibit. "In terms of the preparation, is this a document you reviewed in preparation for your deposition?"

"Yes," Dodson said, "In addition to the emails."

"Good to know that. Do you understand the function of this document was to elicit information from Global Airlines concerning this case?"

"Objection. Calls for a legal conclusion, Von Dietrich said.

"I don't know the exact uh… I don't know the purpose of this document," Dodson said, setting it on the table.

"When you reviewed it, was there any information contained therein with respect to Global's responses that you considered to be erroneous?"

"Objection," Von Dietrich said. "It might be helpful for us to go off the record for a moment. I think the witness may be confused about documents he reviewed."

Darby wanted to laugh. Confused was an understatement for Dodson.

"I prefer to proceed," Robert said, calmly.

"Let's go off the record so I can talk to you for a second," Von

Dietrich said abrasively.

Darby so wanted to tell him to ask nicely but remained silent.

Robert had been dealing with Von Dietrich's shit all day in the shadow of his learning that Wyatt had not been truthful during his deposition, and a storm had been brewing. The clouds were about to break free. *This is going to be fun,* Darby thought.

"I'm asking to *not* go off the record," Robert said calmly.

"Then, I'll say it on the record. If you want me to state it in front of the witness on the record," Von Dietrich warned.

"I don't want you to coach the witness because that's violating Rule 30," Robert replied.

"Exactly!" Von Dietrich spat so loudly that Darby jumped, and her chair almost tipped backwards. He glanced at her then back to Robert.

"Please stop," Robert said firmly.

"I will note for the record that Mr. Allen is affirmatively asking that I not take steps to make a clear record and allow him to accurately get information in this deposition," Von Dietrich began, and spoke for another two minutes with his assertions. Darby looked at her wrist theatrically and then rolled her eyes for Wendel. He appeared confused, probably because she wasn't wearing a watch.

When Von Dietrich was done pontificating, Robert asked Dodson again, "When you reviewed this document, was there, more specifically, when you reviewed Global's responses contained in this document did you determine there was anything erroneous in the responses?"

"To be very clear, the document is *Global's* responses to Ms. Bradshaw's interrogatories," Von Dietrich said. "It is not Ms. Bradshaw's responses to Global's interrogatories. Is that correct, Mr. Allen?"

"Objection," Robert said, dropping his pen. "I'm going to ask you to please—"

"I'm describing the document and you're objecting to that?" Von Dietrich said, his face reddening.

"I'm asking you to lower your voice and to stop disrupting the process. And, yes, I would like to videotape Mr. Clark's deposition. I'm going to accept your invitation for that because this is enough. You have been long talking, speaking objections and it's very clear to me you're coaching the witness. So I'm asking you to please stop and let me ask my questions to the witness."

"I'm neither coaching the witness nor giving long speaking objections," Von Dietrich said. "I literally described the document. So how that can be a speaking objection is beyond me. You can videotape or not. They're your depositions."

"I saw you paging through the document," Robert said to Dodson. "I wasn't asking you to do that this time. My request was, as you reviewed it previously did anything in Global's responses strike you as erroneous?"

"Mr. Allen is not telling you not to review the document," Von Dietrich said to Dodson. "If you want to review it to answer his question you can certainly do so."

"He's already reviewed it," Robert said. "I'm asking you, when you reviewed it *before* did you come across anything that you considered to be erroneous in terms of the Global response?"

"Objection. Lacks foundation. Assumes facts not in evidence," Von Dietrich said.

"Actually, I'm not even sure I did review this yesterday," Dodson said, scratching his head. Wendel was actively nodding, and Darby was sure she saw an incongruent flicker of Von Dietrich's lips holding back a smile with the scowl still engraved into his brow.

"Let's consider that a coached response," Robert said. "Let's move forward, and—"

"I offered to talk with you off the record, Mr. Allen to clear anything up."

"Would you please stop interrupting?" Robert asked.

"And I'll object to you making remarks that are offensive and badgering the witness and being disparaging to counsel, then," Von Dietrich said glaring at him instead of the table.

Robert ignored his comment and said to Dodson, "I'm going to direct your attention to Interrogatory Number 10 at the bottom of the page. Interrogatory Number 10 reads, *identify each person who participated in the decision to refer Complainant for a Fitness For Duty Evaluation pursuant to Section 8 as directed by Captain Robert Dodson's letter dated December 15, 2016.* Did I read that correctly?"

"You're talking about the response to Interrogatory Number 10?" Dodson asked.

"I think he just read the Interrogatory Number 10 to start with," Von Dietrich said.

"Did I read that correctly," Robert asked Dodson.

"Okay. Could you read it again?" Dodson asked.

Is he fucking kidding? Darby thought. If this were not so serious, she would laugh. *Dodson could not really be that ignorant, could he?* she wondered, as Robert read the statement for the second time, and Dodson confirmed it was read correctly.

Robert handed him a second document. "I've just handed you a document dated December 15, 2016, with your signature at the bottom with a Bates Stamp C-065. Is that a letter that you gave to Ms. Bradshaw on December 15, 2016?"

"Yes."

"That's your signature under the word Sincerely?" Robert asked again.

"Yes…" Dodson said hesitantly, looking confused. He glanced

toward his legal team, but their attention was elsewhere.

Finally, a question he could answer, Darby thought, fighting a laugh.

"Going back to Dodson Exhibit 1, the response to that interrogatory reads, *Respondent objects to the Interrogatory's use of the term 'participated' as vague and ambiguous. Subject to the foregoing and without waiving the same, the decision to refer Complainant for a Section 8 evaluation was made by Rich Clark. Rich Clark's decision was made in consultation with Joe Wolfe, and based on information received from Dr. Tom Marsh and Anne Abbott.*"

Dodson just stared at Robert. His face blank, more than likely mirroring what was happening inside his head. He really is that ignorant, Darby thought. And passengers' lives were in his hands. Absolutely Incredible.

"Did you hear the question?" Robert finally asked.

"No. Could you repeat it, please?" Dodson asked, looking more confused than he had all day.

"Captain Dodson, is it correct that you did not participate in the decision to refer Ms. Bradshaw for a Section 8 evaluation?" Robert reworded the question so Dodson might understand what was being asked.

"That's correct!" Dodson responded quickly with a nod.

"Someone wrote this letter for you?" Robert asked.

"Yes."

"Who wrote the letter for you?"

"Objection," Von Dietrich said. "Foundation."

"I don't know exactly who wrote it," Dodson said.

"Did someone give this letter to you and instruct you to sign it?"

"Objection. Compound," Von Dietrich said.

"Someone gave it to me. I didn't require any instruction to sign it."

"Who was that person who gave this to you?"

"It was an attorney," Dodson said.

"What's the name of that attorney?" Robert asked.

"Attorney Joe Wolfe."

"Have you ever previously signed a Section 8 referral letter?"

"I don't recall," Dodson said.

"And have you ever signed a pilot termination letter?"

"No."

"And have you ever signed a pilot disciplinary letter?"

"To my recollection, yes."

"Just once?" Robert asked.

"I don't know, sir," Dodson said.

"Do you recall any other time where in any instance in which you signed a pilot disciplinary letter, prior to your being a participant in the decision-making process to issue it?" Robert asked.

"Can you *define* participant?" Dodson asked.

Robert removed his glasses and stared at him a moment. He withdrew the question and then asked, "Did Ms. Bradshaw give you a safety assessment relating to Global Airlines at some point?"

"Objection. Vague," Von Dietrich said.

"Could you please define safety assessment?" Dodson asked.

Chapter 36

Oklahoma City
Global Corporate Office
October 25, 2018

Play by play the text message created the picture of the deposition. Joe Wolfe leaned back in his chair and read them as they poured into his computer. Dodson was holding his own and evading the questions better than Wolfe had thought he could. His testimony, however, was going to be a problem just as was Wyatt's. Unfortunately, there was another issue on the horizon.

He lifted the phone and called Clark. "Sir, Wolfe here. I have something you need to read."

"What is it?"

"I would recommend you join me sooner than later."

Wolfe did not wait for a response and ended the call. He knew that would be enough to infuriate Clark and propel him down the hall. He didn't care. That man was making his life far too complicated. At least Croft had come to him with this information.

Within five minutes Clark entered his office without knocking. He closed the door firmly behind him. "This better be important."

"Have a seat please," Wolfe said, wiping his hands on his pants. "I'd like you to read this." Wolfe handed Clark the document.

Clark remained standing, and after reading it and said, "So?" tossing it on the desk.

"You claimed you sent Bradshaw in for a mental health evaluation because of Abbott's report. This was your decision," Wolfe said, extending a hand to the document. "Yet that document states that one of our female captains reported another pilot for placing a gun into his mouth and had threatened suicide months ago, and nothing was done."

"He's a first officer," Clark said placing his hands on his hips. "One of our instructors."

"Did you do anything about it?" Wolfe asked.

"No. He's our only *black* instructor," Clark snapped. "What the fuck did you expect me to do?"

"What do you expect to do now?" Wolfe asked.

"Lose the tone," Clark said.

"I apologize, sir, but you've put your nuts in a vice and mine are with them. If these two women find each other, and they will, we have no case against Bradshaw. You've compromised everything."

"How do you figure?" Clark said, a tinge of red working up his neck.

"Our entire case with Bradshaw is that we *had to* do this because of the Germanwings pilot. Yet, that Germanwings pilot was mentally unstable, in and out of the hospital with mental health issues and training problems versus a pilot promoting safety.

"Now we have been notified that one of our instructors placed a gun into his mouth, reported by a captain no less, and you did nothing." Wolfe walked around his desk and stood in front of Clark.

It infuriated him that Clark withheld this information from him. How the hell was he supposed protect the company if he didn't have all the details?

"Please tell me how we intend to take care of this," Wolfe said.

"Fuck. The captain who reported it was one of our female pilots," Clark said, and walked across the room and stared out the window with his hands on his hips. Then he stated, "We can get rid of her."

"She's doesn't have a husband to answer to," Wolfe said, "But—"

"But what?" Clark snapped, turning his way. "Nobody would give it a second thought if she had an accident. Shed a few tears, get on with life sort of thing."

"She's got a couple kids," Wolfe said.

"Compassion doesn't work in this industry," Clark said.

"Jesus Rich, this would be a news media nightmare with Wyatt's announcement, and the pending Bradshaw case. Not to mention Branson's death."

"Now there's an idea," Clark said. "We'll put her into *the program*."

"How?"

"There's some Women in Aviation event this weekend in New York. We'll get someone to slip a mickey into her drink. By the time he's done with her, hell, she'll put herself into the program. Talk to Pete, she works with him. He and Steve will know what to do."

Wolfe sighed and stuck his hands into his pockets as he thought about Clark's proposition. The ramifications were many, but it could work. "Let's say that happens. But the program is only five weeks. Then what?"

"When's the trial scheduled?" Clark asked.

"March 25th."

"Once she's signed up for the program, we make sure she gets the extended stay," Clark said. "They'll break her, and we'll own her. She'll be too scared to say anything after that. Who'll listen to a drunk anyway? They're all liars. This will be over and there won't be a damn thing anyone can do."

Chapter 37

Dodson Deposition Continues

ROBERT RETURNED HIS glasses to his face and calmly asked, "Did Ms. Bradshaw give you a written document in which she evaluated the safety of operations at Global?"

"She did give me an email where she had a comment about safety, I believe. But I don't recall a full-up document that was a *safety* report."

"Did you have any concern about Ms. Bradshaw's mental health after reading this email?"

"I'm not a doctor. I can't judge someone's mental health."

"But isn't it true, after the Germanwings accident, that the FAA said pilots are also responsible for assessing their fellow crewmembers?"

"Objection. Relevance!" Von Dietrich snapped. "Calls for a legal conclusion. I direct you not to answer."

Dodson glanced at Darby and their eyes locked, and then he smiled.

"Is this an email that you wrote to Ms. Bradshaw on September 10th, 2015?" Robert asked.

"Yes."

"And you wrote, *The last time we talked I mentioned that I appreciate your energy for our great profession.* Can you explain what you meant by that?"

"I meant what I said, I appreciate Captain Bradshaw's efforts to make our profession better."

"What efforts were those?"

"She had a lot of efforts. I think she was trying to inspire people to work for us. She was trying to shed good light on professional pilots."

"And how was she doing that?"

"She had a lot of interactions with groups like Women in Aviation and I believe that those efforts would have furthered our profession."

"I've handed you a document we've identified as Dodson Exhibit 8. If you could turn to page 96, Bates stamp 96, there's an email that reads—*The afternoon thunderstorm is cooling things nicely and putting me in the mood for something with an umbrella in it. The rum and fruit cocktails have done wonders for my mood this week. Anyway always good to hear a lot of different aspects on the contract. I still think the best road is to pass it, bank the pay rates, and get right back to work trying to make $8 billion. Then if this pattern continues we will be right back at the table in 30 months for another slice. Look forward to meeting you.* Did you write that to Ms. Bradshaw?"

"Yes."

"Then another note—*Thanks Darby, I appreciate the note and hope all is going well for you. I have been on a rare week of vacation the past seven days (fishing off the Florida Keys.) Hope your health and all is fine.* Is that an email that you wrote to Ms. Bradshaw?"

"Yes."

"Why were you writing Ms. Bradshaw personal emails?" Robert asked.

"I don't remember."

Do you think your memory problems have something to do with your alcohol consumption? Darby thought, drumming her nails on her leg.

"Now, looking at the second email, from you to Director Oliver

Miller, it begins with the statement—*Darby Bradshaw is busy again.* What did you mean by that, busy again?"

"Just what it says, she's busy."

"Did you mean that in a negative sense?"

"No."

"Can you explain to me the second to last sentence—*I will try and talk her back down again but just wanted you to beware of this in case she contacts Rich or George.* What were you trying to talk her back down again about?"

"I don't recall exactly what I was implying there."

"Are you familiar with the acronym SMS, as it applies to Air Carrier Policy?"

"Yes."

"Would you agree with me that that refers to Safety Management Systems?"

"Yes."

"And is it a policy that the FAA requires an air carrier to adopt?

"Objection."

"I'm not an expert on exactly what the FAA requires with regard to SMS, but I am familiar with the presence of that term and that an SMS program or system is in place. Yes."

"Would you agree that part of the SMS program is the development of a safety culture?"

"I'm aware of that, yes… but I'm not a real… uh… I'm not an expert on the Safety Management System and the components of it, though."

"So you don't know why a safety culture is a requirement of SMS?"

"Not specifically, no."

Robert continued to press him on his level of knowledge of a Federal Regulation that Global Air Lines was required by law to have implemented with requisite training for all pilots.

Dodson did not know whether Global's program was in compliance or not. He did not know any specifics on the program. He did not even know who the SMS manager was, what his required duties were, and when asked if he had received the requisite SMS training, he said, "I don't know."

"Are you familiar with the mental health standards applicable to a pilot who wishes to obtain a first-class medical?"

"No."

"Would you agree that significant indicators of poor mental health could include tardiness, absenteeism, and sick-leave abuse?"

"Objection. Calls for speculation," Von Dietrich said. Then added with increased intensity, "Lacks foundation."

"Again, I'm not familiar with that," Dodson said.

Robert questioned Dodson on his conducting a lookback at pilots and he conveyed that there were circumstances that he might have some reason to believe that an individual was violating some flight operations policy concerning sick leave.

"Did you ever conduct a lookback for Ms. Bradshaw?"

"Not... Well, I looked at her schedules. So, in that regard, yes, I did look at her schedules."

Dodson could not recall what year he looked at Darby's schedule, but stated it was simply to see her flight history and where she was based and on what airplane she flew. When asked why he would do that, Dodson answered, "Just to gather information for general awareness." He finally admitted that he'd done this process more than a dozen times regarding Darby. He had been stalking her.

"Now, would you agree Ms. Bradshaw is not a frequent user of sick leave?"

"I don't know what you mean by frequent," Dodson said.

"I don't have a definition of frequent," Robert said, removing his glasses. "How about a regular user. Is she a regular user of sick leave?"

"I guess that I would say the same thing, sir, I don't know what you mean by a regular user of sick leave?" Dodson said.

"Okay then," Robert said. "If you turn to Dodson Exhibit 8, and within that go to Bates stamp 108, page 23. If you go about two-thirds down, there's an email on December 29th, 2015, from you, that says, *Hi Darby not checking on you or anything but just noticed you called in sick for some time in January. As you are not a regular user of sick leave, I hope everything is okay and by all means let me/us know if you need anything.*

"What did you mean when you said, *regular user of sick leave* in this email?"

Dodson stared at the copy of his email for a few moments turning a slight shade of red, and then looked up. "I don't recall. I didn't quantify it in any way."

Chapter 38

ROBERT'S SLACK-JAWED EXPRESSION was punctuated with Wendel's and Betty's fingers rapidly tapping on their cell phones. If Darby wasn't mistaken, they had become in sync. Betty had even left an unopened bag of candy laying helplessly waiting to be eaten. *God forbid, uneaten candy,* Darby thought. Robert had hit a nerve.

She wondered if Dodson realized that his words would be etched into permanence in the form of transcripts. If she hadn't heard his responses firsthand, she might not have believed it herself. Then she wondered if moron was a politically correct term.

Dodson's transcript could appear as lines in a murder comedy. The plot—*Corporate stupidity causes plane crash killing hundreds.* The Regional Director and key person in charge of safety, would be played by Ben Stiller, male model, from Zoolander. Not that Dodson was even close to model material, but his look of stupidity followed by idiocy that flowed from his mouth paralleled Zoolander's pose on the same level of absurdity.

It was hard to believe he was a Regional Director at the largest international airline in the world. He was nothing short of ridiculous, albeit a likeable guy.

Darby glanced at Von Dietrich and wondered if Global's entire defense was based upon witnesses playing dumb or if they had something else up their sleeves. One thing she knew to be true—there was no way in hell this was going to trial.

She shifted her attention to Wendel and then to Betty, both of them still busy texting. This testimony was required to be confidential from all other witnesses; the very reason that Martha Jones was no longer allowed to be in the depositions. She could be a witness due to her level of involvement and wasn't allowed to hear what others said. She wondered who and what they were texting. *How could that even be legal?* she wondered.

Robert smiled kindly at Dodson and continued to ask questions.

"When Ms. Bradshaw met with you on December 13, she raised concerns to you about Global pilot scheduling practices, correct?"

"When she met with me *when*?" Dodson asked.

"On December 13, 2016."

"Yes."

"She expressed concern that Global Air Lines scheduling was not in compliance with Federal Aviation Regulations, correct?"

"Correct."

"And she expressed concern about whether pilots at Global were flying in a fatigued condition, correct?"

"Correct."

"At Global, do you have experience with pilots feeling pressured to continue flying when they're fatigued?"

"Objection. Overbroad. Vague," Von Dietrich stated not raising his eyes. His voice was another thing.

Darby wasn't sure what was vague about that question. It could not have been more specific. Fatigue was one of the most critical safety concerns, and was the most difficult to address. There was no way any international pilot could fly without being fatigued. It came with the job. But to force a pilot to fly who was on the other side of fatigue, that was another story.

"Can you repeat the question?" Dodson asked.

"Do you have any experience with pilots expressing their concern that they're flying while fatigued?" Robert asked patiently.

"Same objections," Von Dietrich said.

"Yes, I've heard pilots express that they felt like they were flying while fatigued."

"And Global has an obligation under Federal Aviation Regulations to train their pilots with respect to their obligation to remove themselves from flight duty when they feel fatigued, correct?"

"I'm not certain what exactly the regulation says."

Seriously? Darby thought. He was a check airman and an effing pilot manager.

"Isn't it true that Ms. Bradshaw advised you that Global was failing to treat deadheading time as flight time for the purpose of compliance for determining compliance with FAR flight duty limitations?"

"I recall a discussion with Darby about deadheading," Dodson said calmly. He leaned back and folded his arms. "I recall a discussion where she was concerned that there was… or that pilots would be reporting fatigued. We talked about different scenarios. So, I do recall a discussion about that issue, yes."

"Are you aware of instances in which Global has scheduled its pilots in a manner that violates FAA duty limits?"

"No."

"I'm handing you a document dated April 7, 2017, from the FAA. Did you ever receive a copy of this letter?"

"Not that I recall," Dodson said reading the document identifying a Global violation.

"Did anyone within Global ever tell you the FAA had made a

determination that, as a result of Ms. Bradshaw's report, the FAA had substantiated that a violation of an order regulation, or standard of the FAA related to air carrier safety, had indeed occurred?"

"Not that I recall," he said setting the document on the table and looking up.

He didn't know Global had received a violation of order, either? Darby thought. Wyatt couldn't recall, and now Dodson had no clue that the FAA had violated them for pilot pushing. If the company was taking this seriously and applying the necessary fixes, then everyone should have known about this violation. If they didn't know, then it was nothing but a paper shuffle at the top of airline management.

"Did you and Mr. Wolfe meet with Dr. Wood the Company Medical Examiner, prior to Dr. Wood's meeting with Ms. Bradshaw?" Robert asked, shifting gears.

"Yes."

"And what was the purpose of the meeting with Dr. Wood prior to his meeting with Ms. Bradshaw?"

"Objection."

"I was asked to attend to explain some of the flight operations policies."

Policies that Dodson had no clue what they meant, where he had never been trained and did not even know if the FAA approved them or not. Darby leaned back, folding her arms and mirroring Dodson again. Her attention fell to her phone.

Darby glanced at her phone. Neal had texted—*Yes, I heard about Stan. We need to talk ASAP.*

"Where did that meeting take place?" Robert asked.

Dodson glanced Darby's way and shifted uncomfortably in his seat. He unfolded his arms and placed them on the table and leaned forward. "It happened in a hotel in Chicago," he said softly.

"That meeting went over 10 hours, right?"

"I don't recall exactly how many hours it went. We started in the morning, and we ended up I think around four or five in the afternoon."

"But Dr. Wood billed you for a 10.5-hour meeting," Robert said, handing Dodson the invoice. "Are you saying that he did not bill correctly, and he overcharged Global?"

"Objection."

"No. I'm not saying that," Dodson said. "I just don't remember exactly. It could have been over ten hours."

"You said you were there to explain flight operations policy?"

"Yes. I was asked to go along to just answer questions that Dr. Wood might have regarding Ms. Bradshaw."

"Was the purpose of the visit by you and Mr. Wolfe, to assist Dr. Wood with his mental health evaluation of Ms. Bradshaw?"

"That was my understanding."

"Can you recall what company documents were provided to Dr. Wood during this meeting in Chicago?"

"I recall Dr. Wood had requested some of my communications with Ms. Bradshaw, the emails that I had back and forth with her. But I don't remember if I gave them to him at that meeting, but I do know they were there and discussed."

"Did you communicate to Dr. Wood, during your meeting with him, that any of Ms. Bradshaw's communications were indicative of mental health concerns?"

"No."

Darby glanced at her copy of the Robert's questions. This was the list of documents that Dr. Wood provided in discovery, that had absolutely nothing to do with her mental health. *Perhaps that of those who provided them though,* Darby mused.

"Are you familiar with the acronym, RVSM?"

"Yes."

"What does that relate to in terms of flight operations?"

"Reduced separation… I'm not positive… vertical, I think, is what the V is. I don't remember what the M stands for."

Darby shook her head, as she responded to Neal's text—*in a deposition and will call later. BTW… Dodson's clueless.* She was stunned that he didn't know that the acronym stood for Reduced Vertical Separation Minimum.

Robert removed a document from the pile and handed it to Dodson. "Here is an email from Joe Wolfe to Dr. Wood copied to you with a subject matter reading *for discussion today,* with the attachment referenced as Bradshaw—RVSM airspace, with an attachment of Advisory Circular Number 91-85. Does that accurately reflect that Mr. Wolfe sent to you and Dr. Wood the Advisory Circular 91-85?"

"Yes."

"Do you recall why this document was sent by Mr. Wolfe to Dr. Wood?"

"Not—no, not completely. I know at some point there was… Ms. Bradshaw had identified a situation where she was stating an airplane flew in RVSM airspace when it shouldn't have, or something like that. I don't remember the specifics of it."

"Where would she have stated that?"

"I don't recall, sir."

"So did you have discussions with Dr. Wood about RVSM?"

"I think at some point I did, sir, but I don't recall the exact conversation."

"Can you recall any of it?"

"Not really."

Chapter 39

DARBY TOOK HER pen and lined through the words *excellent memory* that she had written on the pad of paper. Dodson's selective memory was only for what served Global and him. What she couldn't figure out was if he was honestly that ignorant, or just playing with them. If it was the latter, then he was ignorant enough to not know that he came off as a fool.

"So, your recollection is that Ms. Bradshaw had raised with Global issues relating to non-compliance with the FAA standards relating to RVSM?"

"I do believe that at some point she did, yes, sir."

"Were you and Mr. Wolfe engaged in an effort to discredit Ms. Bradshaw's position with respect to the RVSM issues?"

"Objection."

"No," Dodson said, with a sideways glance to his counsel.

"Do you recall Ms. Bradshaw asking for a copy of your notes from the grievance meeting?"

"I recall Ms. Bradshaw asking me for notes in a meeting. I don't recall if it was the grievance meeting or not."

"Did you give them to her?"

"No."

"But you provided the notes of the grievance meeting to Dr.

Wood, correct?"

"I don't recall. I think I did but I don't recall."

"Why would you have provided him with your grievance notes?"

"I don't recall."

Robert handed Dodson a copy of an email referencing the presentation she had given to senior leadership after she had been pulled for mental health, and two articles she had provided to improve training. The Subject line was—*29th Meeting, Structural Redesign of Pilot Training, Pilot Training and Safety Culture SMS.*

"Would you agree with me that this correspondence relates to SMS compliance issues?" Robert asked.

"Did you say FMS?"

"SMS," Robert said, with a sigh.

"SMS, yes," Dodson said.

"Do you know why this was transmitted to Dr. Wood?"

"No, I don't know why it was sent."

Robert shifted his attention from Dodson to his list of questions, and Wendel glanced at his watch. Robert wrote something on the page, and then handed Dodson another document.

"I've handed you a document marked as Dodson 17, and going about halfway down, there is an email from Dr. Wood to you reading—*Did you say you have a transcript of her resent presentation? I know it would be long but it might provide useful data.*" Robert leaned back and removed his glasses. "Did you read the presentation that Ms. Bradshaw gave to Global, that Dr. Wood is requesting you provide him?"

"I don't know, sir."

"Do you recall Ms. Bradshaw raising an issue about the adequacy of stall-related training for the A330 aircraft?"

"I'm aware she did raise that. I don't recall the exact instance of her doing it."

"Do you recall reaching any conclusion one way or the other as to the merits of the issue that she raised?"

"No."

"So he also writes here starting with the second paragraph—*I have annotated the training, her Air France blog, and different changes and updates based on the Air France crash. Can you look it over and see if I have interpreted the data correctly?* Did you do that for him? Did you look it over and see if he interpreted the data correctly?"

"I presume I did, but I don't recall it."

"So do you know how this issue of the Air France blog related to Ms. Bradshaw's mental health?"

"No. Again, I'm not a doctor," Dodson said.

Darby's attention was caught by the immediate silence of Betty's previous conflict with a Raisinet bag. She was now texting with two hands. Her fat thumbs tap-danced on her phone. Wendel was doing the same. Darby's eyebrow raised and she returned her attention to Dodson.

"Did you read Ms. Bradshaw's Air France blog?" Robert asked.

"I think I read parts of it. I don't recall that I read it in its entirety. That involved Flight 447 that had a fatal accident with all persons onboard perishing. Correct?"

"Correct," Robert said. "That was of an aircraft type that Global uses, correct?"

"Correct."

"That accident involved a stall, correct?

"To my recollection, yes."

"Do you recall whether that blog and part of that blog publication was to advise pilots on how to respond to a stall in order to avoid aircraft accidents, correct?"

"That part I don't recall."

"Do you recall in what way, if any, the blog violated company policy?

"No, I don't recall."

"Do you recall at some point in Dr. Wood's evaluation process that it became very important for Dr. Wood to know Ms. Bradshaw's flight hours?"

"I recall that he did request her flight hours. I don't recall him assigning a level of importance to it."

"I'm handing you a document marked as Dodson Exhibit 20. It's Bates stamped DW245 and 246. It's from Dr. Wood to you and Joe Wolfe. Do you recall ever receiving this email from Dr. Wood?"

"Yes."

"If I can direct your attention to the bottom of the page, it says—*with this data, it is possible to answer the question. Over time is Captain Bradshaw changing the amount of time flying and the number of times is piloting the plane? The strategy is to graph time against cumulative hours or cumulative flights.* What was your understanding of what Dr. Wood meant by this reference to strategy?"

"I don't know. I really don't know exactly what he was referring to when he said this strategy."

"Well, did it not give you pause when you got a letter from a psychiatrist referring to a *strategy* for evaluating Ms. Bradshaw?"

"Objection."

"I don't recall."

"Well, how is knowledge of her flight hours going to contribute to a better understanding of her mental health?"

"Objection. Lacks foundation. Calls for speculation," Von Dietrich snapped.

"I don't know. I am not a doctor," Dodson said more quickly than he had done all day. "I don't understand fully what he was trying to establish there."

"But you were there. Your role was to give Dr. Wood advice on operational issues, is that right?"

"Objection."

"My position was to answer the best I could Dr. Wood's questions," Dodson contended.

"And so, wasn't it clear to you through your conversations with Dr. Wood, that his goal was to discredit the compliance issues Ms. Bradshaw had raised?"

"Objection."

"No," Dodson said, with a quick glance to Von Dietrich. But Von Dietrich's focus remained at the table, his attention, however, was tuned into to every word spoken.

"It's your testimony that there was never any communication either written or oral from Dr. Wood indicating he was trying to discredit her opinion?"

"Objection. Vague. Argumentative."

"My recollection is… that Dr. Wood was trying to establish the facts so that he might reach an accurate conclusion," Dodson said with a tone of defensiveness.

"Was there ever any communication from Dr. Wood that indicated that it was a goal of his to discredit Ms. Bradshaw's opinions?" Robert asked again.

"Not to my knowledge."

"In this first paragraph where it reads, *Dear Joe and Robert, the issue of how much Ms. Bradshaw is flying continues to be an issue*—what was your understanding as to why how much Ms. Bradshaw was flying continued to be an issue?"

"I don't know, sir."

"In the second to last sentence of the paragraph, it reads—*I thought of a strategy which has the possibility of confirming her opinion or refuting it. The problem is it is very labor intensive.* So did you and Mr. Wolfe ever have a discussion about the appropriateness of Dr. Wood's request for additional data that it would be labor intensive to procure?"

"Not that I recall."

"Here, again, Dr. Wood refers to a strategy. Do you know what strategy he was referring to?"

"No."

"But you were participating in the strategy, correct?"

"Objection. Foundation. Misstates the evidence," Von Dietrich said. This time he flashed a glare toward Wendel.

"I would say no," Dodson said, assertively, but then implored, "I was just providing him with information."

"You were providing him with information in order for him to achieve the implementation of his strategy, correct?"

"Objection."

"I don't know what he was doing with the information. That is a possibility. I don't know what he was doing with it."

"If you go to the second to last paragraph, it reads—*With this data, a qualitative opinion could be made or it could be turned over to a person with a statistical background for a more rigorous opinion. Let me know if this is possible.* Did you *ever* get back to him as to whether his idea was possible?"

"No. I don't recall."

"What relationship do Ms. Bradshaw's flight hours have to her performance?"

"Objection. Calls for speculation."

"I don't know what Dr. Wood was moving towards. Again, I'm

not a doctor so I don't know what he was trying to do with this."

"Do you use flight hours as a determinant in terms of a pilot's expertise on flight-operation issues?"

"No. Either we are qualified or we are not. I think," Dodson said.

Darby fought to not laugh at his addition of, *I think*. A line check airman should possess a full understanding of the qualifications of proficiency.

"Did you do an extensive investigation into Ms. Bradshaw's employment history with Coastal and Global?"

"I don't know what you mean by *extensive* investigation."

"Objection," Von Dietrich said.

"Did you do *any* investigation into her employment history, in response to a request from Dr. Wood?"

"Yes."

"What information did you convey to Dr. Wood?"

"A lot of it we just looked at, like her, uh… some of her flight history."

"How did any of that information relate to the mental health evaluation?"

"Again, I'm not a doctor. I don't know what Dr. Wood would've done with it."

"Are you aware that Ms. Bradshaw began as a simulator instructor within six months of her employment at Coastal and maintained that position until she upgraded to the Boeing 757 Captain?"

"At the time, I was quite aware of her history and then I did review it. But I'm not familiar with it again right now."

"Okay. Are pilots allowed to log their flight time while instructing in the simulator?"

"I think so. I've never been an instructor, but I think so."

Oh my God!, Darby thought. A pilot could not log flight time sitting in the back of a simulator. Unless it was Parker pen time—those mythical hours to bolster a resume.

"Did you ever tell Dr. Wood that Captain Bradshaw worked in the simulator 80 hours a month on an average of 7 to 8 months a year for a 12-year period?"

"I don't recall, sir."

"So, at the time of preparing this, you were aware that she had been a simulator instructor?"

"I don't recall when I was made aware of that."

"But omitting that information would be omitting a significant portion of her flight experience, wouldn't you agree?"

"Objection. Vague. Overbroad." Von Dietrich said, repeating his mantra.

"I don't know, sir," Dodson said. "I don't know if it would be or not because I'm also not an attorney." He leaned back and clasped his hands atop his gut, then glanced Darby's way with a glint in his eye.

Chapter 40

THE DEPOSITION HAD ended 20 minutes later, and Darby and Robert walked to their hotel. They parted ways with plans to meet thirty minutes later at the restaurant. Darby went to her room to drop off her computer and change clothes. She called Neal as she walked off the elevator. He answered just as she entered her room.

"How's it going?" Neal asked.

"Dodson is the most incompetent person I have ever known," Darby said dropping to her bed and kicking off her shoes. "He's a buffoon who has no knowledge of the most basic things."

"He's Global management, what can I say?" Neal said with a chuckle. "We knew that."

"I'm honestly thinking that Global's employment profile is to place highly incompetent pilots in management positions because they don't have enough brains to challenge anything," Darby said while unzipping her pants and allowing them to drop to the floor. She grabbed her jeans, and added, "At least in Dodson's case."

"You've got that pegged," Neal said. "Unfortunately, the guys on the line who don't know any better really like flying with him."

"I can see that," she said zipping up her jeans, "but I know too much to ever trust that man. So, what did you find out about Stan?"

"Turns out they were going to send him back into the HIMS

program," Neal said. "Apparently he offed himself because of that."

"No way," Darby said reaching for her shoes. "He would *not* have killed himself for being required to stop drinking, again. Besides, he was drinking Coke in the bar."

"I'm not saying he did," Neal said. "I'm just saying they were forcing him back in. You know how that program is. Once you get sucked in, the company controls you. You look at someone wrong, they'll get rid of you and blame it on drinking even if you didn't. You go in a second time that's the path out of the company."

"ALPO sucks. Have you ever been to a union meeting to see their open bar?" Darby asked pulling on a tennis shoe. "Hell, the union reps show no mercy when they're drinking at our expense."

"That's what I mean," Neal said. "I believe they *were* doing this to him as a threat. But I agree with you, I'm not sure that was enough to get him to take his life. Someone was pissed he was going to support you. There was something else going on, but I have no specifics."

"Who was pissed?" Darby asked.

"I'm not sure. But there's quite a buzz. Not about his being dead, but the fact that he committed suicide. The company announced it was a tragic accident. Everyone has clammed up because he was chairman of the HIMS program."

"Kill the messenger to send a message to everyone to stay silent, and they comply," Darby said.

"I'll keep digging," Neal said.

"Thanks. But don't get them hunting you."

"I won't. Now what?"

"Tomorrow we're deposing Clark and videotaping him."

"Seriously?" Neal said. "Is that normal?"

"I don't think so, only due to the added expense. But Global's lead attorney is an ass. He listens intently and then he yells. What's interesting is that he objects often, and I think only to create a distraction to the line of questioning," Darby said pulling on her other shoe. "When there's something he should object to, he doesn't because he doesn't want to flag the judge."

"Like what?" Neal asked.

"Well." Darby thought for a moment and said, "The other day Robert questioned George Wyatt about the LCWB on his ring and the term making it harder not longer, and Von Dietrich said absolutely nothing. That ring had nothing to do with the case other than it reflected his character. But Von Dietrich objects if Robert breathes wrong. This one he let slide."

Neal laughed. He had told Darby about both those events. "Glad those stories are coming back to haunt him. How many attorneys do they have?"

"Three. I thought Von Dickface, the yeller, was going to have a heart attack today," Darby said. "I'm thinking he needs to get laid before he bursts. The other guy, Wendel, simply texts all day, yawns, looks and his watch and displays excessive boredom. Then the stringy haired fat lady attorney, who belongs to Global's in-house team, does nothing but eat candy and text."

"How do you *really* feel about her?" Neal asked with a chuckle.

"I know that's not very nice to say," Darby said, "I'm just really tired, and she is a condescending bitch. Granted she has a Gucci bag, but I can fly a raw data approach to minimums, and she couldn't operate an exercise bike."

Neal laughed hard. When he stopped, he said, "Do you want me to buy you a Gucci bag?"

"Hell, no," Darby said with a chuckle.

"Videotaping Clark," Neil said, "that'll add to the price tag, huh?"

"Yep, but I think we need to. From what Wyatt said the other day, all fingers point to him. Not that we didn't know that before," Darby said. "I'm actually looking forward to recording his reaction when he learns that we have his email stating he had planned my demise, months before my meeting with Abbott."

"You have that in an email?" Neal said. "Holy shit!"

"You'd be surprised what we got in discovery. Can I fill you in another time? I need to meet Robert for dinner," Darby said grabbing her purse and rushing out the door.

Chapter 41

Oklahoma City
SVP Flight Operations Richard Clark Deposition
October 26, 2018

INTERNATIONAL FLYING GAVE Darby the ability to function anywhere, at any time, regardless of the location or time zone. But she had never imagined how draining depositions could be. Granted the shock of Stan's death had taken its toll. She and Robert spoke at length over dinner regarding Dodson, longer than they'd planned. This morning she felt like she'd flown an illegally scheduled back-to-back Sydney turn. Settling into her chair in the all-too-familiar room, she sipped her third cup of horrific coffee and waited for the deposition to begin.

She did her best to maintain her composure when she heard him approach, but her body had a reaction all its own. Her heart uncontrollably raced when Captain Rich Clark walked into the room. There had been a time when she was certified to carry a gun as a Federal Flight Deck Officer. Thankfully she did not have access to that weapon now.

Once everyone was seated the videographer introduced himself to the group. He then asked everyone to please introduce themselves for the recording. Wendel Kowalski, Karen Sherwin, Betty Dickson and Rich Clark were present on one side of the table. Darby sat beside Robert across from them.

Wendel's presence without the stressed-out leader spoke volumes. Von Dietrich was nowhere to be seen. The strategy of leaving Wendel in charge was something else. There was also an addition of a new female attorney, Karen Sherwin.

Robert opened with the preliminaries as he did during Wyatt's and Dodson's depositions. Rich Clark's body held a tension that Wyatt's had not exhibited, and his eyes reflected a level of intelligence where Dodson's had been vacant. He was, however, clearly irritated to be sitting at this table. When he looked in Darby's direction, he glared. She gave him a fake smile, her heart running a marathon, but when their eyes locked, she winked. No way in hell would she look away first. Within moments, he shifted his eyes back to Robert. Then she took a slow, deep and calming breath,

"One of the purposes of this deposition is for the Complainant's side to determine your knowledge of certain facts and events," Robert said to Clark. "Do you understand?"

"Yes."

"If you subsequently testify in a different manner before a court, we will use this deposition to impeach your testimony," Robert said. "Do you understand?"

"Yes," Clark said, with growing irritation.

Robert began by asking questions on the investigation of her safety report that Clark purportedly had conducted. Clark said he had broken the investigation of the report up into sections and had portioned it out to others to investigate. He talked non-stop for ten minutes while Karen simply took up space, and Betty ate M&M's. Wendel just sat there half-listening while he fiddled with his phone.

When Clark finally stopped talking, Robert asked, "Who would have investigated the safety and compliance issues raised by Ms. Bradshaw?"

"Corporate safety, compliance and security," Clark said.

"Who specifically investigated these concerns," Robert asked

"Well, I'm the one who started the investigation on the safety concerns."

"You say *you* started it?" Robert asked surprised.

"That's correct," Clark said leaning back and folding his arms.

"Did you delegate elements of the investigation to others?" Robert asked.

"Yes," Clark said. "There were several parts to the investigation and the concerns over safety culture and how our program was operating from safety through the operation, and that was delegated to corporate safety, compliance and security."

"Safety culture issues were delegated to whom?" Robert asked.

"Corporate safety, compliance and security," Clark said. "CSCS."

"So, who within in CSCS investigated those issues?"

"Essentially it was turned over to John Lyons," Clark said.

"Who else was involved in investigating issues raised by Ms. Bradshaw?"

"Our... well, so we had three different parts of the report that we investigated. The first was the safety concerns that she had, which for the majority were turned over to CSCS. John Lyons took those. Then I contacted Julie Christy at HR for the EO complaints, and then Bradshaw's Regional Director, Dodson, looked into contractual issues."

"What issues were you investigating?"

"I would have to look at my report," Clark said. "But they were, uh... they dealt with policies in our flight operations manual, and the pilot working agreement including harassment."

"Harassment wouldn't go to HR?" Robert asked.

"Well, yes. Yes, it would," Clark said, becoming flustered.

"You identified HR was investigating safety culture?"

"Well, safety culture is a very broad brush. What I *actually* said was, we were investigating the points that Captain Bradshaw brought forward in her report. And I'm sure you have that report somewhere in your file over there so if you want to go through specifics, I am happy to talk about those, but I won't do it from memory."

"Sorry. You *won't* do it from memory?" Robert asked, removing his glasses.

"No, I can't do it from memory."

"You *can't* do it from memory?" Robert repeated. "I really just had a preliminary question. Is there a requirement for Global to have a safety culture?"

"There is a requirement for Global to maintain safety as its highest priority. That's first and always has been that way at Global," Clark said.

"Are you familiar with SMS?"

"Yes. Safety Management Systems," Clark said. "We have a very robust culture. We've always had a very, very strong safety culture. Global was the first to qualify for SMS with the FAA. Can't remember the date, but we have the greatest SMS anywhere."

"Is having an SMS, then an FAA requirement?" Robert asked, establishing protected activity.

"The FAA does *embrace* SMS as the favored way for any airline, for any operator to operate," Clark said.

"Are you saying it's a voluntary program?" Robert asked incredulously.

"No, I didn't say that. I said that there are variations of SMS programs throughout all of the different airlines, all of the different charter outfits, and of the different flight training schools, anything having to do with aviation, because as a reporting structure up through the FAA, they do want to have a safety management system established at the company. The question really is how elaborate is the system," he emphasized. "How well does it work. And Global has been recognized as one of the top in the industry."

Darby grinned. That was not what he said. He said it was a favored way. *What a dipshit,* she thought. Her heartrate now completely under control.

Robert stared for a moment assessing Clark. Darby wasn't sure if it was because he was waiting for something else to come out of Clark's mouth, or because he was trying to figure out how to get this putz to answer a question.

Then Robert finally said, "My question was, though, does the FAA require Global to adopt an SMS program?"

"Yes."

"And the question more specifically was, are you required to comply with your FAA-approved SMS program?"

"Objection to the extent it calls for a legal conclusion," Wendel said emerging from his phone. "But you can answer to your knowledge."

This time Darby wanted to laugh. A legal conclusion for the Senior VP of flight operations to know if he was required to follow their FAA approved program, regardless that SMS was a federal regulation. She wondered if Wendel knew that Clark was required by law to know these facts due to his position. Dodson might have a bit of leeway, but the Senior Vice President of an international airline was another story.

"The FAA partners with the airline as part of the SMS process," Clark said. "That allows us to be able to work directly with the FAA on things like AQP, on compliance philosophy, on ASAP and FOQA, so they actually are a partner in the SMS program. So, they are not only the ones that are approving the program, they are also participants in the program. So, they get a chance to validate our SMS program every day."

"But that was not my question," Robert said. "My question was not whether they were a partner or whether they participated. My question is—Does the FAA require Global to comply with its published SMS program?"

"Same objection," Wendel said.

Clark's face turned a shade of crimson. He clearly wasn't used to being challenged.

"At Global the compliance is something that is… that we gladly and willfully do with the FAA. I mean, compliance is part of the SMS. If you didn't comply with the SMS policy, you would not have an SMS program. The question is, is it effective, and Global's *is* quite effective. The greatest in the industry."

What a fucking idiot, Darby thought.

She was kind of embarrassed for the guy, and while Dodson's stupidity would be in the form of a written word, Clark's would create more accurate picture, literally. Darby glanced at the camera and smiled as it focused only on Rich Clark. Regardless, she wished he would just answer the questions. But this was all being recorded, and the world would see his stupidity.

"What's your title?" Robert asked.

"Well, I was the Vice President until Wyatt's retirement and then I was promoted to Senior Vice President of flight operations," he said proudly, sitting up a little straighter.

"What were your duties under that Vice President title?"

"The safe conduct of Global's 3,500 flights per day as well as administrative oversight of Global's 14,000 pilots. I also ran the standards program and the special airport theater qualification program."

"What is the standards program?" Robert asked.

"The standards program is the extension of the FAA that qualifies pilots once they complete their simulator training."

"Were you responsible for compliance with applicable federal aviation regulations?"

"Yes."

Oh my God. He finally answered a question with a single word, Darby thought. *Good boy.* She wanted to pat him on the head.

They talked about compliance, and Robert questioned Clark long enough that he finally admitted he was obligated to comply with the FAA-approved program. Getting straight answers out of him was like pulling gum from your hair after you slept in it for eight hours.

He admitted, however, that whenever the program was in place, regardless of if it had been a regulation at the time of implementation, it was an FAA-approved program, and the airline was required to follow it. A key point since Global did have an SMS in place at the time of her writing, despite it not becoming regulation until January 2018.

When Robert asked what the components of SMS were, Clark babbled on about embracing SMS from the top, starting with the CEO and going down the organizational ladder, with a robust reporting culture that started at the ground level with the front-line employees. If they found any problem, they would cease the operation and communicate that to the employees to mitigate risk.

Darby wished she could mitigate his ass. Despite spouting buzz words that sounded good, he didn't have a clue about SMS or aviation safety in general. He was correct in that the CEO was the accountable executive, and the ground floor employees were the eyes and ears of safety. The problem was when those voices spoke their heads were cutoff. Therefore, everyone remained silent.

She was glad that Clark was embarrassing himself on camera. If they had to go to court, then the price would be worth it.

"Reporting culture is, therefore, an SMS component that Global was required to maintain," Robert asked. "Correct?"

"Objection to the extent it calls for a legal conclusion," Wendel said. "You can answer if you know."

"A reporting culture is something that Global has always embraced. As a matter of fact, Global has the most robust ASAP reporting program of any air carrier in the world, 25,000 reports per year that come through. I—"

"No, no, you are not answering the question." Robert said with far more patience than Darby felt.

"Objection," Wendel said. "Let the witness be permitted to answer."

"I am going to," Robert said. "But I am just going to advise counsel and the witness that if the witness answers the questions posed to him, this will go much faster. If you want to finish what you were saying, go ahead, and then I will re-ask the question."

"You should please let the witness answer the questions before you interrupt him," Wendel said. "Go ahead."

Betty was crinkling a wrapper and Darby glanced her way. Starbucks chocolate covered almonds. They were Darby's favorite, and she felt a touch of jealousy.

"So, as part of the reporting culture, certainly that is the basis of an SMS program," Clark said. "Global has always had that, so it is vital to the SMS program, yes."

Robert stared for a moment. He then looked at his paper and silently read through his questions, lining through some. More than likely figuring out how to extract juice from this turnup.

Wendel sighed heavily, and theatrically looked at his watch by raising his arm, then he rolled his eyes. What was once humorous behavior the first couple times had long lived its useful life. Somewhat like a two-year-old doing something funny followed by laughter, so they did it again and again. Wendel's antics were getting old.

Karen was busily writing on her legal pad. Betty was oblivious to it all. She texted with one hand and popped chocolate into her mouth with the other. Darby's legs were crossed under the table and she bounced her foot in frustration.

Robert finally looked up from his papers and asked, "Would you all like to take a break?"

Chapter 42

THEY WALKED INTO the briefing room and Robert closed the door. He turned and said, "That arrogant asshole."

Darby laughed. "And now this makes so much more sense, doesn't it?"

"I have nothing I need to talk to you about," Robert said. "I just needed to get out of there for a moment."

She understood perfectly. They talked about Clark for a moment, used the restrooms and then returned to the deposition room. The ten-minute break turned into fifteen by the time the opposing counsel returned. Clark appeared with what Darby could not overlook to be a permanent shade of red. Within minutes they went back on the record and Robert asked Clark if he had ever testified in court before, and he said no. Robert reminded him of the AIR21 trial with Captain Keith Smith, where he had recently testified.

"Pardon me for not knowing all the legalese here," Clark said. "This is something that I tried very hard *not* to specialize in."

His attempt to slam Robert was juvenile. Regardless, she wanted to laugh that he'd stated his appearance in court to be a legalese term that he was unfamiliar with. *Yes, he runs an airline,* Darby wanted to add for the record. However, that was a well-documented fact.

Clark spoke dismissively of Captain Smith's AIR21 case, of which he was highly involved. Then he admitted to the Section 8 case with Captain Hill, who had a lawsuit against the airline and had also named Clark in that case. Perhaps that was something that Darby should have done as well.

"What reason did Dr. Marsh give you for suggesting that he might consider a Section 8 for Ms. Bradshaw?"

"He took the input from the EO person that spoke with her."

"Who was that?" Robert asked.

"Ms. Abbott."

"He took *her* input?"

"He took her input, and he reviewed the set of circumstances that led up to Ms. Abbott speaking with Captain Bradshaw and he came forward with a recommendation that there may be concerns here that we needed to have reviewed before she returned to the cockpit."

"What facts did he identify for this recommendation?" Robert asked.

"The biggest concern really was the concern that flight operations was actually out to in some way harm Captain Bradshaw. There was also the lack of understanding of what I would consider policies and procedures, and lastly I would say harboring or the inability to release things that happened in the past that drove a behavioral, I don't know how quite best to say, a behavioral anomaly."

Darby placed a hand over her mouth and suppressed a laugh. Her eyes sparkled with the humor. She was thankful she wasn't on the video. Clark glared her way. While he answered Robert's questions his eyes shifted between Robert and Darby. Any movement Darby made, even the slightest, the motion caught his attention.

"All those, all the elements you just identified, are the reasons that Dr. Marsh brought it to your attention?"

"That's not a complete list. You asked me what were the *major* things that he asked and that's it, as I think back on the specifics that we talked about, those were the first three, yes."

Wow, Darby thought. Clark confirmed that Dr. Marsh had talked to the leadership structure, in addition to Abbott. He was digging his hole deeper with each word he spoke. But then he expressed his deep concern for Darby's social media violations and wearing of her uniform with the press.

What the hell? Darby thought. There were no social media violations, and she never wore her uniform any place but the flight deck, or a grade school and only after she had received permission. She had never even spoken to the media. Just because he said so, apparently that made it fact. Truth be told, had she done that, they would have had reason to terminate her, and wouldn't have needed to go down the crazy path.

Regardless, as angry as she was about his lies, Clark was simply helping her case. The interrogatories stated the *only* reason they did this was because of what she had said to Ms. Abbott. Now he expanded that to another story. He was changing his original assertions.

"When did Dr. Marsh get his information regarding those issues from Regional Director Dodson?"

"We discussed her history in a meeting prior to the… as the recommendation came forward as Ms. Abbott was recounting the interview that she had with Captain Bradshaw."

Clark proceeded to testify that they had spoken to Dr. Marsh about her inability to harbor things from the past. This is when Darby wished she was the attorney and could ask him if he understood the meaning of ethnographic. Her report was an eight-year historic view of consistent violations compared to the FAA's regulatory requirements regarding a safety culture that opposed safety management systems. Clark conveyed Ms. Abbott's fears and how she did not sleep that night after meeting with Darby, because of Darby's fear that management was out to get her. That statement received an eyebrow raise and smirk from Darby with a response in the form of a scowl from Clark.

"Had Ms. Bradshaw ever communicated to you that she was fearful of harm coming to her from the flight department?"

"I wouldn't say that she came out and told me she was fearful of that. She did indicate to me that she had given her friend a copy of the safety report. I didn't think much at the time."

Darby had not told him about giving the report to Linda. He was parroting that from Abbott, thinking that it could help bolster his case if he, too, had those concerns. However, what he did not understand that this assertion, albeit false, strengthened her case, not his.

Robert wrote something on his legal pad and then shifted directions and delved into Clark's experience. Clark clearly enjoyed talking about himself. They had a question-and-answer session on Clark's experience with the Navy, Global, and his relationship with George Wyatt.

"Would you consider Captain Wyatt to be an honest man?"

"Most definitely."

"Have you ever known him to be untruthful?"

"No."

"Do you know that Captain Wyatt is a contender for a high position for the FAA?"

Clark's eyes narrowed and his body stiffened. He shifted in his seat and glanced at Wendel who was diddling with his phone again. Nothing had been announced yet, and Clark's wheels were turning regarding what to say.

Kathryn had told Darby his plans, and Darby knew that was the very reason Wyatt had cut Robert off at the knees when he had asked him the prospect about a future job.

With no guidance, Clark finally answered, "Yes."

"What position is that?"

"Uh," Clark shifted in his seat again and glanced at Wendel who was busy with his cell phone. He waited for the objection that never came, and he finally said, "I believe he's in… he has been nominated to be the FAA Administrator."

Chapter 43

Des Moines Washington
FAA Office
October 26, 2018

KATHRYN STEPPED FROM behind her desk and advanced toward John McCallister as he entered the room. She took both his hands and squeezed. "Thank you so much for stopping by."

"I'm not sure I had much of a choice," he said with a grin. He glanced at his watch. "I do have to catch a flight in a couple hours."

"I won't keep you long."

John sat in an armchair at her coffee table in the corner of her office, and Kathryn walked to her credenza and poured two cups of coffee. She added two cubes of sugar to John's cup, hers remained black. She handed him his coffee and sat across from him.

"Thank you," he said and took a sip.

Kathryn sipped her coffee, assessing him as she did. Then she decided to cut through to the chase. She set her cup on the table and said, "John, what the hell is going on?"

"Would you believe me if I said nothing?"

Kathryn folded her arms and made no comment.

He broke her stare by closing his eyes for a moment and when he opened them, he said, "Nothing can go out of this room."

Kathryn nodded. The only reason John came to see her was to answer that question. He knew what she wanted, and he was there to provide it. Now a wave of nausea rolled through her gut in fear of what he would say.

She and John had been through a great deal together and trust was their cornerstone. He had called her out of retirement from the NTSB and pulled her into an investigation years ago, after three fatal airline crashes. She'd done it behind her husband's back, so she thought. Nothing had been what it appeared, and Bill had actually orchestrated those events.

John had been investigating her husband, Bill Jacobs, at the time. Despite the details of events, Kathryn showed him what she was capable of. In the process, they'd lost Jackie's husband who had been like a brother to Kathryn. They had almost lost Darby. And tragedy brought Linda into their lives. John and Jackie eventually married.

Kathryn had been offered a top position at the NTSB, but she turned it down, naively thinking she could prevent accidents from occurring if she went to the FAA. She thought she could stop them instead of cleaning up the carnage at the NTSB. Yet, planes continued to crash and there was not a damn thing she could do to prevent any of it, despite her position.

John set his cup on the table and stood. He walked across her office and looked out the window, overlooking SeaTac airport, and stuck his hands deep into his pockets. He stood that way far too long.

"You're scaring me," Kathryn said.

John turned. "We have bigger problems than we imagined."

"Bigger than Wyatt becoming the aviation administrator?"

"I believe he's just a pawn in the game," John said. "Which places Global in the heart of this."

Afraid to ask what *this* was, she asked, "How much of it has to do with Darby's safety report?"

"I believe, everything." John returned to his chair and sat heavily. He leaned forward with arms on his knees and said, "Her report was more than just what Global was doing incorrectly. It was her research that hit a chord. If they don't discredit her and it finds its way into someone's hands who cares, she will be a metal rod in the center of a rotating engine."

"Is she in danger?" Kathryn asked.

He stared for a moment and said, "No."

John had hesitated a bit too long and Kathryn knew otherwise

"Airbus is in the process of releasing an aircraft for single pilot operations," John finally said, "but with the ability to fly without a pilot."

"Releasing?" Kathryn said, surprised. "I'd heard they were planning to build one."

"This has been under development for years," John said. "It won't be long. With Wyatt as the administrator, he will be the person to approve that technology in the U.S."

Kathryn leaned back and raised a hand to her mouth. Multiple alarms went off in her head. She finally said, "Darby was right, then. The reduction of pilot training and increasing number of ASAP reports could be an effort to reduce public confidence in the pilot force."

John nodded. "More than that, I believe that there is more to the MAX crashes than what we see on the surface. Who would have the motivation and ability to build and disperse knock-off parts?"

Drake Industries, Kathryn thought. But this had Bill Jacobs written all over it. Bill had forced planes down to take control of the industry on behalf of the pilots. History was repeating itself, but this time to remove pilots from the equation.

"If the industry builds automated planes that don't need pilots, they'll be removed." Kathryn sighed heavily and said sarcastically, "Besides, pilots make errors, so what do we need them for anyway."

"That's what they'll contend."

"Is Bill involved?" she asked.

Nodding, John said, "I believe Drake Industries is, too, and Bill is now connected. We imagine the parts on the MAX originated from Drake Industries. We have no substantive proof, but believe that's the case."

"That was the first thought that crossed my mind," Kathryn said. She could not believe they were reliving the same nightmare, but it looked as if they were. "What about Darby's case? They were not able to discredit her with that doctor, but I would think a case like this in the media would kill Wyatt's chances of that position."

"We can only hope," John said. "Historically, the administrator's position has been bipartisan. If that's the case, there is no way in hell he'll get that position based on what he's been involved in."

"Unless Darby loses her case," Kathryn added.

John nodded. "With that said, I would suspect they would buy her off to silence her first."

Kathryn laughed. "How well do you think that would work?"

John grinned. "You'd think they'd at least try."

"Darby would be amicable to creating change and holding those involved accountable, and if they did that, then I think she would end it."

"But what if those involved run all the way up to the CEO, or the board? How deep does this go?" John asked. "I am uncertain who all the players are. Therein lies the problem."

"If this goes all the way to the top, then they might want to fight it out in court," Kathryn said. Then she shook her head. "No, they wouldn't. I can't see it going that way. Even if the CEO was involved, he would not want the exposure. The discovery they acquired from Dr. Wood gave her everything to win her case."

"We think that, but the law is the law," John said. "If Global is as powerful as I think they are and has as much invested as they do, putting our faith into a legal system that will be determined by one man, there is no guarantee."

John's words were everything that Kathryn had thought of but had refused to give power to by voicing those fears. Darby's AIR21 case would be heard and adjudicated by an administrative law judge and not by a jury of her peers. There was nothing she could do now but have faith.

Darby had made it this far because there were people who had done right by her along the way. There were honest people in the world and Kathryn needed to believe they would continue providing her a path to success. But she wasn't so sure those people worked in the airline industry. She hoped the ALJ was an exception.

"We might be facing a war on the future of aviation," Kathryn said. "But now, Darby's in the middle of Global's attack on her."

"That's not too far off spectrum," John said. "This might also be the beginning of an attack on the world. For all those who are pushing for automation to take over the skies for financial gain, will shortly thereafter see an actual global… as in worldwide attack."

John stared at her for moment, then glanced at his watch and stood. "Darby was spot on. It they remove pilots from the flight deck we will be facing the next level of terrorism with thousands of flying bombs taking to the sky. With a flick of a button, they could fly into any building worldwide."

A chill like none other took over Kathryn at the thought. "But they have to see that coming," she said standing. She walked toward the door with John.

"They do," John said. "But war and terrorism are big business. Not unlike cancer. Nobody profiting from either will *ever* allow the billion-dollar revenue generator to cease operation."

"The very reason cigarettes are legal, despite the knowledge they cause cancer," Kathryn said softly.

"Exactly," John said.

Kathryn reached for the doorknob. Instead of opening the door, she turned toward John, and stood in front of it blocking his path and asked, "What's going on with you and Tom?"

Chapter 44

Oklahoma City
Clark Deposition Continues
October 26, 2018

IF LOOKS COULD kill, Darby would have been dead many times over. If she hadn't been on Clark's hit list before, she most certainly was now. At first Clark said there was a chain of command policy, but that was not written anywhere. There was, however, an open-door policy which *was* written. The unwritten portion was, however, how they did business, and that became the culture of the airline. He looked like the fool that he was, but they got it all sorted out.

Robert finally established that Global had an open-door policy and anyone could speak to anyone in the company—something that infuriated Clark to admit.

"Do you ever confer with Walt Croft?" Robert asked.

"When you say confer with Walt Croft, Walt doesn't call me up to ask my opinion on things, typically," Clark said. "I do know Walt, certainly, and I have had a chance to be in meetings with Walt that center on operational issues, on finance issues, budget and so forth. But no, I am not on his speed dial list."

"Have you ever had *any* communications with Mr. Croft concerning Ms. Bradshaw?"

"No, I have not."

"Did you ever make any kind of report to Croft concerning Ms. Bradshaw?"

"No."

How the hell can he sit here and lie? Darby wondered. More than that, why the hell didn't Wendel brief him on the fact they had the memo regarding the Clark and Croft's meeting? She had proof that they had met and discussed her. For thirty minutes no less. Robert asked a few more questions feeding Clark enough rope to hang himself.

"When was the first time you spoke to Ms. Abbott after her interview of Ms. Bradshaw?"

"I believe November 24th."

"Was that in person or on telephone?"

"As I recall, it was in person."

"Who else participated?"

"Dr. Marsh, Joe Wolfe, the labor relations attorney, and then the corporate attorney, Martha Jones."

Darby glanced at Betty Dickson. She looked up from her phone when she heard Martha's name and glanced at Darby. Darby winked, and then made a point of looking at the pile of candy wrappers in front of her before she looked away.

"Did you have another meeting?" Robert asked.

"I don't recall another meeting. We definitely had that one on the 24th."

"Did you engage in any further investigation of what Ms. Abbott reported prior to the Section 8 decision for Ms. Bradshaw?"

"I don't quite understand."

"Prior to your issuance of the Section 8 letter, did you conduct any further investigation whether the Section 8 was warranted?"

"No."

"You never called Ms. Bradshaw to get her version of her conversation with Ms. Abbott, correct?"

"No, I did not."

"Did you authorize anyone else to contact Ms. Bradshaw to get her account of what transpired between her and Ms. Bradshaw?"

"No, I did not."

As the question and answers continued, it turned out that Clark also had a teleconference on November 28th with Abbott, Dr. Marsh, and Dr. Wood that lasted no longer than an hour. There had been reference to some meeting in the emails that she had received in discovery, and now she understood. Dr. Wood agreed at that meeting that they should give Darby a mental health evaluation. That very recommendation would increase his bank account by $74,000. Regardless, that's not how the contractual process worked.

"Did Martha Jones express her opinion?"

"Objection. I direct you not to answer any legal advice that you were provided."

"I don't want to be contentious about this," Robert said, removing his glasses. "But Dr. Wood is on the phone and he's an independent contractor, and Dr. Marsh is on the phone and/or in the meeting, and he is an independent contractor, so it is our position there is no privilege that applies. Having stated that position, is it counsel's directive that the witness is being directed not to answer that question?"

"I made my statement," Wendell said.

"I'm sorry, could you do me the favor of reading back what counsel directed the witness to do? I am not receiving the courtesy of confirmation whether he was directed not to answer this question."

"I disagree that I wasn't courteous," Wendel said with a distinct whine. "But go ahead," he said with a flick of his hand.

"Would you please tell me whether he is directed not to answer questions about what Martha Jones said?" Robert asked the court reporter.

The court reporter tried to find the spot and read a couple statements in doing so. But Wendel was losing his patience with her. He finally said, "It depends on what your question is. What is the pending question?"

"What did Ms. Jones say at that meeting?"

"Objection. It is too broad for him to answer without asking him to potentially divulge information that would be privileged."

"Are you directing him not to answer?"

"I am directing him not to answer."

They took another break and when they returned, Robert's focus was to get admissions of Clark's involvement in forcing the evaluation.

"Is it correct, that the Section 8 decision was made by you?"

"Yes, all Section 8 decisions to go forward are made by me."

"Did Mr. Wolfe participate in the decision to make the Section 8 referral?"

"Objection to the form," Wendel said. "You can answer."

"I didn't ask for his advice, no."

"And is that correct that you based your decision on information from Dr. Marsh and Ms. Abbott?"

"That's correct."

"Did Dr. Marsh provide you facts beyond what he heard from Ms. Abbott?"

"Objection," Wendel said.

"I'm not sure I understand the additional facts. If you can hum a few bars," Clark said with sardonic smile.

"Was his role to provide you with facts concerning Ms. Bradshaw's conduct, or was it to interpret Ms. Abbott's report?"

"Objection," Wendel said. "You can answer."

"Essentially he heard Ms. Abbott's report, based on that information that he had recommended an assessment was appropriate and I agreed that we needed the assessment before she could return to the cockpit."

The next fifteen minutes Robert established, according to Clark, that Dr. Marsh had made his recommendation and decision during their conference call with Dr. Wood present. Attorney Wolfe was there because he was the expert on the process. However, Clark assured Robert that the process was very distinct.

In this very distinct process, Dr. Marsh was supposed to have met with Darby prior to his decision. She did not meet with him for another six weeks *after* that management meeting that sent her into the process. Second, Marsh was supposed to have consulted with the ALPO doctor on the selection of the psychiatrist to be used. Dr. Wood was at that meeting and he had been selected by Joe Wolfe, bastardizing the process.

The branches were getting thicker as they moved deep into the weeds with Clark's deposition, and he was snagging the company's case on every thorn. Darby now wondered if Clark was more arrogant or ignorant. At the very least they all should have read the contractual process and tried to follow it, regardless of his plan to nail her.

"Had you previously considered referring Ms. Bradshaw for a Section 8 referral?"

"I wouldn't say that I had considered referring her for a Section 8. I had seen some things in her behavior dating back to as early as my first interaction with her that I felt was somewhat peculiar."

"Did you bring up that prior conduct during the teleconference?"

"I did not."

"Why did you not?" Robert asked.

Wendel objected, and said he was confused with which meeting on which date, or both. Robert clarified he was curious as to the teleconference, during the point they made the decision to send Darby into a Section 8. Wendel apologized because he was not trying to interfere but thought he was being helpful. This time it was Darby who rolled her eyes.

His interjection was nothing but a delay, giving Clark time to figure out what to say. This process was nothing short of a poker game and learning the signs of those at the table. Clark, however, was simply a blowhard that liked to hear himself talk. Darby sat with arms folded and grinned as he rambled on.

He kept glancing her way and her smile unnerved him. He pressed on and said that he didn't think she had a problem when they first met, but reflecting back, he changed his mind. Where Wyatt said that Darby brought everything forward in good faith, Clark said she brought it forward with unintentional bad faith. He did confirm that Dodson had no idea why Darby was given the Section 8, even though he had been tasked to sign the letter.

"Have you ever heard of the Aviation Rulemaking Committee on mental health?"

"Yes. We had a pilot on that committee."

Interesting that Wyatt didn't know anything about it, Darby thought.

Robert asked him a few questions about the committee, and Clark alleged that the committee was for pilot hiring. Clark could not recall if Wolfe was on the committee. Wolfe's covert presence was under the guise of representing Airlines for Americas. Robert finally stuck the email under Clark's nose that Darby had been waiting for all day.

He allowed Clark to review it, and red began at his neck and moved up to his big head. His jaw tightened, but he retained his fake plastic smile. He spent a long time reading that short email, no doubt trying to figure out how to get out of it.

"This email that you took some time to review reflects that July 11th, you were considering a potential referral of Ms. Bradshaw for a Section 8 review, correct?"

"Actually... what I was *trying* to do was to ensure that we understood what her actions were and why she could or could not understand what might be appropriate. In the administrative place, and if she couldn't do that, brought into question whether or not she would be able to appropriately execute her duties as a flight crewmember. So therefore, we may need to consider a Section 8, yes."

What the hell did he just say? Darby wondered, as she stifled another laugh with her fist. His eyes flashed warning and she winked.

"It says here in the last paragraph, *I also think we should consider whether a Section 8 is appropriate.* Why were you considering a Section 8?"

"I actually state we should consider whether a Section 8 is appropriate, and I think that my sentence stands, and I still believe that to this day, it stands to reason she might not be able to make appropriate decisions for the safe operation of a flight as a crew member."

Robert questioned Clark about the email he had sent to Wyatt and his kid gloves comment, and the briefing of HR. Clark couldn't remember briefing HR, or why he even wrote that to Wyatt, or what his words meant. His memory was now failing miserably.

Perhaps he, too, needs a mental health evaluation, Darby thought.

The day pressed on slowly while Robert asked the same safety issues he had with Wyatt. Clark attempted to bullshit his way through things in which he purported to have great knowledge. But he knew nothing about the Airbus and couldn't answer the questions, whereas at least Wyatt was able to because he had flown an Airbus. Clark looked like a fool.

While Wyatt was calm and intelligent, Dodson was ignorant and evasive. Clark was hostile and arrogant. He laughed at some questions Robert asked, clearly mocking him, but in truth that laughter was a defense mechanism. His expressions were priceless. *Thank God we are videotaping,* Darby thought again.

"As you sit here today, do you have any concerns about Ms. Bradshaw's proficiency as a professional airline pilot for Global?"

"Well, I still have concerns for her decision making and judgement to a certain degree, yes. And I followed the process appropriately, and the Section 8, and wanted a fair and accurate assessment to be done. I think that the process worked, certainly not without some bumps in the road in terms of… uh… so she was returned to flying, but I can certainly say that the result does leave me with a lingering question of decision making from time to time."

"And that's based on social media issues and her research?"

"No. More to do, I would say, with letters that have been written regarding our upset recovery training program and her feelings that we are not following the FAA mandate."

"You have concerns for mental health based on her reporting your training processes?" Robert asked incredulously.

"No. I have concern with her ability to execute the procedure, that is … that has been trained. In an emergency situation, the one thing you cannot have is unpredictability and that's why we go through extensive training in the simulator. I'm afraid she won't perform as required."

"What was her position?" Robert asked.

"The language that we were using a *process*. We called it a *strategy*. In her mind there were flaws. But she hadn't even trained at the time."

Clark continued for another five minutes explaining their procedures and defending them. She wondered if he understood aerodynamics, or the fact that anyone could read the procedure and know it was not sound, did not follow the FAA mandate, and was going to kill someone. He clearly had been spending too much time in an office.

"So, she was concerned about the upset recovery training. Is that an FAA-approved program?" Robert asked.

"Yes, it is required by the FAA."

"And she went through training as part of a Global B777 checkout, correct?"

"She did not when she wrote the letter. She hadn't gone to training at all!"

"But she has since gone through training?"

"I believe so, right," Clark said.

"And she passed training. Correct?" Robert asked.

"Yes."

"So… she must have done it correctly. Correct?"

Clark stared with acknowledgment of what he had just admitted, the red returning. "I guess," he finally said.

They spent a few minutes discussing training and stalls. Clark argued that Airbus A330 had a stick shaker because the manual said so, but often procedures are changed with bulletins. There was no stick shaker on the Airbus. The fact this man was the SVP of flight operations at an international airline was simply amazing. Robert then directed him to go to page nine of Exhibit 4.

"I want you to look at the first three bullet points at the bottom of the page which reads "Pilot writes a blog post, how to perform a stall recovery, to educate other pilots after AF447, was pulled from the ocean due to the fact that this pilot never received stall training on the A330."

"Did you understand that Ms. Bradshaw had not received stall training on the A330?"

"No, I did not."

"So, you never asked her about her stall training related to the A330?"

"I don't specifically recall asking her about her stall training. I do know she wrote a blog outside the purview of Global and I had no exposure to that blog or understanding that any of the information on it was true or accurate."

She was more relaxed now realizing the intelligence in his eyes ended there, and she crossed a leg over the other. He still had concerns for her, but she certainly had concerns for him as well. As should the FAA.

"This was the blog related to the fatal accident for the Air France Flight 447?" Robert asked.

"No, I don't know that! All I know is there was a website or page that A330 pilots went to and I'm not exactly sure where that blog post came from."

Darby wondered if he were as clueless about the Air France crash and her post or if he was trying to cover his ass. She didn't know that Global had 14 events when she'd written that blog. All she had wanted to do was educate fellow pilots on how to fly out of a stall in alternate law.

Clark and Wyatt knew that there had been a problem, and that problem killed 228 people at another airline because they did nothing. The FAA was equally complicit because they had received the ASAP reports and took no action. Now Wyatt was destined to become the head of the FAA. *Where the hell is justice?* she wondered. Clark and Wyatt as much as killed everyone on Air France Flight 447.

Chapter 45

Oklahoma City
Corporate Office
October 26, 2018

WALTER CROFT READ the text messages populating his computer from Clark's deposition regarding the AF447 crash. "Shit," he said. He removed his glasses while closing his eyes and pinched the bridge of his nose. If this becomes the story, Wyatt's name would be all over it. They could lose everything.

He pushed away from his desk and stood; thankful that Clark's deposition was done. Then he walked across the room with a single focus in mind. He was reaching for a bottle of Scotch when his secretary buzzed. Returning to his desk, he pressed the button and said, "Yes, Rose."

"Mr. Johnson Von Dietrich has arrived."

"Please send him in."

Walter turned as the door opened. He stepped forward and extended his hand. "Johnson, thank you for joining me. Please. Have a seat," he said motioning toward the seating area. "Can I get you anything to drink?"

"No, sir. Thank you," Von Dietrich said.

Croft had been told that Goldman, Goldman, and Epstein was

the only law firm that could handle this case. He was assured he would have the top legal team. Von Dietrich was the leader of that team, and if anyone could pull this off, they said he could. *So, they said.* With so much riding on this, they'd better damn well be right.

"How's it going?" Walt said sitting across from him.

"I'm not going to lie. This is going to be tough. We have a singular way to win this." He held Croft's gaze for a moment, and then continued. "That is to convincingly plea that Global *had* to do this in the interest of safety." Von Dietrich remained upright with tension about him that Walt found disconcerting. Von Dietrich folded his hands and stared at them for a moment, then looked up. "That other report must *never* come out."

"It's being taken care of," Walt said. He stood and walked to the credenza and lifted the bottle. He held it toward Von Dietrich, who shook his head no. Croft unscrewed the lid. "What I really want to know," he said as he poured a couple fingers into a glass, "is can you bury that deposition regarding the Air France situation?"

"It will never find its way into court," Von Dietrich said. "Allen is simply establishing protected activity. But…"

Walt replaced the lid on the bottle and returned it to the shelf while waiting for Von Dietrich to finish his statement. He sipped his drink as if it were a calming breath, and then turned. "But what?" he asked when nothing followed Von Dietrich's statement.

"The concern is that the Air France blog became a part of her medical report."

"Can we undo that?" Walt asked returning to his seat.

"Somebody at Global gave the data to that doctor." Von Dietrich shook his head. "We'll diffuse it the best we can."

"I hope so," Walt said. "But Bradshaw has it."

"Yes," Von Dietrich said. "Legally she could provide it to the media, because it came directly from Dr. Wood and is not protected."

"But it mentions Global and would make us look bad," Croft said. "That's a violation of the social media policy."

Von Dietrich stared for a moment and then said, "It could be argued that Wyatt and Clark's decisions made the company look bad, not the dissemination of information."

"We'll deal with that if the time comes," Walt said, appreciating his candor.

Von Dietrich was correct, but a termination took two years to resolve in the grievance process, or longer if they decided to extend. At the end of the day, they controlled the arbitrator and there was a little thing regarding collateral stopple that would prevent her from retrying the case. She'd never return, despite Global having a legal argument or not. Bradshaw was not an issue, simply an irritation.

"I understand you're representing Boeing in the 737 MAX lawsuit," Croft said.

"Our firm has accepted that case, yes," Von Dietrich said. "I believe they plan to make me lead attorney."

"Good," Walt said, and then tipped back his drink. "Very good."

Chapter 46

Oklahoma City
December 19, 2018
Dr. Thomas Marsh Deposition
Oklahoma City

THE BENEFIT OF returning to flying prior to litigation could not be overlooked. Darby was able to finance this fight for discovery. Unfortunately, the battle was draining both her time and resources and had become one of the most physically, mentally, and completely exhausting things she had ever done. Never had she been pulled in so many directions at one time.

Granted, she could have taken a less active role and allowed Robert to pursue discovery without her involvement. But she refused to be the passenger of her life. To give up control while being attacked would be like giving up her plane to the hijackers on 911. She would have fought to the end there too. This battle was no longer for her survival. This fight was for her fellow pilots and passengers worldwide. If she failed, the world could multiply the deaths of 911 by thousands.

Thankfully, Robert was able to accommodate the depositions around her schedule so she could be present. Regrettably the depositions combined with her flight schedule found her home only a couple of days each month. The extended travel across the country was nothing but an expense. Yet, life's balance sheet identified that when effort exceeded expense the bottom line was success.

Robert Allen also reminded her the value of money when he said that his father always told him, "This family spends money on experience, not things." This was undoubtedly an experience of a lifetime. She sighed as they waited for Dr. Marsh to arrive for his deposition.

Dr. Marsh was Global's inhouse doctor. She had initially trusted him, and her misplaced trust proved that she could be a very bad judge of character. Everyone made a mistake now and again, but she'd made many by trusting Global management. Despite what had happened, she resolved to err on the side of maintaining faith in people, even if they proved her wrong. A world without trust was a world of despair, and not where she wanted to live.

Darby sipped her Venti Starbucks. Bringing your own brew was a much better option to deposition coffee. She carried her cup to the window and looked outside and then up between the buildings. Despite whatever was going on, she knew there was a higher power protecting her along this journey. She had thought often how close she came to losing her career. The man they were about to depose could have ended this before it started. But he didn't. He'd lied to her, and then he manipulated the record. And yet she still survived.

She closed her eyes for a moment in gratitude for all she had in her life, especially for the strength she had acquired through this process. The very strength that enabled her to survive the journey to hell and back. After Dodson and Clark's depositions, she wasn't sure what was worse—the actual evaluation process with Dr. Wood or the litigation process. That was open for debate. But she was still standing, and they could not break her.

Where her strength came from, she had no idea. But she knew

she wasn't alone despite the many times she felt her dark nights of the soul during the two years that she was grounded. Yet each time she arrived at the proverbial river's end without a paddle and a waterfall looming in the distance, someone came into her life and gave her an outboard motor to power to safety. Everything always worked out. She just needed to maintain the faith.

The voices behind her were a stark reminder of what was about to occur. She turned, then walked over to the fridge and grabbed a bottle of water for Robert and set it in front of him. He was in his zone reading documents preparing for the day. Darby sat to his right and sipped her coffee as she watched Dr. Marsh get settled.

Marsh was wearing a floral Tommy Bahama shirt. It was mid-December, and the highs wouldn't be above 45 degrees Fahrenheit. Opening his computer, he had a wildly animated expression that continually changed as if he was having a conversation with himself and added the expressiveness to match the voices in his head. She had never seen such behavior.

It had been over three years since she had met him, but this was not the man she remembered. The doctor that Darby had met years earlier was calm, respectful, professional and he had reminded her of Marcus Welby M.D. This guy was a Rodney Dangerfield reenactment from Caddyshack. Only Marsh wasn't funny.

"Robert," Darby whispered. "Is that okay for him to have his laptop?"

Robert looked up from his document and toward Marsh. "Sir, you have to put that away for the deposition."

"I do? Why?" Dr. Marsh asked with the annoyance of a thirteen-year-old who was just asked to put his phone away at the dinner table.

"It's the law," Robert said, glancing to Wendel, who looked at Marsh and nodded.

Today Wendel Kowalski was present and flanked by Betty Dickson and Ms. Karen Sherwin from Texas. Karen was the perky little blonde who had sat quietly at Clark's deposition, taking in the activity. She was clearly new to this process, and perhaps they brought her on the team to ensure that someone would pay attention to the proceedings. Darby couldn't be sure, but last time she was the only person with a pen and paper instead of a phone.

After introductions were made and Dr. Marsh was sworn in, Robert gave his standard explanations on the procedural process and then began.

"Have you ever testified in court before?" Robert asked.

"Yes."

"How many times?"

"Since I've been a physician, I'd say probably twelve."

"What were the circumstances?"

Dr. Marsh explained that there had been three child abuse cases, one auto accident, one malpractice suit, and the rest were airman actions, but there had been no FAA proceedings. When asked the circumstance of the airman actions, he said that beyond the malpractice claims, there was a divorce where the pilot was out on disability, and he had to testify as to why the pilot couldn't fly.

"Were you qualified as an expert witness in any of these proceedings?" Robert asked.

"I don't know what that definition means," he stated, with a furrowed brow. "I was speaking as an aviation medical examiner."

"Do you understand that you have been sworn to tell the truth and if you fail to do so there could be adverse consequences?" Robert asked.

"Yes."

"Are you taking any medication or any other drugs that might impair your ability to testify?"

"Not to my knowledge," Marsh said folding his arms.

Not to his knowledge that he was taking them? Or not to his knowledge that they might impair him? Darby wondered, perplexed by his answer. If she was gambling on this, she would bet he was on drugs now and he was impaired.

"Are you suffering from any kind of *illness* that might affect your ability to testify today?" Robert asked, sliding past Marsh's previous response.

"Not to my knowledge," he said and looked directly at Darby with a smile as broad as he could make it with his lips closed. The edges upturning high on his face. Instantly Darby understood what she had originally thought as an irrational fear of clowns by others, now to be a justified horror.

"Do you understand everything I have said up until now?" Robert asked.

"Yes," Dr. Marsh said nodding rapidly and repeatedly in confirmation of his spoken word.

"Have you ever been treated for a mental health issue?"

"Yes."

Darby's eyebrow rose. *Now this will be interesting,* she thought. She had doubted the rumors were true, but nothing surprised her anymore.

"What did the treatment consist of?" Robert asked with compassion.

"It was a general anxiety disorder after the passing of my mother."

"How long ago was that?"

"She died in 2004, so since that time."

"Was the treatment complete?" Robert asked.

"No, ongoing."

"Ongoing. Since 2004 did you at any time suspend your practice?"

"No."

What the hell? Darby thought. He had been taking anti-anxiety drugs for over 14 years for a sadness that occurred with the passing of his mother. Dr. Marsh was a drug addict.

Robert pressed on with his questioning, while Darby observed his behavior.

The word on the street was that Dr. Marsh was an addict and that was the reason he lost his job at FedEx. He was well-liked by most pilots who knew him, while others felt he was lazy. Darby now changed her original opinion. He was not on drugs, he had to be *off* his meds today and needed them.

The expressions, body language, and animations he put into his statements were unnecessary and displayed what she could only determine to be a lack of control. If she had known this would be the case, she would have spent the money and videotaped him also.

The response that he lacked knowledge as to how those drugs impacted his testimony was interesting as well. As a medical professional he should know how they impacted the brain. Yet he had testified that he lacked knowledge that if he was taking drugs that would impact his ability to testify. His long-term drug use could also explain the difference in his personality between now and when she had first met him.

This man should be removed from his position as an AME. He was a danger to society in the capacity that he held. He was probably a danger to himself.

Chapter 47

HIS ANSWERS TO the simplest questions were an effort for Dr. Marsh, undoubtedly because of his previous admissions of long-term drug use. He was clearly thinking about what he'd just said and was not in the present moment.

Darby had seen excellent pilots fail check rides for the same thing. An error that could not be forgotten which ultimately destroyed the pilot's performance. If this had been a check ride, Dr. Marsh was headed for remedial training.

After questioning his involvement in the process and what he did to prepare, he finally admitted to reading the records he had regarding his evaluation process with Darby. He also confirmed reading emails and the reports from Ms. Abbott and Dr. Wood. Following this hour and a half exchange, which hardly moved them over the starting line, Robert suggested they take a fifteen-minute break. A much-needed break for Dr. Marsh to gain some composure.

Darby went outside and called Linda. She wanted to know what she was dealing with regarding Marsh.

"I read something in the Journal of Clinical Psychology not too long ago that people on anti-anxiety meds have a 36% higher mortality rate," Linda said, "Meaning that 40% are more likely to die who use them than not."

"But are there side effects beyond death?" Darby asked with a chuckle. "Not that death to the bad guys isn't a positive option. What I mean is, if you don't die, what are the long-term effects?"

"Dizziness, fatigue, high blood pressure, and such," Linda said. "But the real problem is addiction. After the urgent situation has passed, those who continue to take them, it's because they don't know how to wean themselves off."

"What would happen if Dr. Marsh stopped them now?" Darby asked. "Like cold turkey."

"He would go directly back into the pain he felt at the time. He could plummet into complete depression without the ability to cope," Linda said. "His anxiety would be as if time had never passed."

"Maybe it's better to stay on them," Darby said.

"No. Not at all. Those drugs hinder his coping skills."

"He's certainly not coping well this morning," Darby said. "He probably forgot to take them, or perhaps tried to get off them short-term. I'm not sure, but he's not the same person I met three years ago."

"I imagine he's not," Linda said. "Look at it this way, when you go to the gym, how do you gain strength?"

"I lift weights. The muscles more or less tear and they rebuild stronger."

"The brain is much the same," Linda said. "The psychological experience you have gone through with Global has actually given you more mental strength, like working out. Therefore, by experiencing the hell that you did, going forward you'll be stronger next time because of that growth. You actually built resilience."

"But Dr. Marsh can't get there because his brain is blunted by the drugs," Darby said.

"Exactly," Linda said. "But at some point, Dr. Marsh is going to have to process his grief otherwise, as you say, he'll crash and burn."

"Are you sure he's not Prozac deficient?" Darby asked with a grin and then said, "I guess people medicate with alcohol. Perhaps taking drugs is the better option."

"Yes. But not a permanent solution," Linda said. "These drugs are best if not taken longer than a year. Not fourteen."

"I kind of feel sorry for the guy," Darby said.

"Don't," Linda said.

"But don't they say that possessions turn to dust and food turns to shit and the only thing that really matters in the end are people's feelings?"

"Screw his feelings, he has none. He didn't do this to you because he was on those drugs," Linda said. "He did this because he was asked by Global management to proceed down this path."

"He did this because he was asked by Global management to proceed down this path."

"I know. But if the company knows about his drug addiction, they could be holding that over his head. If they terminated him, he'd have a hard time getting a job elsewhere."

"Stop right there, young lady!" Linda snapped, followed by a laugh. "Seriously. You are not going to experience the Stockholm syndrome with this one. Keep focused, and don't feel empathy for a bad guy who tried to throw you into a shallow grave while you were still alive."

"Interesting visual," Darby said. "Empathy aside, how does someone get off those drugs?"

"There are some naturopathic methods that could help. Simply sleeping, exercising, eating right and perhaps meditation and yoga. Anything that helps reduce the stress hormone and raises serotonin levels. Research has also identified that being around trees lowers stress hormones."

"I knew there was something I loved about trees," Darby said. Then she asked, "Could what he's doing to pilots be causing his stress? Maybe the reason he can't get off the drugs?"

"Absolutely," Linda said. "I think they help him cope all the way around."

Darby said goodbye to Linda, and then returned to the deposition room just as they were about to start. She settled into her seat, and Robert began.

"Who is your current employer?"

"Medical Inception LLC," Dr. Marsh said, "as well as Thomas Marsh, M.D., AME, and I'm still in the Navy Reserve."

"Do you have a contractual relationship with Global?"

"Yes," Dr. Marsh said.

"In what capacity?"

"We are an aeromedical and occupational medical and safety consultant to Global, several other airlines, and... I will say a loss of license insurance company," he said folding his arms, unfolding them, and then folding them again while he spoke.

"How long have you had contract services with Global?"

"I would say at least twelve years," he said glancing toward Wendel. But Wendel was texting and not paying attention to him. Betty was eating chocolate covered raisins again today. As much as her eating candy irritated Darby, a chocolate buzz would be most appreciated right about now. Instead, she finished her coffee that had gone cold.

"What other airlines?" Robert asked, pulling her attention back to Marsh.

"United, Express Jet, let me think... Uh, One Sky, Atlas, SkyWest and indirectly with FedEx."

"Why do you say indirectly with FedEx?" Robert asked.

"Through the insurance company portion. HW Alliance Insurance,"

Dr. Marsh said, glancing toward Wendel again. This line of questioning was clearly making him nervous, and yet Wendel still was not paying attention. Little Miss Karen, however, sat there ever so perky with her pen perched ready to write something. So far, her page was blank.

"What is HW Alliance Insurance?" Robert asked.

"They are a loss of license company, uh… basically an insurance company."

"What does HW stand for?" Robert asked.

"I don't know!" Dr. Marsh snapped. "Does it have to stand for something? If you let me have my computer, I could look it up, but I think it's just initials."

"That's quite all right," Robert said, calmly.

Darby folded her arms and her eyebrow shot up again. Drugs or not, she knew somebody named that insurance company after him—*Half-Wit*.

Chapter 48

There was an argument going on in his head, and Darby wasn't sure who was winning. Dr. Marsh shifted in his chair, raised his hands, widened his eyes, grinned, scowled, and showed more expressions than Darby had ever seen in one sitting. The crackling paper pulled her attention back to the legal team.

Betty fought to get her chocolate out of the bag with one hand, while she texted with the other. Attorney Sherwin stared at Dr. Marsh with the oddest expression—a mixture of confusion laced with disbelief. Perhaps there was a splash of horror flashing through her eyes. Darby grinned.

She could only imagine Sherwin wondering if Dr. Marsh had released the pilot who would be flying her home tonight, and how much an Uber from Oklahoma to Texas would cost.

While Robert assessed his list of questions, Darby glanced at Wendel. Where Von Dietrich was pegging the stress meter, Wendel was nothing but a spectator who had no interest in the event and was being inconvenienced by having to be there. Perhaps, however, today his habit of looking at his watch was in anticipation for it to end and get Marsh off the hot seat.

"How long have you known Dr. Wood?" Robert asked.

"I have known of him and worked with him since 2013."

Robert established that Dr. Marsh had referred four pilots to Dr. Wood. Two from Global, a United pilot, and a FedEx pilot. Marsh said there were too many to count that he had recommended to other psychiatrists, but he made a point of sending pilots to locations geographically close to home. In Darby's case, he sent her non-stop to Skokie, Illinois, a couple thousand miles away from Seattle, when there were psychiatrists in her own back yard.

"How many company-directed mental health evaluations have you been involved with, with respect to pilots since 2013?"

"Total?" Dr. Marsh asked.

"Yes, sir."

"Not just mental nervous, psychiatric?" Dr. Marsh asked.

"Yes, psychiatric," Robert said patiently.

"So how many have I referred for evaluations to a specialist?" Dr. Marsh asked.

"Correct," Robert said, removing his glasses.

"Hundreds," he finally said.

"Hundreds of pilots who were required by their respective airlines to—"

"No," Dr. Marsh interrupted. "We contracted with their airlines to assist them in getting evaluated for recertification issues."

"My question was narrower." Robert sighed. "How many company directed or mandated psychiatric evaluations have you—"

"Since 2013?" Dr. Marsh asked.

"Correct," Robert said, rubbing his eyes.

"Probably 18."

Darby covered her face with both her hands for a moment and shook her head. She was paying for this expose, and he was an effing moron, drugs or not. She dropped her hands and glanced at Betty, who had switched her poison to a Hershey bar. Two points for Betty.

It was much easier to break off a square without looking up from her phone. Wendel was also engaged with his phone, ignoring Marsh. This was a proverbial Groundhog Day. Yet Karen was finally writing something on her legal pad.

Robert handed Dr. Marsh the letter of Darby's removal and asked, "Can you recall whether you had consultations concerning Ms. Bradshaw with Dr. Wood prior to issuance of that letter?"

"Direct," he said. "I don't believe so."

"You specified direct. Were there contacts with him which you characterize as *indirect*?"

"I believe there was a call where I was invited to discuss Ms. Bradshaw."

"What would have been the purpose of his being on a call prior to the issuance of the mental health directive?" Robert asked.

"I believe at the time there were concerns raised… well, the crux of it, uh… there were concern's raised about Ms. Bradshaw's mental health, and at the time this was coming from an employee with her, and she mentioned some concerns, and so I think that was the reason in terms of having him come on board to listen, to see, get his two cents on what he thought this impression was of this employee, Ms. Bradshaw," Dr. Marsh said without taking a breath between words.

"To borrow your expression," Robert said, "what were his two cents?"

"I think at the, uh… I am trying to think when we discussed," Dr. Marsh said, scratching the back of his head and furrowing his brow. "Or it was a conference call that eventually occurred, and Ms. Abbott was on the call, and she uh… well, she gave more detail about what happened." He shifted in his seat and glanced to this legal team, none of whom were about to help him. He returned his attention to Robert. "I also think at that we had Abbott's report of the meeting, and I believe he supported that there were concerns here to look further into it and he recommended the Section 8 process."

"Are you saying *Dr. Wood* recommended it?" Robert asked.

"No, I think he… uh, I was the eventual one that recommended that," Dr. Marsh said, ringing his hands together. "But I asked his opinion in terms of if he felt there were concerns there that were raised."

"I'm sorry, you asked his opinion?"

"Right."

"What did Ms. Abbott say about her meeting with Ms. Bradshaw?"

"That during several hours of a meeting, I believe Ms. Bradshaw was anxious, tearful, concerned about her wellbeing and safety, suggesting that someone at Global could harm her. And this was quite an experience for Ms. Abbott, that frightened her to come back and report to Global. And they got me involved to see if there is a medical reason."

You're not paranoid if they really are out to get you, Darby thought.

The oddity was how Dr. Marsh could form an opinion based only on the hearsay of one woman, and not take the time to meet with Darby first, or check any of her medical records. He was an FAA representative issuing first-class medical certificates to pilots worldwide, he owed the public more. None of that mattered now.

Robert needed to ensure that Darby's safety report was connected to the adverse action of forcing her into a psychiatric evaluation. Darby thought that was obvious because the only reason she was meeting with Abbott was because of her safety report, which Abbott had brought to the meeting. Global, however, was alleging that Abbott was there because of EO complaints buried within that safety report, which had been a surprise to Darby.

"Did Ms. Abbott discuss the subject matter that she and Ms. Bradshaw were discussing?"

"I don't believe in detail, no," Dr. Marsh said.

"So, Ms. Abbott made no comment about the issues related to the incidents of harassment that Ms. Bradshaw had suffered or alleged that she had suffered?"

"I don't think specifics were mentioned," Dr. Marsh said leaning back in his chair. "I know she was sent out there to interview Ms. Bradshaw regarding some EO concerns."

"So, you don't know, or she never articulated what those concerns were?" Robert pressed.

"In her written statement she did, but on this call, I believe it was just I wanted to get more of the observations she had, the behavior she witnessed, and the statements that brought concern to her," Dr. Marsh said, glancing at Wendel, during a moment of attention. Wendel nodded at Marsh with a smile of encouragement.

"On this call did Ms. Abbott ever identify the subject matter context in which Ms. Bradshaw become tearful?"

"No, I can't recall. I don't believe so."

"Did she ever mention the subject matter context in which she expressed concern for her well-being and safety?" Robert asked, pushing for an answer.

"Yes," Dr. Marsh said.

"So, what subject matter context did Ms. Abbott provide?" Robert asked with the patience of Job.

"That, I think she said Ms. Bradshaw told her she had some documentation about Global's safety that she had given to her friend. Ms. Bradshaw had given to her friend to lock up, and in the event of harm coming to her that her friend was supposed to release it and give it to her… uh, to give to the media or a third party, I guess to get it out."

"Documentation about Global's flight operation safety?"

"I believe so," Dr. Marsh said.

They had thought she was going to take her safety concerns to the media. Exposure that they could not afford. Had that happened while Wyatt oversaw Global flight operations, he would never have been considered for the FAA position. But, then again, that didn't explain why Clark had premeditated it months earlier. Perhaps they had been privileged to her research prior to the report. The potential media exposure explained the privileged logs and why marketing was communicating with the legal department at the highest levels regarding Darby.

She *had* told Ms. Abbott if an accident occurred due to *any* event in her safety report that was not addressed, she would go to the media if Global knew and took no action to prevent it. She then had asked Ms. Abbott a singular question—*Why should we have to kill people before we impact change?* Something she had left Ms. Abbott to think about. *Bingo!* Darby thought. But then, isn't that what happened with the MAX and Air France 447? People had to die before they did anything.

Whatever Ms. Abbott had relayed to management, they feared Darby was a loose cannon and was going to tell the world. What she could not figure out is why they thought this was the route to silence her. If she had said anything, they could have fired her for a social media violation. Then again, terminating her would have freed her from Global's social media policy and she could have been interviewed. If they pulled her medical, that would have seen the same result. Perhaps if she was diagnosed as crazy, they figured the media wouldn't listen.

Maybe she had to stop trying to figure the rationale of sociopaths or she would drive herself crazy.

What Global management never expected, was that no matter

what they did to her she would not roll over. She couldn't with what was at stake. They made her an opponent instead of an ally, and then totally underestimated her. If this ended up in court, these safety issues would become public knowledge.

Darby leaned back and folded her arms with a sigh. This time when Wendel looked her way she narrowed her eyes ever so slightly and locked them with his, and he quickly looked away. If silence was their motivation, this was not the path.

Chapter 49

Minneapolis Minnesota
December 19, 2018

MICHELLE DANFORD ROCKED on her couch, her arms hugging her legs tucked up tight. *"God, how could this have happened?"* she cried. Her eyes were swollen from tears that had been falling for days. Reaching for her beer and wishing she had something harder, she was thankful the kids were with her ex-husband. She was devastated and did not know what to do.

Wiping her nose, she dropped the tissue to the floor with the others and reached for her phone. She pressed speed dial. Within seconds it was answered.

"Michelle," Pete said, as he answered. "I've been meaning to call you."

With that statement, she began sobbing. "Pete, I'm in trouble."

"What happened," he asked.

"I don't… I don't know how to say this, but… but… I was raped!" With that disclosure, the tears fell harder than ever.

"What? When?" he said. "Are you drinking?"

"I'm so humiliated," she said. "I awoke in some guy's room in New York and I was being raped. Over and over." She sobbed. "It was horrible. I screamed to stop. I screamed and fought, but he didn't care."

"Do you know who it was?" Pete asked.

"I have no idea. I was at the Women in Aviation event, and I think someone slipped something into my drink. I went from having fun to a total blackout and awake in…" then tears flowed again.

"You need to talk to Steve," Pete said. "I'm going to have him call you right back." He ended the call without as much as a goodbye.

Michelle stared at the phone, not knowing if she should have called him or not. But she didn't know what else to do, or who to call. She was embarrassed, violated, and felt sick to her stomach. Burying her feelings in beer before noon was not that answer. She needed help.

Pete Graham was the chairman of the Pilot Assistance Network of which she was a member. Their goal was to help pilots in crisis. She never imagined that she would be one of those pilots. Steve Owens was the new chairman of the HIMS program since Stan Branson's death. Michelle had no idea why Pete said she needed to talk to Steve, but she could only imagine he had experienced something like this with another pilot.

Steve had been a cocaine addict and still found his way back to the flight deck. He would know exactly what to do. Maybe he could get her help. He had to know people. Then the night came rushing back, and she began bawling all over again. She stared at her beer, and then threw the bottle against the wall and rolled to her side on the couch, and smacked her fist into the pillow.

"Why did this happen?!" she cried. "Why? Why?"

The ringing of her phone startled her. She sat up and grabbed a tissue and blew her nose. Then wiped her eyes with the sleeves of her robe and answered. "Hello."

"Michelle, this is Steve. Pete said that you have a problem."

"I was raped," she said. Realizing that the admission was easier each time she spoke the words. But the sheer pain would never disappear.

"Can you tell me what happened?"

"I don't know what happened," she said. "I was at an event and drinking wine with a bunch of friends, and the next thing I knew I was in some hotel room being repeatedly raped."

"So, you *were* drinking."

"I just told you I was drinking wine with my friends. That's the last thing I remember. So yes, but not that—"

"Michelle, alcoholics will always deny that drinking causes their problems," he said. "The first step is admitting you have a problem."

"I have a fucking problem because I was raped!" she yelled and cried even harder.

"Are you drinking now?"

"What the hell do you think?" she said. "Of course, I'm drinking. Hiding from what happened in a bottle. You should know that more than anyone."

"I understand you're upset," Steve said. "But we can fix this."

"How can we *ever* fix this?" she cried.

There was no way she could ever undo what happened. She had no idea how to process it. The guilt was overwhelming, thinking there had to have been something she could have done to avoid it. But she didn't know how it even happened. How she got there. How the hell could she have avoided it? She had no idea. But this was not her fault!

"I want you to enter the HIMS program," he said. "If you remove the alcohol, you will solve all your problems."

"How in the hell is stopping drinking going to help me deal with what happened?" she cried. That was the only thing that was getting her through what happened.

She didn't really care about having to give up alcohol. She enjoyed drinking for the fun of it with her fellow crewmembers, and at times to relax at the end of the day. But she couldn't imagine facing the humiliation and violation of her body without numbing the pain.

"The reason you were raped was because you're an alcoholic."

"Someone could have put something in a Coke!" Michelle wailed.

"Michelle, we have counselors in the rehab program. You'll go into the pilot program, with other pilots. You'll get rape counseling."

"I will?" she said, at the first glimmer of hope. The first hope she'd had since the rape.

"Of course," he said. "You won't have to pay for a thing. You'll be pay protected, *and* you'll have the time to work through what happened with a professional counselor. This will be a good thing, I promise."

She wiped her eyes and thought about having access to a rape counselor. She knew that was what she needed. That's what she would have advised anyone else in the same circumstance. Her head was still buzzing from her morning beer, and she shook it in an effort to think more clearly. This was the answer. It had to be. She could get help by talking to a rape counselor.

"Michelle, are you still there?"

"Yes," she sniffed and blew her nose on a tissue.

"I'm going to email you a contract. Do you have a way you can print and scan it back to me?"

"Yes."

"Okay good. I've just sent it. Go open your computer and print it. I'll wait."

Michelle stood and stumbled, steadying herself against the door frame as she headed to her room to find her laptop. It was already running. She had been searching online for solutions to no avail. She had no idea how to deal with this, without working and no pay, or how long it would take. Logging into Yahoo, she saw his email and downloaded the document. Closing one eye to minimize her double vision, she pressed print.

"I've got it," she said.

"There's nothing to this contract. It's simply just saying you agree to not drink again. Just outlines the requirements of the Global program. This is such a powerful benefit to the pilot group," he said. "If you turn to the last page, that's where you'll sign the contract."

"Now?"

"Yes, now," he said. "It's not going to get *any* better. The quicker we get you in, the quicker we can get you help."

She was nodding as he spoke. She knew he was right. After a couple of moments of rustling through her desk, she found a pen, closed one eye again, this time to focus on the signature line, and then signed the document. "I signed. Now what?"

"Do you have a scanner?"

"Yeah," she said.

"Good. Place the page you signed on the computer, and I'll give you an email to send it to."

Waiting for his confirmation, she walked to her bed and laid down. Logistics now rolling through her mind. She would be gone for three weeks. Her ex-husband would have to understand and keep the kids. She was so tired. God, she would miss her boys. But she needed to deal with this rape, or she would be no good to them.

"Michelle?" he said startling her. "I've got it."

"Now what?" she asked.

Chapter 50

Oklahoma City
Marsh Deposition Continues
December 19, 2018

ONE EMAIL AFTER another was being shoved under Dr. Marsh's nose as he waffled between cocky and nervousness. The nerves were winning as he evaluated emails that he had written and or received, clearly surprised that Robert had them.

"If you could turn back to Marsh Exhibit 17 to confirm the second paragraph, following the salutation Dr. Wood, it states, *I did inform her that the evaluation could very well end up being the result of a misunderstanding between Ms. Bradshaw and the HR rep.* Is that a fair characterization of what you told Ms. Bradshaw in your face-to-face meeting?"

"Stress the word *could*," Dr. Marsh said, followed by, "yes." And then he grinned with his clown smile.

Compassion shifted to irritation and Darby wished she could stress something else and pop his balloons. The worst part of this was that she had trusted him, and he had defied that trust. More than that, he defied the trust of the traveling public who believed he was a gatekeeper to safety. Not to mention he was a doctor.

"Isn't it true that you contacted the FAA to advise them of Dr.

Wood's report?"

"Isn't it true that Ms. Bradshaw contacted the FAA?" Marsh retorted, widening his eyes.

"I'm asking you to answer my question, please."

"I'm sorry." Marsh folded his arms and said, "I did contact the FAA when I found out Ms. Bradshaw got a first-class medical."

"Why did you do that?"

"I wanted to make sure they knew what was going on here. This was… uh… first of all… who contacted them and why she was getting a first-class medical." Marsh sat up straight and he placed a hand on the desk and raised the other, waving it as he spoke. "Again, this was going outside the Section 8 process which was agreed upon by the pilots' union and Global, and to keep the FAA out of it, and suddenly the FAA is fully informed, and I had documentation reflecting that this individual had a medical condition that did not meet the medical standards!"

"Was it *your* understanding that Section 8 precluded Ms. Bradshaw from renewing her first-class medical?" Robert asked.

"She could do whatever she wanted but the contract had… uh, that had been enforced and used so many times before. We wanted to keep the FAA out of this until the last minute, if at all."

This was fascinating that he was so furious because Darby had invited the FAA to the party by the issuance of another first-class medical. *Why did he care?* she wondered. Global had not allowed her to fly regardless of if she held a medical or not.

He was correct, the contract stated the company was not allowed to tell the FAA until the process was complete. The only reason they withheld this information was to sink the pilot to a point where it would be too late for the FAA to get involved. If a pilot lost medical certification due to mental health from a certified psychiatrist, it would be a hell of a lot more difficult to get it back, and the FAA would typically not challenge the doctor who removed it.

"So, it was your view that Ms. Bradshaw involved the FAA in the Section 8 process?"

"No," Marsh said placing a hand on his hip, stabbing the air with the other and said, "She went and got a first-class medical and really didn't share with the FAA the whole Section 8 process!"

"Do you know what she disclosed to the FAA?"

"All I can say is that when we eventually got the documentation... well, uh, she did share the report with the Mayo Clinic. That was mentioned in her 8500, but nothing mentioned, as I recall, about Dr. Wood."

The 8500 document was the application for a medical certificate. Darby had documented that she had been seeing a psychiatrist and stated it was due to a corporate political action. The FAA never denied her first-class medical. Because the Mayo Clinic doctors overruled Dr. Wood's assertion she did not disclose the bipolar disorder on the form. If she had been misdiagnosed with cancer, she certainly would not have told the FAA that she had cancer if she did not.

"Before you went to the FAA, did you contact Ms. Bradshaw?"

"I did not."

"Before you went to the FAA, did you contact anyone at Global concerning your intention to contact the FAA?"

"I don't believe, I just let them know I received a first-class medical certificate for Ms. Bradshaw, a current first-class medical certificate."

"Who did you inform of this?"

"I imagine, Joe Wolfe," Marsh said, his voice lowering, glancing at his legal team.

"But you did not discuss with any of them your intention to contact the FAA?"

"I *may* have asked them, because now what do we do? This had now compromised the Section 8 process. This was again new territory. So…"

"And one of them authorized you to contact the FAA?" Robert asked.

"I can't recall specifics but again they were contacted."

"Would you have contacted the FAA without the approval of Global?"

"Probably not."

"And did you contact flight surgeon Michael Banks?"

"I don't recall directly talking to him, no."

"Who did you contact at the FAA?"

"I think eventually it was Dr. Christopher Cantwell, the Northwest Regional Flight Surgeon."

"What did you advise him?"

"Concerns I had given the evaluation process that was going on for Ms. Bradshaw and what their decision was based on."

"How did Dr. Cantwell respond to your expression of concern?"

"I believe he was unaware of this, and we subsequently got a request for information from Dr. Cantwell's office," Dr. Marsh said. "He was unaware that Ms. Bradshaw had undergone an evaluation under the Section 8 process including an evaluation by Dr. Wood."

Darby's eyes widened as Marsh spoke. His confusion was evident, but she couldn't believe he would lie about something that was so readily provable.

She shifted between empathy and disgust. Marsh had completely twisted the facts, of which Darby attributed to an actual memory issue. She was certain he simply couldn't remember what transpired regarding all this, and there was more than likely no malicious intent in this deception.

A Federal Air Surgeon had warned Dr. Johnson, Darby's AME, not to support her because Dr. Wood was highly respected in Washington. He also told Dr. Johnson not to get backed into a corner because Darby's case was a timebomb, and he referred to Global as *the baddies*. Therefore, Dr. Johnson had reached out to the Western Division, Regional Flight Surgeon, Dr. Christopher Cantwell, explained the situation and asked for his advice and help. It was Cantwell who issued Darby her first-class medical certificate based upon Dr. Johnson's current medical examination and the Mayo Clinic's report, that over-ruled Dr. Wood's diagnosis. Dr. Cantwell had been aware of everything.

Dr. Cantwell also knew of Darby's bipolar diagnosis from Dr. Wood, but he was in the possession of the report from a panel of doctors at the Mayo Clinic who had subsequently cleared her. It wasn't until Dr. Marsh reached out to the FAA that Deputy Federal Flight Surgeon, Michael Banks, Cantwell's boss, challenged Cantwell for the issuance of Darby's medical certificate and forced him to review Wood's report in its entirety.

Thanks to Cantwell standing strong on his position and fully reviewing Wood's report, determining that it was shady, the FAA medical appeals board sent her a letter that she could retain her medical certificate. Perfect timing, too, because it was a week before her Global-mandated, no expense spared, second evaluation with the neutral doctor. A little influence from the FAA never hurt.

The neutral doctor was requested to conduct a second evaluation, outside the bounds of the contract and without ALPO's objection, because Global said so. While he doubled his price from the first evaluation, she wondered if he knew that he could have added a few more zeros.

Despite Global inviting the FAA into the process and her clearance, management still would not allow Darby to return to work. If that wasn't proof enough that they were playing by their own rules, Darby wasn't sure what was.

Robert handed Marsh another document. "You have been provided with a document we have identified as Marsh Exhibit 25 Bates stamped 8422 to 8438. Would you agree that this is a first-class medical for Ms. Bradshaw?"

"Yes."

"Was it this first-class medical that prompted you to contact the FAA?"

"Yes."

"And was it the receipt of this actual document that prompted you to contact the FAA?"

"No, the one that started out was her first-class medical which had no restriction on it."

"So, there was a document prior to this?"

"Yes."

"I am sorry, so this one dates from August 27, 2016, and the one you were concerned about was the subsequent February of 2017, or was it this document?"

"No, I believe it was this one," he said looking at it. He scratched the back of his head. "I can't recall the specifics, but I believe I got an email from Ms. Bradshaw announcing congratulations I got a first-class medical."

"This was prior to any diagnosis from Dr. Wood, correct?"

"Objection, 'this' is vague. Do you know what 'this' means in that question?" Wendel asked.

"What... this medical here?" Marsh asked.

"Yes, correct," Robert said. "Isn't it true you didn't get the diagnosis from Dr. Wood until December 2016?"

"Yes," he said hesitantly, looking more confused than ever.

"And this document discloses that she had been subject to evaluation by Dr. Wood, correct?" Robert said referencing one of her medical certificates.

"Yes. There was no diagnosis made, of course. And Grant didn't seem to follow up on that either," Dr. Marsh said.

"I'm sorry. Grant?" Robert asked.

"Her aviation medical examiner. Doctor Grant Johnson. In his explanations he didn't seem to follow up with that either," Marsh said.

"Do you know that her doctor *did not* ask that question?"

"It isn't written on the comments here," Marsh said. "I don't know if he wrote it, but he certainly didn't document it."

"And you ascribed that lack of information to wrongdoing by Ms. Bradshaw?"

"No."

"Did you contact Ms. Bradshaw's AME?"

"I did not."

"Why not contact Ms. Bradshaw with respect to your concerns arising from this document?"

"I don't know."

"Would you agree with me that the FAA has the final say in terms of medical certification of a pilot?"

"From a medical certification, but not for Global."

"Did you receive this email?" Robert asked sliding another document under his nose.

"It looks like I was cc'd on it, correct," Marsh said, folding his arms and looking away from the document, as if he had just received an F on his report card and if he didn't look at it, it didn't exist.

"The first three sentences from Joe Wolfe read, *We have done things like this before. I think before we go down this road we should discuss where we are in the process and figure out how important this type of analysis is to the evaluation. In any event, probably a good time for a status check including Dr. Marsh.*

"And that followed an email from Dr. Wood that reads, *Dear Joe and Robert, this issue of how much CaptainBradshaw is flying continues to be an issue. I have thought of a strategy. The problem is labor intensive.*" Robert hesitated. Leaning back in his chair he asked, "Did you have a discussion with Mr. Wolfe and Dr. Wood concerning this flying information?"

"This is hieroglyphics to me," Marsh said. "I need a break."

Chapter 51

Oklahoma City
December 19, 2018

A QUICKLY DEVOURED LUNCH and they were back in the deposition room. Darby wished Dr. Marsh had taken his meds because this process would have been much easier for him. It certainly would have been for her. He was now standing behind his chair, wringing his hands and tapping his foot. His Tommy Bahama shirt was an illusion of relaxation that screamed contradiction to the man wearing it. Within no time they were back on the record.

"Is it part of your responsibilities to review Dr. Wood's medical invoices?"

"Not really," Marsh said.

Two different invoices were on his table, totaling $73,923.45. Sixty thousand had been billed directly to Dr. Marsh and the other was billed to Joe Wolfe.

"In your experience, how does that dollar figure compare with dollar figures of other psychiatric evaluations that you are familiar with?"

"It was high," Dr. Marsh said, giving the invoices a sideways glance.

"In your experience what's an average cost for a psychiatric evaluation of a pilot?"

"For a Section 8?" Dr. Marsh asked.

Darby rolled her eyes.

"Yes," Robert said with fortitude that Darby no longer held.

"So, probably $15,000 to $16,000 as I recall."

"Was that including cognitive testing?"

"I believe so," Marsh said. "Be advised that every case varies. I can't say cookie cutter. The doc has to get whatever they want in terms of the investigation if they wanted that and that's the hours. We want to make sure it is done thoroughly to their… we can't say, this month, no more, sorry, we are done." Marsh's volume and cadence increased with each word.

"We have to make sure it is brought to a conclusion. They are given everything there. So yes, that was a high bill. But again, that's what Dr. Wood needs to do, you will need to talk to *him* about it!"

"What is the average cost of cognitive testing?"

"That can vary. Just from my rough swag that can be $2500 to $6000. And that would be the initial evaluation. They may have to follow up down the line and have testing done again."

That swag was a little off. Darby had been told that her series of tests would have been a little over ten thousand dollars. If Michael Hackman had approved mental health evaluations, that would have cost Global Air Lines $140,000,000.00 every six months based on 14,000 pilots. *Two hundred and eighty million dollars a year,* Darby thought.

"Are you familiar with the Hippocratic Oath?" Robert asked.

"Correct."

"You took one as an MD?" Robert asked.

"Yes."

"Did that Hippocratic Oath apply to a Section 8 process and your role therein?"

"Objection," Wendel said. "If you have a view on that, you can answer."

"Do no harm, is that what you are getting at there?" he snapped. "I'm sorry if I gave *any* impression I was harming anyone on this," he said with disdain, his voice rising. "I was doing my job to make sure that things were safe! I'm not there to be used as some axeman or whatever like that. So, yes, I took the Hippocratic Oath in this case, what are you referring?"

Robert hit a nerve, and Dr. Marsh was about to blow a gasket. If only Von Dietrich was here, too, they could have a fireworks display.

"I am just asking a question whether it was applicable, in your mind, to the Section 8 process."

"I wasn't actually delivering care, I was doing an evaluation. But I wasn't trying to hurt this individual. And I am just trying to think where you are coming from on that one," Marsh said. "Sorry, but again, Hippocratic Oath absolutely!" He hesitated a few minutes, and then glared at Darby and asked, "Where did I let Ms. Bradshaw *down* under the Hippocratic Oath?" His face reddening.

"This process is, that I am asking questions rather than you asking them," Robert said.

"I got it! Understood!" Marsh snapped, and folded his arms, and pouted.

"I objected to that question as you heard," Wendel said, "Judge Geraghty will be able to review all the questions that are asked here eventually. So, you can answer the questions that are asked. And I will object when I find it suitable, okay?"

"It was a very narrow question. I am not sure I got an answer. And I am not trying to put you on the defensive but rather just to get your understanding whether the Hippocratic Oath applied to your role—"

"Asked and answered. I'm going to direct you not to go further on that. It is an offensive question, and it was answered," Wendel spat as if he, too, were offended. "You can ask him the next question."

"Could you tell me what his answer was?" Robert asked.

"Read back the record," Wendel said.

While the court reporter looked for the response, Robert commented, "There was a lot of anger."

"The Rules of Federal Procedure require that you ask questions that are not designed to harass the witness, that are appropriate to the subject matter of the case," Wendel said. "I think that question went beyond it, in my opinion. But in any event, he could answer the question, and I believe the answer is clear, over an objection."

"Rule 30 provides that a person may instruct the deponent not to answer—"

"Rule 37 also applies." Wendel said threatening Robert.

Wendle is finally paying attention and growing a pair with a threat like that, Darby thought. Rule 37 authorized the court to direct that party's attorney who failed to participate in good faith in the discovery process to pay the expenses, including attorney's fees incurred by other parties as a result of that failure.

"Could you please not interrupt me?" Robert said.

"No, I am not interested in your recitation of Rule 30, so you can take it up with Judge Geraghty if you are not *too* tired," Wendel said.

Darby raised an eyebrow. Threatening was one thing, but that was a low blow. Robert had made an error on a name earlier, and he had apologized by stating he was a bit fatigued. He had flown in early that morning and then he had to deal with Dr. Marsh. Wendel Kowalski was now becoming a schoolyard bully. Lazy and theatrical was a better look for him.

"I want to state for the record that under Rule 30 a person may instruct a deponent to answer only when necessary to preserve privilege, to enforce a limitation ordered by the court, or to present a motion under Rule 30 (b) (3)," Robert said. "And I am asking as a courtesy which of those—"

"I will file if you require us to file a motion on this subject," Wendel said interrupting Robert once again.

"Okay," Robert said, flatly.

Wendel stared at Robert with his mouth open for a moment, perhaps not knowing what to do with Robert's 'okay', and then he said, "But I don't think you should require us to do that. And if you have another question, you should ask it." His voice had shifted back to pleading.

"I didn't hear the answer and I will accept for the time being, given I have no alternative at this point, to ask the court reporter to read the response back," Robert said.

"Why don't you ask the witness if he has anything else to say in answer to your question, and then he can decide whether or not he thinks he has more to say in answer to your question," Wendel said. "That seems like a fair way to get the answer to your question since you believe that this is actually relevant to your case, that you are representing your client and not a violation of Rule 37."

"I asked the witness whether it was his understanding that the Hippocratic Oath applied to his role in the Section 8 process," Robert said.

"I will withdraw my direction to the witness to not answer the question," Wendel said, setting his phone on the desk with force. "I would suggest that you listen to, if you want to listen to the answer again because maybe you are just not focused this morning on the words that are coming out of the witness' lips, but if you want to hear it again and you still believe that he has not answered the question, my suggestion is you ask him whether he has anything else that he would add to answer that question."

Wendel had just moved from a bully to an ass. For an easy answer to a simple question, this had certainly gotten out of hand.

"That's not my question," Robert said.

"You are citing an oath that goes back 2,000 years to Athens, Greece," Wendel began. "You haven't cited what that oath is. You are basing it on some layperson's knowledge of medical practice without foundation, and you are asking the witness to answer a question of whether or not that oath applied, a legal conclusion to his conversation with your client.

"He did his best to answer that question, inappropriate as it was, as *offensive* as it was, and if you want to pursue that line of questioning, I am suggesting a way that you can pursue it without having to create any motion practice. If you don't like my suggestion, you can try something else and ask a question. I won't speak further on the subject, so you are free to do what you see fit at this point." He theatrically threw up his hands and Darby slowly shook her head when he looked her way.

"I will follow your prior suggestion that we see if he did answer that question or not. So, could you read the answer?" Robert said to the court reporter.

They went off the record and read the transcripts. They went back on the record and Robert and Wendel discussed whether he was allowed to answer or not. Wendel said that he had already withdrawn the direction to not answer, and that he could. But then he argued more about Rule 37. Finally, Wendel told Robert to ask the question again, but he didn't think it was fair he'd have to write a motion.

Darby didn't think that Judge Geraghty would like such a frivolous motion, but what did she know. She also thought it was a fair question to ask if a doctor's duty to cause no harm to a patient was the same duty under Global's Section 8 process. Dr. Marsh was not Darby's doctor but was fulfilling a contractual role for Global Air Lines in the capacity of a doctor. She also wanted to know the answer to that question.

"Dr. Marsh, the time you were performing your duties pursuant to Section 8 of the collective bargaining agreement, did you have an understanding as to whether the Hippocratic Oath applied to the services you were rendering to Global?" Robert asked again.

"Could I see a copy of the Hippocratic Oath, please?" Dr. Marsh said sarcastically.

"I don't have one, so if you can't answer the question then—"

"Then in general I can't answer that," Dr. Marsh said, folding his arms and giving Darby his tight-lipped clown smile.

Chapter 52

HAD THIS BEEN a padded room, Dr. Marsh would have looked more like the inpatient than the doctor. Robert asked him the simplest of questions, but Marsh would not provide simple answers. Darby wasn't sure if he couldn't remember, or if he was changing his story to fit what he thought he was supposed to say. He was sarcastic at times, disrespectful at others, and was easily and often offended.

The Hippocratic Oath question had almost pushed him over the edge. However, he later admitted that Darby had told him during their meeting, that the only harm she believed would come to her was them messing with her in the simulator or giving her line checks. Yet, he had failed to admit that she also told him the Section 8 process had been threatened if she met with Wyatt and Clark. He had admitted she relayed training concerns and flight operations behaviors as questionable and unsafe practices at Global.

To state Dr. Marsh was an odd character was an understatement that left Darby perplexed, wishing more now than ever that they had videotaped his deposition. Nobody would believe this. She didn't believe it and she was watching the live show.

"Did you take all she told you at face value, or did you just discredit her representations?" Robert asked.

"No, why would I… no! Forgive me, I wouldn't discredit her," Dr. Marsh said in offense.

"It is one or the other, I suppose," Robert said.

"But understand, please, please," Marsh said. "This is a she-said she-said, okay. She said I've got mental health concerns with this individual there. She said, I'm fit as a fiddle. We are talking with the people that operate the aircraft up there, still living in the time of Germanwings and EgyptAir. So, when in doubt, knowing the FAA… uh, we lean towards, we got to figure this out to make absolutely sure… go above and beyond and make sure there is not a problem here. So, I did not disregard—"

Robert said, "I want to—"

"Wait. Did the witness finish?" Wendel asked.

"Please finish," Robert said, with a sigh.

"That's why I talk to these individuals. I know it's stressful for them there. I want to get it taken care of appropriately. And I'm giving the individual, the pilot, in this case, Ms. Bradshaw, to tell her side of the story," Dr. Marsh said. "So, you know, if I gave her the impression… that I was discrediting her, that's an hour-and-a-half of discrediting her that listened to her both when she met with me and also on the phone call afterwards."

Darby had not spent more than 40 minutes with him. Maybe he was combining their call the next day, she wasn't sure. Robert's question, however, was designed to clarify if Marsh discredited what Darby had said, yet now he says he believed her.

Then why proceed solely on the medical opinion of the pass travel complaint department lady? Darby wondered. One reason. He, too, had been given marching orders.

"That wasn't my purpose," Robert began. "And I assume that sometimes in your position, in your evaluations you make credibility assessments, correct, you decide whether you think someone is telling the truth or not, in your—"

"That can be, yes," Dr. Marsh said.

"But in this particular instance, you did not assess whether Ms. Bradshaw was telling the truth or not in terms of her account?"

"I could only assume she *was* telling me the truth," Dr. Marsh said emphatically.

Darby believed that. That was exactly the feeling she had in his office. He appeared to be trying to figure out what was going on because he knew she did not have a problem. He had given her a name and number of a specific doctor at ALPO's aeromedical department to call, then told her he would call her the next day. As it turned out, that was a setup in itself.

The next day he called and told her some excuse as to why he wasn't allowed to release her and that only the selected psychiatrist had that ability now that it had started. He had changed his tune overnight. That statement was also in conflict with the contract. As it turned out, he had already agreed to use Dr. Wood that morning before they ever talked.

"I'm sorry, tell me again, you went to medical school where?" Robert asked

"Chicago Medical School."

"Was there mental health training at your medical school?"

"Yes."

"What did it consist of?"

"Typically, in med school, if you will, you get, your first two years are mostly book work, your second two years are mostly clinical. You have a required eight-week rotation in psychiatry. Not to say that in some of the other rotations you are doing you may come across mental health issues unique to those patient populations."

"Do you have any mental health obligations as an AME, when you are evaluating a pilot to perform some type of assessment of mental health?"

"As an AME, when a pilot is coming to my office for an aviation medical exam, yes."

"What does that consist of?"

"It is… I can't give you the verbatim word, but it is a general impression based on the behaviors, statements and related… uh, other supporting documentation about the pilots' mental health ability."

"Prior to making your determination to refer Ms. Bradshaw for psychiatric evaluation, did you talk to her AME?"

"No."

"Did you review any of her AME medical records?"

"No."

"Did you review her personnel file?"

"No."

"Did you review workplace records related to attendance, absenteeism, or lateness?"

"No."

"Are you familiar with HIMS?" Robert asked.

"Yes."

"What does that stand for?"

"Human interventional motivation study."

"Have you had HIMS training?"

"I have."

"What did that consist of?"

"That involves additional training. They hold it typically out in Denver, Colorado, or Aurora, I guess, for a four-day-long briefing involving ALPO aeromedical, the FAA, experts in the field of addiction and mental health, I will say psychiatrists, neuropsychologists, representatives from the airline, and then aviation medical examiners," Dr. Marsh said.

"How many Global pilots do you have as clients in your AME capacity?" Robert asked, shifting directions.

"1800, 2,000, I think. That I've seen for physicals and all."

Wow! Darby thought. She lifted her phone and googled the number of workdays in a calendar year. If he were to have 2,000 airline pilots, each of them twice a year, that's 4,000 events. She plugged in the numbers into the calculator. That would be 15.9 pilots a day. In an eight-hour workday. Notwithstanding that he was conducting evaluations for the HW medical insurance, conducting Section 8 evaluations for Global, and spending time in court. She typed in his low end at 1,800, and that was 14 pilots a day. *No way in hell,* she thought.

Either Dr. Marsh was exaggerating, or he was pencil-whipping his evaluations. Then she did the math of $250 per evaluation. This was a million-dollar-a-year goldmine for medical certifications alone. Quite the money machine for Dr. Marsh, and the very reason he was motivated to work with Global. He had to play their game. Darby's career was not worth what he would lose by standing to her defense.

"That is not a conflict of interest to represent both Global Air Lines and individual pilots?" Robert asked.

"I object to the extent it calls for a legal conclusion," Wendel said. "But if you have an opinion, you can answer."

"This was worked out with Global and agreed upon that I could do this on Global pilots."

Robert shifted his attention to Darby's medical application, and then glanced at his list of questions. Wendel and Betty were up to the same behaviors, but the blonde appeared to be listening intently with fascination.

Robert continued to question Marsh as to the requirement of entries on the medical certificate form, the 8500 document. Wendel continued to object, due to drawing a legal conclusion, but he allowed him to answer.

"And if the FAA had ever determined that she had misrepresented relevant information, that would be a basis for revoking her medical, correct?" Robert asked.

"Sure, it's their call," Dr. Marsh said.

Robert leaned back and assessed Dr. Marsh. He too noted the behavior anomalies and confusion in statements. They were now on the tail end of the day, and they had learned enough from him, but there was one more thing Darby wanted to know. She knew Robert felt uncomfortable with the question, but it was important that she understood Marsh's behavior for doing what he had done to her.

Setting down his pencil, Robert paused for a moment. "Were you on anxiety-related medication when you gave your opinion to place Bradshaw into a Section 8?" Robert asked with gentleness and concern that he'd shared with Wyatt regarding his feelings towards retirement.

"Objection!" Wendel snapped.

"I will object too!" Dr. Marsh said.

"I direct you not to answer," Wendel said.

Robert accepted his objection and looked at his paper for the next question. Darby suspected that he was more than likely relieved at the response. However, red was growing up Dr. Marsh's neck toward his face.

Dr. Marsh opened and closed his mouth, but nothing came out. The storm was brewing. *This is going to be good,* Darby thought watching him. She glanced at Robert who was reviewing his questions, oblivious to Dr. Marsh's antics.

"Of the top ten prescription medications in this country, three of them are antidepressants, antipsychotic or antianxiety medications!" Marsh spat.

Robert looked up in surprise.

Dr. Marsh continued. "Pilots can't have them. I don't write those rules! If they do, they have to get them on a special issuance. Please go out there and tell probably a third of the country they shouldn't be doing their stuff or shouldn't be testifying, shouldn't be caring for people because they are on these medications!" He yelled, "You like courts? Enjoy that one! Next question please."

Marsh folded his arms with a humph. He looked directly at Darby and gave her that creepy closed-mouth clown grin. Darby returned the smile, but hers was one of compassion. She truly felt sorry for this sad little man and hoped he would get the help he needed.

"Is anxious the same as anxiety?" Robert asked.

"No," Marsh said.

"Objection," Wendel said.

"What is more severe?"

"Objection. I direct you not to answer," Wendel said.

Darby's eyes flashed from Marsh to Wendel and back to Marsh. His arms still folded, he gave her an even bigger grin, and tipped his head side to side, as if saying—*I don't have to answer. Ha. Ha.* Darby returned his smile this time thinking, *you're such an ass.*

"Counsel, please tell your client to stop smiling at us," Wendel said. "Mr. Allen, I find that very upsetting to be smiled at by your client when you are engaged in the types of questioning that you are. So, I would like you to instructor her, or we can leave now."

Darby wished they *would* leave now. Instead, Robert finished the questions that took another 30 minutes, and they took a break.

After they returned, Robert said, "Before I pass the witness, I would want to make the comment for the record, since counsel made a comment on the record about my client smiling at the witness, and I didn't see what she had done, so I didn't feel I needed to instruct her with respect to something I haven't seen."

"Fair enough," Wendel said.

"In any case, she told me, and I don't want to be contentious about this, but she told me during our break that her smile was responsive to a smile that she received from the deponent. I don't know if we are going to resolve that here."

"So, credibility is what it is," Wendel said.

"Good," Robert said. "No questions from you?"

"None," Wendel said.

They ended the deposition and went off the record. Darby walked over to Wendel.

"Don't you *ever* disparage me like that again by challenging my credibility, when you don't know what the hell is going on. Dr. Marsh was grinning at me, and I returned his smile."

"I'm sorry, I didn't know," Wendel said. "I apologize."

"Well, you should have apologized on the record."

"I simply didn't see what happened, and only saw you."

"Well, I've been watching your antics this entire time, and perhaps if you were paying closer attention to your witness and less time on your cell phone—"

"That's not—"

"Please *do not* interrupt me," Darby said. "Your lack of professionalism with the audible sighs, rolling your eyes and theatrically looking at your watch as if we're wasting *your* time is uncalled for. I understand Global is paying you a large sum of money for an outcome. But I am most *certain* they are not paying you *extra* to be a whiny, theatrical, malicious ass."

Chapter 53

Oklahoma City
Embassy Suites
ALPO Meeting
January 14, 2019

Throughout her two years of hell and the ensuing battle for truth, Darby had never questioned anything she had done in pursuit of safety—until now. She thought depositions were painful, but this process was staggering.

Tables lined the left side of the room facing the opposite side of the room, with tables configured in the same manner on the other side. A row of tables across the back connected the two sides. This is what they called the horseshoe. The podium was on an elevated platform in front of the congregation.

Darby sat against the far back wall with one leg crossed over the other with her arms folded, and the horseshoe well in front of her. Her foot bounced, for no other reason than she held a bit of nervous energy.

A grin spread across her face. The irony of what she was about to do, could in fact be construed as crazy. Dr. Wood could have a field day with this one.

The current speaker was reading his speech. She wasn't sure what shook more—his hands or his voice. His nerves were interesting because he sat in the horseshoe on a regular basis. These were people he worked with and knew well. As a matter of fact, the *only* other people running for office were already union representatives and part of this group. They simply rotated in and out of positions as they were all vying for power. *The Lord of the Flies* came to mind.

This union meeting was to elect the officers to the master executive council, known as the MEC. Unfortunately, 14,000 pilots were prohibited from voting for their MEC leadership. The best they could do was elect their local representatives, who were supposed to represent them. Instead, the representatives within this room voted each other into position by negotiations at an open bar the night before the election, and often to the detriment of the constituency.

These meetings were in the most luxurious of hotels. The outer lobby hosted a buffet for breakfast, then cookies, pastries, and snacks were available until the lunch buffet was produced. Sandwiches, pasta, fruit, chips, cupcakes, and a cooler filled with Coke products. This went on for an entire week, funded by those pilots who were actually working for a living.

When the speaker was done, questions began. Some questions were polite, while others were clearly an attack. She had been told the night before that the union was divided. Half represented the company, and the other half supported the pilots. The two sides were in a bitter fight against each other. Sadly, the decisions of those on behalf of the company were self-serving. The participants knew if they played ball with the company, even at the sacrifice of a pilot or two, then they, too, could move into a lucrative management position.

Darby glanced around the room and thought, *if this isn't a lucrative enough position, I don't know what is.* She sighed heavily.

The next speaker walked up on stage, equally as nervous as the first as he read his speech. Darby extended her fingers, glancing at her nails, glad she had taken the time for a manicure with a fresh coat of Crimson Red. She smiled at the thought of Clark's face during his deposition.

After the question-and-answer session, Darby was asked to leave the room. The next two speeches would be for the MEC chairman, the same position she was running for, and they were not allowed to hear what the others had to say. Darby would be the last speaker of the day. As the first of the three candidates walked to the microphone with a speech in hand, Darby exited the room.

She had no idea where the incumbent was, but he was on her shit list and probably hiding from her. He had allowed Global to escort her through hell without union support and then played dumb. Denying he'd been in receipt of a letter she submitted in request for his help, six hours later he forgot he'd told her he'd never received it, and began talking about his impression of that very letter he asserted to never have received. Not a smart move. She didn't call him out at the time because he was giving her a ride to the airport, but that event was something she would not forget.

Darby knew she had less than a zero chance to win. Hell, she would not even get a vote. There were two contingencies and even one vote could take the election one direction or the other. Darby didn't know much of the other guy running, but if they could rid themselves of the incumbent, they would be far better off than before this election.

She walked out the door to the lobby. Stopping short with her mouth agape, she peeked inside the coffin. *Oh my God!* she thought. There was a grocery store-sized chest freezer filled with ice cream bars and ice cream sandwiches, which explained so much. Everyone in that room had moved beyond the freshmen ten, to the union thirty. Tables were also filled with fruit and cheese, slices of cake and brownies. Lots and lots of brownies. Gluttony at its best, funded by her dues.

Darby called Kathryn and the call went to voicemail, so she left a message. She sat for a moment and glanced through a magazine, then went to the bathroom and brushed her hair, and added a fresh coat of lipstick. She assessed herself in the mirror and shrugged. *Good enough,* she thought. She headed out of the bathroom wondering if maybe she should have written a speech.

She was not here to win the election; she was here to communicate a message on behalf of her fellow pilots. It was a shame, however, that everyone in that room only voted for those who were part of the club. They were missing some talented help from people who cared. There were many qualified pilots that would be outstanding in this position; yet, would never be accepted because they were outsiders.

She returned to the lobby as the door opened. A head poked out and looked left and right. "Darby, you're up," the man said.

Chapter 54

SHE HAD TEN minutes and not a second more. Once inside the conference room, she walked behind the tables, down the right side of the room, and up to the stage. Darby approached the microphone. She assessed the room for a moment. A few guys were looking at her, most were looking at their phones or playing on their computers. Less than half were paying attention.

After she introduced herself, Darby said, "When I took my first flight, I was hooked. I loved it. I knew that flying would be more than an occupation. It was something that would become my life. Each, and *every* one of you had that first flight experience. You became pilots because you loved it or believed that the job of flying to be a worthy career. I am most certain that you did not become a pilot because you wanted to become a union representative.

"You made your dreams come true, and then some of you realized that things could be better. Better wages, better working conditions, better schedules, and much needed protections for our careers. Those of you who got involved for the right reasons, jumped into the river to help. But that current was strong. And as hard as you tried, the effort became an uphill battle due to politics. Eventually you began going with the flow, and now you are drifting backward with the current. I'm telling you, at the end of that river is a waterfall! We must do something to regain control of this union.

"Last night at your social where alcohol flowed at the union members' expense, I learned how divided this group is. How in the hell do *any* of you expect to achieve unity among our fourteen thousand pilots when you can't even get along amongst yourselves? This concern is more than just about a contract. This is about the survival of our careers.

"I was removed for two years because of my being overly concerned for safety. Safety concerns, as a result of substandard training at Global Air Lines. Manufacturers are creating pilotless aircraft. This will be a future where pilots will be monitoring automated systems managed by kids in a warehouse on the ground. The FAA induced a pilot shortage by increasing flight time requirements. Due to the pilot shortage, it won't be long until they change the four-crew requirement to three pilot, the three-pilot requirement to two, and the domestic system will be flown by single pilot operations. This will be the future with 50% of the pilot jobs gone, until they go fully automated.

"Our airline is reducing training to a dangerous level, by lowering standards. We are not even allowed to disengage the autothrust on the triple seven. Nobody flies anymore. We are required to manage the automation. ASAP reports are at their highest level because pilots' lack understanding of our highly automated equipment."

Darby scanned the room while she spoke until her eyes landed on the training chairman and held his attention. "Making training easy for pilots is not the answer to survivability of the job. Allowing the company to deny manual flight creates automation reliance, and not the path we should be going."

She paused and then returned her attention to the group.

"Captain George Wyatt testified that we had close to 27,000 ASAP reports this year alone. These errors will be the very ammunition the company, manufacturers, and the FAA will use to justify removing the pilot from the equation. For those of you who are playing into the company's hands, shame on you! You owe your constituents better than that. This is about the survivability of the pilot job. You may not have given a damn about *my* career, but I assure you that when they cut 50% of the pilot force that will reduce ALPO's income by 50%.

"I took a stand for safety on behalf of my fellow pilots and passengers alike, and nearly lost my career. Where was my union?" She paused and assessed the group before she continued. "What happened to me, should never happen to anyone. But I'm not here about me. I stand before you, not as Darby Bradshaw, but as the voice and representative of those fourteen thousand pilots who you are *supposed to* be representing. I'm asking for your vote so we can sustain the pilot job and be the voice our pilots deserve. Thank you."

Darby received a few applauses, and then the questions began. She grinned at the thought of questions, as this would be more of an attack.

"You pointed out how we are divided," a representative said. "How do you think you're going to get unity within our group?"

"I don't know. Maybe I'll make you sit in the middle of the room, hold hands, and sing Kumbaya," Darby said. "For God's sake, you're adults! If you can't get along, how the hell do you expect the pilots to unify and vote in a contract?"

"What do you view your role as the chairman," another representative asked.

"To listen to you as a group. Yours is to listen to the pilots."

"Have you even read the MEC manual?" the first officer representative from Memphis asked. "I mean… I have it here," he said extending his hand to his computer. "If I quizzed you, could you answer the questions?"

"I have not read the manual," Darby said.

"How do you expect to do your job if you don't know what it says?" he spat with theatrics for the group.

"Sir, I am a B777 type-rated pilot," Darby began with the intent of emasculating him with the size her plane compared to his light twin. "I did *not* read the manual or learn that aircraft until *after* I was awarded the position. That seemed to work out just fine."

There were a few laughs, and then someone to the left said, "Darby, I first want to thank you for taking your time here. Have you ever held any ALPO offices in the past?"

"Not as a representative," Darby said. "I assisted in starting the pilot assistant network, PAN, to help pilots in crisis. I was a volunteer on the critical incident response team, CIRP, and during the strike prior to the merger, I was a Seattle command center representative."

Darby did the work without the title. What she did not say was that she had left PAN because the Chairman, Pete Zowalski, refused to train volunteers how to identify and or deal with suicidal pilots. She had been trained through CIRP and knew what was needed.

Instead, she was ordered to take a potentially suicidal pilot's name and phone number, then tell him someone would call him back. She would not be part of a pilot's death sentence.

Shortly after she'd returned to work from her mental health stint, she had requested ALPO leadership to investigate two ALPO attorneys for their behavior during her lack of representation. She was subsequently kicked out of CIRP. She was blackballed from the union for trying to fix it. Now she made one more effort to speak some sense into them.

Darby now wondered if Stan had in fact killed himself, if he had called for help and was put on hold and told that someone would call him back.

Chapter 55

Seattle Washington
January 17, 2019

Kathryn had made a lasagna for Darby and had invited Linda and Jackie. Her twins were at a basketball practice, and this was a much-needed break for them all. Darby all but missed the Holidays by dropping trips to make the depositions work and be able to pay for it all. She needed some down time and Kathryn would give it to her. Kathryn could not help but feel responsible for much of what Darby was going through.

They had all laughed uncontrollably during dinner when she told them about Dr. Marsh's deposition. The other depositions were equally laughable, albeit in a pathetic way. None of this was amusing. Kathryn felt guilty, however, for not confiding in Darby with what John had shared, but then there was nothing she could do.

They had finished dinner and moved to the living room. Kathryn refilled Darby's glass and set the wine bottle on the table, and then sat beside her on the couch.

"Thanks," Darby said. She then told them what she'd said at the union meeting.

"It kind of reminds me when Bill was running," Jackie said.

"Yes, but we definitely had different agendas," Darby said. "It amazes me how nobody in the union can see what's happening to the industry."

"People don't comprehend unless their paycheck is attached to that understanding," Linda said.

"It will bite them in the ass one day," Darby said. "Unfortunately, those in charge will pull up the ladder to protect themselves."

Kathryn remained silent. She couldn't tell Darby what John had conveyed. Besides, Darby knew what was happening. Most of it anyway. Instead, she asked, "When do you expect the summary decision?"

"I'm not sure," Darby said. "It would be nice if we could get it before we spend another penny on depositions. But with Wyatt's and Clark's testimony, we should win this thing."

"Then no court?" Linda asked.

"Nope, it would be over, and the judge would award what he deemed appropriate."

"Why would it be over?" Jackie asked.

"Both sides filed a motion for summary decision," Darby explained "Meaning, based on the facts that we currently have; we are asking for a judgment without a trial."

"So the judge could rule in their favor?" Jackie asked.

"They won't win this," Darby said. "But I'm not too sure about the preemption."

"Okay, *I* don't even know what that means," Linda said, with a chuckle.

"They're arguing this belongs in the grievance process," Darby said. "But the AIR21 statute was created because the judicial system asserts that safety should not be placed in the hands of an arbitrator, who is nothing but a businessman. An arbitrator's decision depends upon his next paycheck."

"They can be bought?" Linda asked.

"Yep," Darby said. "The very reason I dropped my grievance."

"What I don't understand is how Wyatt could become the FAA administrator if he violated the whistleblower law," Jackie said.

"Good question," Darby said. "Could you imagine if he was running the FAA. The thought gives me chills."

"Any way we can keep him out?" Linda asked.

"Tell the committee what he did at Global," Darby answered. "If anyone on the Senate Committee knew of his dozens of federal violations to include retaliation against an employee for reporting safety, they would never confirm him."

"Can't you talk to a reporter?" Jackie asked.

"If I want to get terminated," Darby said.

"But this is about the FAA inspector, not the company," Jackie said.

"It would be difficult to tell this story without implicating Global," Linda said. She looked at Kathryn. "But you could."

"Not this time," Darby said. "If he were to get in, despite our efforts, then Kat would lose her job and never work again. Well, maybe at Starbucks, and that could have benefits."

"It would be worth the risk," Kathryn said. "But it would be difficult to make a difference from the outside."

Kathryn hated that sentiment. Those words were the proverbial excuse for those who were afraid of making change. They did nothing because they wanted to retain the job to make a difference, therefore they never did anything of substance.

"We have months before confirmation," Darby said. "We'll figure something out."

Kathryn glanced at her watch and then excused herself and went to the kitchen to finish cleaning up the dinner dishes. She wanted to warn Darby, but her hands were tied. Her heart broke for what

Darby was going through, and there was not a damn thing she could do. She hated herself for promising John she would remain silent.

"Can I help?" Darby asked as she followed Kathryn to the kitchen. Jackie and Linda joined them. In no time the kitchen was spotless, and the dishwasher was running.

"I did a little research," Kathryn finally said, draping a towel over the edge of the sink. This was nothing that Darby couldn't have learned on her own but had not found the time. She had been so focused on details of her case; the big picture was nothing but a backdrop these days. "I know who the Administrator was when Air France 447 crashed."

"Who?" Darby asked.

"Michael Hackman," she said, taking a seat at the kitchen table.

"He was the administrator who scrapped the mental health evaluations," Darby said.

"The very same," Kathryn said.

"Why's Wyatt replacing him?" Jackie asked.

"He's not," Kathryn said. "There's a temporary in place now, who won't even serve the full term."

"Where's Hackman?" Linda asked

"Sitting on Global's Board of Directors," Kathryn said flatly.

"What the hell?" Darby said and sat heavily at the kitchen table next to Kathryn. "They slipped Hackman onto the Global Board in exchange for the mental health deal. I can't believe I didn't see that. I can't believe I didn't see all of this."

"See all of what?" Jackie asked.

Darby looked from Kathryn to Jackie and sighed. "Michael Hackman made a deal with the devil to abolish the mental health evaluations that would have cost hundreds of millions, for a position on their board."

"But why didn't he just end his term?" Linda asked.

"Because of the MAX," Darby said, opening her phone and typing something into Safari. Then she looked up. "Hackman left the FAA six months before the first crash. The pending MAX crashes were not a surprise."

"All those ASAP reports," Kathryn said. "I suspect he knew the plane was faulty and he looked the other way."

Darby nodded, typing into her phone as she said, "Hackman knew this was coming down the chute. A hundred bucks says there was a cover-up at Boeing with the FAA's hand right in the middle of it and Hackman needed to get out, or he'd get his hand burned."

"So, he went directly to Global," Kathryn said.

"More or less," Darby said looking up from her phone. "Three months after he left the FAA, he joined the board and thus the need for the temporary guy."

"Oh... because Wyatt had to retire and separate from the airline before going to the FAA," Jackie said.

"No," Darby said. "Wyatt didn't need to retire before becoming appointed. He could have stayed as VP and gone directly into the position. He retired for a purpose. Global needed to move the chess pieces as covertly as possible to sanitize both Wyatt and Hackman."

"Removing Wyatt from Global, pulled him from your case to avoid accountability," Linda said. "He really couldn't stay at Global with a lawsuit underway and his involvement. They also couldn't swap him with Hackman as that would be too obvious."

"Exactly. Innocence by separation," Darby said. "But they're just rolling out of one bed and into another, cutting deals with each other and writing them up in blood."

"I had no idea," Jackie said. "Honest, John never said anything, or I would have told you."

Darby reached out and took Jackie's hand and squeezed it. "I know." Sighing, she stood. "We'd better get home. It's getting late."

Kathryn walked them to the door. "I'll tell the girls you said hi."

"Thanks," Darby said, pulling her coat on. "Give them a big hug, too."

"Are you going to see Tom tonight?" Jackie asked Darby.

"I wish," Darby said, throwing her purse over her shoulder. "He's out of town for another training class."

"No, he's not," Jackie said looking confused. "On my way here tonight, I forgot the wine so I drove back home and his car was in our driveway. He and John were in John's office arguing about something, so I decided to leave them be. I grabbed the wine and slipped out before they woke the baby."

"Are you sure?" Darby asked. "Why would he be in town and not tell me?"

Kathryn's heart sank, yet she remained silent.

Chapter 56

JOHN AND TOM *barely know each other,* she thought. Wondering what the hell was going on, she tried calling Tom twice and both calls went directly to his voicemail. In her first message Darby had told him she was heading home and heard that he was in town. The second message she'd said she was home. Now soaking in a bubble bath, all she could think about was his being in town and over at the McCallister's house. Arguing no less.

She closed her eyes and slid lower into the tub, allowing the bubbles to touch her chin, then shifted her attention to Global. She wasn't sure which was worse—Wyatt being the leading contender to be the FAA administrator, or Hackman walking onto the Global board after he created legislation to help the airline, safety be damned.

The most perplexing thing was, that Hackman who held a position on the Board of Directors had implemented SMS. Safety management systems was his baby, yet he sat on the sideline overseeing a company who violated that very regulation in every way possible.

Her phone rang and she startled. Breathing deep, she dried her hand and stuck an earbud into her ear and answered.

"I hope it's not too late to call," Robert said. "Can you talk?"

"Of course," Darby said.

"I'm in Los Angeles, and just returned from dinner to an inbox full of notifications from Judge Geraghty's office."

"Good news?" she asked, hopeful.

"Yes, and no," Robert said. "He has denied Global's request for summary decision, denied their pleading complaint for preemption, and he denied their stay of the proceedings."

"That's great news," Darby said, a huge smile spreading across her face, not wanting to ask about the bad part. At this point, she'd be fine without hearing it.

Global had plead preemption under the Railway Labor Act trying to remove her case from federal court and into the grievance process, instead of the courtroom. They also requested a summary judgement to rule in their favor and wanted to stay the proceedings to end it all.

Ha. Ha. They lost, she thought and punched bubbles into the air.

"It is excellent news," Robert said. "But—"

"Our request for summary decision didn't fare so well either?"

"No. He wrote an order denying our motion for summary decision," Robert said. "He said that we satisfied the stipulation that you engaged in protected activity, the parties were subject to the act, *and* that the referral to the psychiatric evaluation was an adverse action."

"Then why did he deny us?" Darby asked tipping her head back and closing her eyes. *Global got to him,* she feared.

"He didn't completely deny us, he only denied causation," Robert said. "Meaning, all we have to prove is that your protected activity was a contributing factor."

"But I thought we had enough case law in our motion supporting causation."

"We did," Robert said, "but he didn't mention any of the cases we cited in his discussion. Not only did he not acknowledge their existence, but he also did not rule on them. He should have."

"I don't understand," Darby said. "We had case law and we should have won it all, but he remained silent as if it didn't exist?" A worry line etched into her forehead. "Do you think Global got to him?"

"No. Of course not," Robert said. "This is one the strangest cases of premeditation, with multiple levels of high executive involvement. My guess is that he wants to better understand what happened before he rules."

"He wants to give them their day in court," Darby said softly.

"I believe so. The way this was written is an oddity too," Robert said. "He should have stated he was awarding partial summary decision, not an order denying the motion."

"Well, regardless of how he wrote it, we're three steps closer."

"That we are," Robert said. "I also had an interesting call with Wendel today."

"Interesting as in ha ha?" Darby asked.

"He wanted to know if you're willing to go to mediation."

"Really?" Darby said, wondering what the hell they were up to now. Not knowing how mediation worked, she asked, "Do we sit at a table like in a negotiation?"

"No. The mediator sits in your room and talks to you, and then will talk to the company's decision maker. He or she will go from room to room."

"Then the mediator decides the ruling?" Darby asked.

"Yes, and it will become binding."

"That sounds like a *really* good deal," Darby said sarcastically, "but *only if* we can have Cheryl Winters do it."

Cheryl Winters had been the arbitrator the union and the company had selected for her grievance, the same woman the Global attorney had ex parte communications with and had made every effort to shove down Darby's throat. She was also the same arbitrator that ruled against Keith Smith. Everything about that woman screamed bought and paid for.

Darby ended up having to drop her grievance because the union would not honor the contractual process and allow for a strike off. Global wanted Cheryl Winters, and ALPO did not object, despite an OSHA mandate enabling Darby to be participatory in the selection of the arbitrator.

"Well... actually they did."

"No way," Darby said sitting upright. "Are you kidding?"

"I'm not."

"Okay, then... On that basis let me think about this for a moment," Darby said, and then added, "Not no, but hell no!"

"I suspected that would be the case," Robert said with a chuckle. "Okay. I'll see you in White Plains in a couple days. We can meet for dinner Sunday night if you're up to it. Just give me a call when you get settled."

Darby said goodbye and she dropped her phone to the floor. If she hadn't known that Global was trying to buy off the process before, she now knew beyond a doubt that to be true. God, she hoped they had not gotten to the judge, too. Despite the warmth of the water, a chill invaded her body.

Her phone rang again, and she glanced at it. *Tom.* She thought about removing her earbud and dropping it to the floor beside her phone, sending him directly to voicemail. Instead, she reached out of the tub and answered.

"Hey," she said, ignoring the fact he had lied to her.

"Sorry I missed your calls earlier," Tom said.

"That's okay. Where are you?" she asked with more tone in her voice than she had planned.

A slight hesitation and Tom said, "Home. My schedule changed and I got back to town earlier than planned." Another moment of silence and he asked, "Are you okay?"

"Yeah," she said. "I had a good dinner. Then a few minutes ago I learned that we lost our summary decision." Darby sighed. "And… Jackie said that you were at her house arguing with John." She hesitated a moment and said, "I think I'm just tired."

"Sounds like we need to talk," Tom said.

"Yeah… probably would be a good idea. But we should wait until after my deposition. I need a day to catch up before I head East."

"Of course, if that works best for you."

"It does. I'll be home on Wednesday, I think."

"I'm really sorry about that decision."

"Yeah, me too." Darby said goodbye, then ended the call. She closed her eyes slid back into the water, but it had cooled considerably.

Chapter 57

White Plains New York
January 19, 2019

THE MORNING BEGAN turbulent with nerves, but by noon Darby was able to turn off the seat belt sign. Attorneys often spent hours prepping their clients for deposition. There had been no prep for Darby. Robert simply told her to answer his questions and be herself. She knew the reasons Wendel was asking what he did because Robert had taught her the law. Wendel was also transparent. Betty Dickson was equally predictable.

Wendel had just spent the previous thirty minutes asking Darby about the grievance process. She suspected he was angling for a collateral stoppel claim, or simply trying to build a case that if she had dropped her grievance, then how could she have had an AIR21 claim. But the judge already ruled on that, so she wasn't sure as to his motive.

Unlike Robert, who had written pages of questions, Wendel had a list of words on a sheet of paper. She suspected a two-by-four might be a better memory jogger. But who was she to judge? Wendel had a difficult time getting his words out and he often mumbled. She wanted to ask him if he were tired but refrained.

"Have you filed a grievance under the Pilot Working Agreement?"

"I did," Darby said with a smile. *As a matter of fact, more than one,* she thought.

"I'm just going to show you a document that we'll mark it as, I guess, Exhibit… uh… we'll call it Bradshaw one, if that's okay." Wendel slid the document towards her. "This is a document that you authorized to have filed on your behalf, correct?"

"I don't know if this is the one that was authorized or not," Darby said looking at it.

"Okay. But did you file it?"

"I can't be 100% positive that this *is* what I filed," Darby said for the record. "But yes, I did initiate a grievance to this extent."

Her union attorneys took it upon themselves to write what they wanted, despite Darby's editing. So, she wasn't quite sure what they had filed and if it was the same document that he held. Scanning it now, there didn't appear to be anything irregular that jumped off the page.

"Okay," Wendel said. "And that grievance has not yet been heard, correct?"

"No. This grievance was cancelled," Darby said, stating the obvious.

"Okay. What is the basis for your… uh… the contention in this grievance that Global violated… uh… it looks like you wrote… Well just leave it at that," Wendel said, and Darby wanted to laugh or at the very least help him to get the words out.

Then he asked, "What is the basis of this grievance?"

"Objection. Document speaks for itself," Robert said.

"May I read the grievance?" Darby asked, restraining her smile. She wanted to read it more closely to ensure they were not setting her up.

"Yeah, you can look at it," he said.

After reading the grievance in total, Darby said. "The basis of the grievance is that they sent me into a Section 8 in retaliation."

"In retaliation for what?" Wendel asked.

"For my reporting safety."

"When particularly did you report safety, if there is a time, that you believe was the cause of the retaliation?"

"The point in time was when I met with both Captains Wyatt and Clark, and gave them a safety report," Darby said.

"Anything… any other basis for this grievance that is in front of you, besides what you have told me?" Wendel asked, and then said, "And take your time."

"Well, this is part of the grievance process, and the document identifies the basis of the grievance," Darby said, not understanding what he was getting at. So, she reiterated, "They retaliated and placed me in a Section 8."

"Any… uh, you said the grievance hasn't been heard yet," Wendel said. Then he added, "That's what you said a minute ago?" Inflection turned his statement into a question.

"Yes, I said it had been cancelled," Darby said. "Dropped."

"Who cancelled it?" Wendel asked.

"I dropped it."

"Why?"

"I dropped it because I was not being fairly represented. Under the collective bargaining agreement, we have the right to due process. First, ALPO delayed that process—"

"Okay," Wendel said.

"I also had the AIR21 ongoing, so I hired Mr. Allen to represent me on this grievance," Darby said, pointing to the document in question. "At which time Global decided they didn't have inhouse counsel that could competently handle it, so they hired Brian Talbott from another law firm—"

"I got it."

"Then attorney Brian Welch gave us four arbitrators and said we could select one of the four—"

"Okay."

"However, the union has a strike off process in the collective bargaining agreement with a list of 13 arbitrators, not 4. They pick, we pick, you know, back and forth until we strike these people off, one by one. So, we told Welch that we didn't want any of the four he selected and to strike them off. Then he just disappeared off the scene and we never heard from him again."

"Who is the *he* in that sentence?"

"Attorney Brian Welch."

"Okay," Wendel said with a sigh.

"So Welch disappeared off the scene and never responded to Robert. Then seven months later, *after* I got my job back on my own, and three days prior to my triple seven training, the ALPO attorney who wrote this," Darby said, motioning toward the grievance, "contacted me and said we needed to immediately get my grievance off the books—"

"I got it," Wendel said.

Darby ignored his injection. "She had said that it had been going on too long. And I said, *no*, I won't do this in the in the middle of training. I had not flown for two years, and I asked her to help someone who didn't have a job, that my grievance could wait. The next day she responded and said, I was right about not doing it right now, but they had already selected an arbitrator—"

"Okay."

"Turns out it was one of the four arbitrators that Brian Welch had selected seven months earlier. One that I had objected to."

"Do you remember the person's name?"

"Yes," Darby said with a smirk, "Cheryl Winters."

"Okay, keep going," Wendel said with no indication of recollection. "I'm sorry to interrupt."

"I told the ALPO attorney I did not want Cheryl Winters. Then the next day we received a letter from the OSHA investigator, who had received a letter from Welch calling off the OSHA investigation."

"Do you know the content of the letter?" Wendel asked. "Let me rephrase, did you read it?"

"Yes, to both questions. He told the investigator that we had a collective bargaining agreement, that I had been made whole and that there was a neutral arbitrator that had been selected—Cheryl Winters," Darby said for emphasis.

"I got it."

Darby wasn't so sure he did get it and continued. "He asked OSHA to drop the AIR21 complaint and OSHA complied. Then my attorney, Robert Allen, reached out to the OSHA investigator and explained why the AIR21 should continue. The investigator said that he had sent a letter to Global that outlined the rules, and he had told them if they wanted to hear the AIR21 complaint in the arbitration process, via the Pilot Working Agreement, that they had to follow the OSHA rules."

"Did the OSHA investigator state what those rules were?" Wendel asked.

"Of course," Darby said. "They are clearly outlined in the OSHA manual, as well. The rules state that I could select my own attorney, receive attorney fees if I win, that we get to do full discovery, and I would be participatory in the selection of the arbitrator."

"Okay."

"It's not okay. I was not allowed to be participatory. I was denied. The arbitrator was being shoved down my throat. I had written numerous emails to the ALPO attorneys and provided them the OSHA manual and stated I did not want Cheryl Winters. I requested a strike off process. ALPO denied. They said that I had to pick a date with that arbitrator."

Darby was sensing the anger she felt at the time and took a deep breath. It infuriated her how her union had worked with the company to such an extent.

"I got it," Wendel said again.

"The ALPO attorney provided dates," Darby said, ignoring him. "She told me to pick one. The funny thing was, this arbitrator wasn't even available for another ten months per her schedule, which contradicted the urgency. I spoke to my captain rep and he agreed that the urgency was odd based upon the delay with her availability. He looked into it, and then miraculously the arbitrator found earlier dates."

"Did you accept those earlier dates?" Wendel asked.

"No. I was not available. I also knew that I was *not* being represented by ALPO, and if Winters was involved in my case I would be done. I decided to put all my faith into the federal court system, and I dropped the grievance," Darby said. "Ironically, I heard a year later that Cheryl Winters was offered to be the mediator in this AIR21 process."

"I'm sorry," Wendel said stuttering a bit. "Told by who?"

"Who told the mediator?" Darby asked.

"Who told *you* that Cheryl Winters was asked to be the mediator?" Wendel asked, knowing precisely that he was the person who offered her on a platter.

"My attorney, Robert Allen," Darby said, sitting back and folding her arms for effect.

"So, uh… I caution you to be cautious about communications

that you had with Mr. Allen," Wendel snapped. "Because… uhhh… you don't want to inadvertently… and I don't want to encourage you to waive any kind of privileged communications—"

"Okay," Darby said flatly, cutting him off.

"You had with Mr. Allen," he continued, ignoring her intent to end his angst.

"Okay," she said again.

"So, I don't consider you to have done that now. I'm just stating that for the record."

"Okay," Darby repeated.

She'd seen many behaviors of Wendel Kowalski from boredom to impatience and even complete and total confusion, as well as hostility, but this was a first time she witnessed him nervous. Darby glanced at Robert who leaned back, apparently providing Wendel all the time he needed to run down this path of defense. Darby wondered if Wendel's reaction was due to his potential violation of Global's privilege with him regarding Winters, or not.

"But if you have any questions about… if any of my questions require you to provide me with information about contact… communications… conversations you had with Mr. Allen, or any other lawyer, then I'd want you to wait and consult with Mr. Allen about that subject before you answer," Wendel said. "Is that understood?"

"That's understood," Darby said. "And so, when I've been speaking about my ALPO lawyer all day long, we're not counting her as *my* lawyer because she's technically a lawyer for ALPO and not for Darby Bradshaw? Or is it because the ALPO was actually working for your client, Global?"

"I will state for the record," Wendel said, "that I don't consider that your client has waived any kind of privilege."

"Just to alleviate your concerns," Robert finally said, "I don't suspect you are improperly probing. But I think this is not testimony concerning conversations about trying to obtain legal advice, but rather the fact that Global had offered Cheryl Winters as the mediator in the AIR21 dispute, she's just reporting the facts, as opposed to any dialog to obtain legal advice."

"That's fine, the record is clear," Wendel said. "So, I interrupted you. I didn't want to interrupt your story. I think the question a ways back was, why did you cancel your grievance, and you have been answering that *at length*."

"So, continue," Robert said with a smile.

Robert had advised her if he asked an open-ended question to go as long as she wished. Darby wasn't sure what was more irritating to Wendel, Robert's methodical asking of questions with time and silence built in, or Darby speaking at length.

"Is there more of that?" Wendel asked.

Darby so wanted to give him *more of that*, but she had a flight to catch, and she had made her point.

"So, in summation," Darby said, "Global had influence into the ALPO's selection of the arbitrator, and I was not going to receive a fair arbitration process. Global and ALPO were jointly violating OSHA's requirements if they wanted this to be carried out through the arbitration process. My only hope was to proceed with this case in a federal court and pray that the ALJ had more ethics than Global management, ALPO, and the arbitrators they were employing."

Chapter 58

After lunch, they jumped back into the ring. Wendel Kowalski had his gloves on, but he circled the ring tight against the ropes, asking nothing of importance and simply wasting her time. Then again, these were billable hours to Global and there was no reason to cut it short from their perspective. She glanced at her watch, hoping she wouldn't miss her flight.

"Okay. And the purpose of you...," Wendel began. "Well, you wanted to speak to Captain... well, first of all, what did you understand Captain Wyatt and Captain Clark's position to be at Global?"

Come on, spit it out, Darby thought waiting for the question to emerge. When he finally asked it, she said, "They were the top two leaders in flight operations."

"Okay. Was there any *other* reason you wanted to speak to them, besides what you wrote in this letter?" Wendel asked.

"The reason is in the first paragraph."

"Okay."

"I felt compelled to speak to them after I listened to Lawrence Patrick speak at an aviation safety conference," Darby said. "Mr. Patrick said that every employee had an unfettered responsibility to bring anything forward that they saw wrong with the airline, and that we could shut down the airline if we identified anything unsafe."

"Okay. And you, at this point, agreed with the statement that… or let me rephrase that, Wendel said. "You would have *approved* of the statement that every employee can shut down this operation at any time for a safety issue. Is that right?"

"The CEO at the time said it," Darby said, "I believed he believed it."

"But my question is whether you *personally* approve of that concept," Wendel challenged.

"Objection. Vague," Robert said. "Go ahead."

"I approve of my CEO stating whatever he wants to state in the interest of safety, yes," Darby said, trying to refrain from laughing.

Throughout the entire deposition she understood why he asked the questions he did. This was no different. Dr. Wood had claimed she was ready to be a CEO, and that grandiose behavior was deemed to be a medical disorder. Kowalski was trying to get her admit to her sickness. This had gone beyond the point of ridiculous.

Darby glanced at the time and hoped the hotel was still available. No way she would make her flight. Then she thought about what she would order to drink with dinner. A steak and scotch were sounding good, but so was a bubble bath.

"Well, I'll ask you hypothetically, if you were a CEO of an airline, is that a comment that you would be comfortable making, hypothetically?" Wendel asked.

"Excuse me?" Darby said, bringing his words into focus as he had become white noise. "Are you asking me, did he make that comment?"

"Clearly, I'm not asking you that!" he snapped. "So, listen to the question, and I'll see if you understand it! And if you don't—"

"I don't understand…" Darby said.

"I want to object, again, to the sarcasm," Robert said. "I think she is being—"

"There was no sarcasm! And your client knows that there was no sarcasm there, nor has there been sarcasm throughout," Wendel said. "But you know you like to do this. If you want to make a speech you can go ahead."

"I'm not going to make a speech," Robert said, flatly.

"I'm going to keep the time on how long it takes," Wendel countered, looking at his watch, not having listened to Robert.

"You made a sarcastic comment that of course she knew of the question, and she didn't," Robert said. "You are accusing her of bad faith, and it's not appropriate, and it's argumentative. And also, so long as I have a moment here, because—"

"Yeah, go ahead," Wendel said leaning back in his chair and folding his arms.

"I don't know if the court reporter is catching the constant interjection of 'I got it' or 'okay' as my client is responding to the questions. But clearly, those interjections of 'okay and okay' that are breathless and hurried, are for the purpose of cutting off her answers," Robert said. "And I would ask that counsel refrain from interrupting with those interjections."

"Mr. Allen, I've given a courtesy to you starting this deposition at a very early time. I've given you the courtesy of starting this deposition at your office in White Plains at a fair amount of personal inconvenience to me and my client," Wendel said.

Who is he kidding? Darby thought. He was distorting the truth on the record again. It was Darby who offered to go back East, ensuring he wouldn't have to travel across the country to Seattle for this blessed event.

"And I've told you that I would do my best to have the deposition be finished so that your client could make her flight home, because I am not sarcastic, and I am not discourteous at all," Wendel continued.

"And I am simply being professional and doing my job. I have no personal issues at all with your client. And I think I've treated her, and the record will reflect, respectfully throughout and courteously throughout, and I will continue to do that, as I told you I would do, no matter the provocations that I feel. I will always take the high road, always, and I will always treat your client with respect. I am never sarcastic. I never intend to be sarcastic.

"If you believe that I'm being sarcastic or believe that I'm cutting her off, then either you are mistaken about that or it's inadvertent. And I will do my best to try to keep that from happening. I will say though that if you interrupt the deposition with speeches that are unnecessary, that it's going to be very difficult to finish it, as I've promised that I would try to do. And if I'm trying to move things more quickly, it's really out of deference to your client's schedule, because I do want to finish the deposition in the time that we've allotted, and I don't want to have to come back and do it again, both for her sake and for our own… for my sake and everyone else's sake.

"So, I've now wasted some time having to make that presentation. I hope we don't have to come back and do this again," Wendel said. "Again, I believe the record will reflect that I have never used any sarcasm or any disrespect throughout this deposition. And I'm happy for the record to be reviewed by any third party for that purpose. Can we continue?"

"I would ask at this point," Robert said. "I know it's going to be very difficult for the court reporter, but I would ask that she do her best to record every time, as my client is answering the question, that there are interruptions such as 'okay' or 'I get it,' or any other indication that her responses are being interrupted or hurried along. Please proceed."

"I apologize. I need a few minutes to think about what I was asking, because my train of thought has been interrupted by your presentation," Wendel said with an expression of anguish.

Is he going to cry? Darby wondered. His eyes were filled with pain, and he placed his hands together as if in prayer and moved them to his lips. He then closed his eyes. Darby glanced at Robert and shrugged. The room was silent. Darby was holding her breath waiting for Wendel to break down in tears.

Minutes later he opened his eyes. "Can you read back the last question," Wendel finally said to the court reporter, and then he looked at Darby. "And answer before the break. Please!"

Chapter 59

Seattle Washington
January 20, 2019

They say that the English language has 112 words for deception, each with a different meaning. Tom tipped back his beer as he glanced at his watch, thinking of a few additional words that could define his behavior.

Darby would be walking in the door any minute. She would be expecting him to answer a question or two. Answers he was not ready to provide. Some things were better left unsaid. If he had known the deception of those in her life that had gone before him, prior to his involvement, he never would have accepted this position nor allowed it to go this far.

But then, look what I'd be missing, he thought staring out the window as Darby's car pulled into view. She turned into her driveway. *Now or never,* he thought. This would be his moment of truth and he had no way in hell to know how it would turn out.

He stood, tossed back his beer, and then threw the empty bottle into the recycling can. He emptied the cartons of Chinese food into dishes as the garage door grinded in the background. A bottle of Merlot had been breathing on the table, and he quickly poured two glasses. He tossed the Chinese food cartons into the trash, and stuck serving spoons into the bowls as the garage door began its downward cycle.

Opening the door, he poked his head into the garage. Smiling he asked, "Can I help you with your bag?"

"I'm good," Darby said, pulling it out of the trunk.

"I hope you're hungry," he said.

She smiled. "Did you cook?" she asked as she walked toward him.

He took her suitcase and said, "Nope. Something better." He gave her a quick kiss.

They stepped into the kitchen, and she closed her eyes and breathed in the aroma wafting from the table. "I've died and gone to heaven." Opening her eyes, she said, "This is exactly what I needed. Chinese food is the perfect meal after flying across the country."

"Do you need a few minutes?" Tom asked setting her suitcase by the kitchen counter.

"Hell no," Darby said. "I'm starving." She went over to the sink and washed her hands.

"Sorry you missed your flight last night," Tom said walking up behind her and wrapping her in an embrace. "Really sorry."

"It was okay," Darby said, turning toward him. She wrapped her arms around him and laid her head on his chest. "I was beat after that deposition anyway, and the sleep was welcome. Besides, Robert and I got a lot of work done today."

"Well let's get you something to eat so I can get you to bed," Tom said, hugging her tight.

"I like the way you think." Darby walked over to the kitchen table and slid into a chair. "This looks so good," she said, scooping a spoon of rice onto her plate. She added a couple of pork slices, and then grabbed a pancake.

The elephant in the room lingered. He stared, amused at the woman before him. Most women would have jumped in his shit three days earlier, and having every right. But not Darby. Tom sat across from her and dished his up his plate. "How was the flight?"

"I watched two movies," she said. She then raised her wine glass and sipped, watching him. "This is nice, thank you."

He raised his glass toward her and said, "Welcome home."

"Sorry. I had to taste test it first," she said with a smirk, and then clinked her glass to his. Then she took another long sip. She set her glass on the table and reached for a barbeque pork and dipped it into a dish of hot mustard. "This is really nice. But it's not getting you out of our talk," she said with grin.

He laughed. "Damn. I was hoping I could distract you with egg rolls," he said, dipping one into sweet and sour sauce. "You want to go first?"

She shrugged and then pushed her rice around the plate with her chopsticks. "I really like what we have," Darby finally said. "And I don't want to get into your business. But it was weird thinking you were out of town, and then I come to find out you were at Jackie's house."

"I'm sorry," he said. "I have no excuse as to why I didn't tell you. But it wasn't anything. Really."

"Jackie said you and John were arguing," Darby said, piling moo shu pork onto her pancake. "That's not a nothing. Are you working on something with John?" she asked folding her pancake around the pork.

Tom watched her create her moo shu pancake and wondered if he should simply tell her the truth. He was torn. He wanted to tell her, but he also knew it was to ease his conscious and would do nothing but hurt her. She was going through far too much to add one more thing to her plate. He also knew that was the coward's way out, but it was as logical as he could get, and it was the truth.

"I dropped in to see how John's investigation against Rich Clark was going about the wine," he lied. "I don't think that his doing nothing when Clark tried to poison you was the right step. You could still be in danger."

"John's not my bodyguard," she said looking directly into his eyes with the intensity that he loved. "Besides, I didn't think there was an investigation. The investigation that needs to be conducted is for Stan."

"That's closed."

"What?" Darby said, dropping her moo shu pork pancake to her plate.

"The evidence says that he killed himself." Tom reached out and placed a hand over hers. "They found gun residue on his hand. His left hand."

"But what about the car? And the people who saw someone go in?" Darby asked.

"Someone did go in and conduct a search of his property," Tom said. "But there is no reason to believe he did not pull the trigger."

"Unless they told him if he didn't, they would get his family."

"I suppose with everything you've experienced, that's not quite out of question in your world."

"I've seen too many people die at the hands of airline management. My brake line has been cut more than once, I've been attacked, left for dead, and there was an attempted poisoning."

"A cat with nine-lives," Tom said.

Darby smiled. "I might be running out of them." She lifted her pancake and took a bite. "Mmm, this is so good," she said with her mouth full. She extended it toward him in offering.

He took a bite and nodded. It was good. Then he leaned back in his chair and lifted his wine. Staring into it for a moment he searched for the words that wouldn't make him a total liar. "I shouldn't get involved in your life more than I have, but I care about you."

"I care about you, too," Darby said, placing the pancake onto her plate. She lifted her glass and sipped, her eyes not leaving his.

God, he wanted to have this conversation naked.

She then said, "I actually thought the worst."

"The worst, huh?" Curious, Tom asked, "What's the worst?"

"Well… I thought you had another girlfriend, and that John found out. And you were arguing with him not to tell me."

Of all the things that he and John had argued about, that was not one of them. He only hoped as things heated up, that John would not defy his trust.

Chapter 60

Oklahoma City
Corporate Office
February 4, 2019

CLARK LEANED BACK in his chair in a mood. "What can I help you with?"

Wolfe tossed the file on his desk, and then stuck his hands into his pockets, unknowing their level of trust. Clark was a timebomb, and Wolfe spent most of his day cleaning up after him. When the tyrant did not get his way, he stamped his feet and ordered it so. *God forbid the day that I will ever tell him no*, Wolfe thought.

"Michelle Danford is going to be a problem," Wolfe said. "A counselor at the Talbott Center said she could get out a week early for graduation."

"We already discussed the timing," Clark said. "Ensure that counselor is overridden."

"That's not the problem," he said, "Danford told multiple counselors about the pilot who placed a gun in his mouth. They have an obligation to report it."

"They have an obligation to Global," Clark said. "Remind them who keeps that place running."

"Policies are in place to report any concerns to their board, and the board is required to carry them forward," Wolfe pushed.

"The very reason our management team sits on the board."

"There is a problem if *you* had anything to do with Branson's death."

Clark's eyes narrowed. "You give me more credit than I deserve." Then he laughed. "They were going to deal with him in the program. He was smart enough to make the wise choice on his own. I had nothing to do with the trigger."

"We're not exactly sure what he told Bradshaw."

"Well, it won't matter now, will it," Clark said. "None of it will."

"As long as he didn't leave a note."

"There was nothing," Clark said flatly.

"Good," Wolfe said. "How do you want to handle Danford?"

Clark opened the file Wolfe set on his desk and began to read. Wolfe pulled up a chair and waited.

Michelle Danford had embraced the program better than anyone they'd seen in years. As is expected of inpatients, they are required to share their deepest secrets. Those files then became leverage in the operation that Global could hold over them. However, with that said, the leverage she provided the company was in fact against the company. She was beautiful and that drew attention; often, unwanted attention that she had reported over the years and Global management had done nothing. Managers sexually harassed her and spoke vulgar terms regarding her body and the fit of her clothes, openly and in meetings. It always got back to her.

She had also been a female activist, fighting for women's rights and motherhood issues. A member of the pilots' assistance program, she was well versed in pilot issues. But none of that was the problem. The issue was, she was in the program and heard that a pilot committed suicide and thought it was the same pilot who told her he stuck a gun in his mouth. She called that pilot from the Talbott Center to see if he was alive. He was, and he told her that he'd done it again. This triggered her grave concern that no one at Global was doing anything to help him. With her newfound strength in sobriety and faith in God from the program, she wanted to tell everyone about this event to get him and others help. Now Branson killed himself and this fueled her fire.

Closing the folder, Clark looked across the desk to Wolfe and sighed. "Move her to MARR for a policy violation in communicating via text messages with the other patients."

"Those text messages were graphic pictures sent *to* her," Wolfe said. "She reported it."

"Well, she gave him her phone number," Clark said. "That means she engaged him."

"No. Talbott's office staff posted everyone's phone numbers on a bulletin board. She even argued against that and asked them to remove hers."

Clark pushed back from his desk and stood. "I don't fucking care about the details. As far as I'm concerned, she violated policy. She will be moved, and make it door to door. No calls to anyone or she will be in violation of the contract and immediately terminated."

"She's got to deal with childcare," Wolfe said.

"Then one call to the ex," Clark said. "You see that she is transferred to MARR, and you keep her there as long as possible. MARR is the toughest inpatient treatment program there is, and she will be broken."

"Okay. Consider it done," Wolfe said, standing. "You're right. If anyone can silence her, the MARR addiction center will."

Clark handed him the folder. "If we get lucky, she'll realize, as Branson did, that there are a few things in life worse than death, and MARR might be one of them."

Chapter 61

Oklahoma City
Ann Abbott Deposition
February 19, 2019

ANN ABBOTT WAS nothing but a tool. *To be precise—A hoe,* Darby thought with a grin. Preliminaries were complete and they were well underway with the Abbott deposition. Everything they had learned in discovery told Darby that she had been wrong to have given her the benefit of the doubt. Abbott had known exactly what she was doing, and that came with a price tag on Darby's head. Now Robert would extract the truth.

Darby glanced at Robert and wondered if he would see through her smoke and mirrors. He had thought she would be a formidable adversary and was Global's strength due to her OSHA interview. She had been calm, collected, and answered the questions perfectly during that interview. But then again, she had not been challenged. The OSHA investigator had also asked leading questions.

Robert was not so sure that Abbott was part of the conspiracy. Darby tried to believe that, too, but she couldn't overlook the deception and the inconsistencies in what Abbott said had happened, and what had actually occurred.

There were always different perceptions in any conversation, dependent upon the psychology of the individual. However, the inconsistencies were many and fact based, and Darby could not overlook Abbott's subsequent promotion. She had found Abbott's report located within her medical report, and it was a complete fabrication of reality.

"I may have misheard you," Robert said. "I thought you had testified that you had HR certification?" Robert said.

"Oh, I apologize if I said that. I'm a *member* of SHRM," Abbott said.

"So, you have no certifications beyond your BA, correct?"

"Correct."

Darby searched SHRM on her phone. The Society for Human Resource Management was a professional membership association that was headquartered in Alexandria Virginia. For $199 anyone could get certified. But the glorified Ms. Abbott was not even certified, she was simply a member. She had been working for Global for 23 years, and now she was a manager in HR.

"What was your position at the time you interviewed Ms. Bradshaw?" Robert asked.

"I was the manager of the Equal Opportunity Department and the Pass Travel Complaint Department."

"What position do you currently hold at Global?" Robert asked.

"I'm the Senior HR manager, Airport Customer Service, in Cedar Rapids."

"How long have you held that position?"

"Since February 1, 2017."

"Was that a promotion?" Robert asked.

"Oh, no. That wasn't a promotion. It's actually the same job classification," Ms. Abbott said, fingering the edges of her sweater.

A very quick and well-rehearsed answer, Darby mused.

"Was there a pay increase?"

"There was," Abbott said glancing at Wendel.

"How much of a pay increase?" Robert asked.

"Five percent."

"So, from what to what?" Robert asked.

"I've received different increases since that time."

"Well, what's your current pay?"

"I… we just got an increase. I… I just got the increase and I'm trying to…" Abbott said, flustered. "I don't want to give you an incorrect amount."

There was a reason she wanted to conceal what she was making now. Regardless, a 5% pay raise for her 'non-promotion' two months after helping to create the pretext against Darby could not be overlooked.

"You said you sent a draft of your report to Mr. Wolfe?" Robert asked.

"I didn't say *who* I sent it to," she said.

"But you said you sent a draft of your report to—"

"To legal," she said. "I sent it to legal."

"Did you send it to anyone specifically?" Robert asked.

"I gave an early draft to Martha Jones."

"Did you have any conversations with anyone else in Global's legal department prior to your November 22nd meeting with Ms. Bradshaw?"

"Not in Global legal," she said, fiddling with her sweater again.

"Well, did you have meetings with *anyone* concerning Ms. Bradshaw prior to the November 22nd meeting with her?"

"Yes."

"With whom did you have meetings?"

"Joe Wolfe."

"And he is an attorney?" Robert asked.

"He is," she said. "He's in labor relations."

"How many HR investigations have you experienced?"

"Over a hundred," Abbott said proudly.

"How many in flight operations?"

"Well, this is the only one. I don't normally do flight operations."

"Who assigned you to this case?" Robert asked.

"Julie Christy," Abbott said.

"Is she an attorney?" Robert asked.

"Yes, she is. But in HR."

"When did you first speak to Martha Jones?" Robert asked

"Just after I spoke to Ms. Bradshaw."

Abbott's fidgety behavior grew. Her hands moved from rubbing the edges of her sweater, to folding them on the table. Then she slid them into her lap. She was uncomfortable with these questions and Darby could not deny that she enjoyed watching her squirm. Not the composed person Robert thought her to be.

The OSHA interview is what had worried Robert. She had been in complete control and was laughing with the investigator. She was not laughing now.

"You spoke to her before you got on your flight back home?" Robert asked.

"No. She didn't answer her phone. I left her a message."

"Just so I have your testimony straight," Robert began. "You spoke with Joe Wolfe, a Labor Relations attorney in flight operations, prior to meeting with Ms. Bradshaw. Correct?"

"Yes."

"Attorney Ms. Christy, from the HR department, assigned you to this case?"

"Correct."

"But it was Martha Jones, a corporate attorney, that you made your first phone call to shortly after meeting with Ms. Bradshaw, and you left her a message?"

"Yes."

"What message did you leave her?"

"I can't recall," Ms. Abbott said.

"Objection," Wendel said. "Attorney-client privilege."

"Why did you call a corporate attorney versus the attorney that assigned you?"

"Objection," Wendel said. "Badgering the witness."

"I'll withdraw the question," Robert said with a sigh. This was an answer that was evident based upon Martha Jones' level of involvement.

Robert flipped through his pages and lined through some questions and circled others. Wendel sighed heavily and exchanged a look with Betty Dickson as she ripped open a package of peanut M&Ms.

"So, do you believe Global is a safe airline?" Robert asked.

"I absolutely do!" Ms. Abbott spoke louder than she had all day, and with such conviction that Darby almost laughed.

"What do you base that on?"

"Our safety record. In the airport customer service job that I work, I know what they're doing from a safety perspective. I know what training they go through. And I know that Global puts safety at the top of their list."

"In what areas of its operations?" Robert asked.

"Every area of operations!"

"And how would you know that with respect to flight operations?"

"From a company perspective, we're very transparent on what we expect and what we do. And the training, I feel though, again, our safety record speaks for itself," she said. "But from a detailed perspective of flight operations in reviewing some of this, and looking at her concerns, I did go back obviously and ask some follow-up questions regarding some of Ms. Bradshaw's concerns. But I don't have specific information."

She held onto the edges of her sweater and rubbed them between her fingers, as if it were a security blanket. Then she said, "You asked if I feel as though the company is safe. I do."

"But you had a problem with Ms. Bradshaw's concern for safety?" Robert asked.

"We have a very safe company and I just feel she was overly concerned for safety," Ms. Abbott said.

Robert handed Ms. Abbott a copy of Darby's safety report. "Did you tell the OSHA investigator that Ms. Bradshaw wanted to discuss this report?"

"Yes. She started talking about the entire thing. And again, I was there only to look at the HR or the EO concerns."

"But isn't it true she never asked for an EO investigation?"

"Yes. But we take our investigations serious, and we had to investigate even if she did not want us to."

Darby wanted to point out that all these safety events had occurred years earlier, up to eight years earlier. Despite her reporting them at the time, they never investigated anything at the time of occurrence.

"Okay. Did she bring up specific safety concerns during your meeting?"

"Yes."

"Which safety concerns?"

"Different ones that she had outlined. And again, I tried to draw the conversation back to the EO concerns."

"But *which* safety concerns did she identify, or did she articulate?" he asked referring to the report.

"I can't tell you specifically, I can't tell you exactly which safety concerns she started talking about."

"Okay. You told the OSHA investigator that Ms. Bradshaw was adamant about *not* meeting you at the airport, correct?"

"She was."

"Did she give you a reason for her adamancy?"

"She did not want anybody from the flight ops group to see her there. And felt that they would be asking questions."

"The rank and file or the leaders of flight ops group?"

"She wasn't specific with me, if I remember correctly."

"Well, did you ask her specifically about whom she was concerned?"

"I specifically said, I secured an area in our airport customer service area in which flight ops was not near. I didn't want her to feel like she had to go there, whether I was anybody in particular."

"But my question was different," Robert said. "My question was, did you ask her about whom she was afraid?"

"I don't remember."

"Objection," Wendel said. "Can I hear the question?"

The court reporter reread the question, and Wendel told her she could answer.

"So, I didn't say she was afraid. I said she was afraid people would see her and I together. So… and if I didn't say that, let me clarify. She didn't want to be seen with me and that people would start asking questions. I did not ask for who she was afraid at that point. If she was going to be uncomfortable, I did not want her to have to meet someplace that she wasn't going to be comfortable."

"Did you say that you've never conducted a flight operations interview before?"

"Yes. That's correct."

"Then her not wanting to meet in flight operations was a bit irrational, in that nobody would know you and—"

"I did not say she was irrational," Ms. Abbott said, interrupting.

Darby wanted to laugh. Not irrational, but emotional, paranoid and overly concerned for safety at an airline that has a safety record that speaks for itself.

"That was not my question. It appears that you could have been a flight attendant or a pilot friend meeting with her. Correct?"

"I suppose so."

"Then there should be no questions, correct?" Robert said.

"But that was *her* fear," Ms. Abbott said.

"Now, you told her you would get a conference room at the hotel, correct?"

"I did tell her that."

"And you ended up conducting the interview in the hotel lobby, correct?"

"It was a sectioned off area," she said.

"Was there a door to close off the area?"

"No."

Darby shook her head slowly at the misrepresentations. They had sat in the hotel lobby seating area with multiple tables and chairs. People came and went at will, ate at the tables within feet of theirs. Some people were clearly listening to their conversation. Abbott admitted to having Darby's report on the table and taking notes on it. She also asserted Darby had cried for three hours.

"And when Ms. Bradshaw became tearful, did it occur to you it would be more appropriate to adjourn the meeting to a more private venue?"

"I didn't have a more private venue that I could offer her," Ms. Abbott said. "As I said, I secured a very private room at the airport. She did not want to have that private room, nor did she say I would rather meet at a different time or someplace else."

"So, at no time did you consider it appropriate to adjourn the meeting until you could get a hotel conference room?"

"Objection," Wendel said.

"She never *asked* for a different room, she never asked to not continue to speak!" Abbott exclaimed in defense. "And I continued the conversation, which I felt was important. Although she was emotional, it was a conversation that she seemed to want to finish, and I felt that was important at that time."

"Why did you think it was important at that time?"

"Because she was emotional. Her passion was very clear! She… we had set aside this time. This was the time I was giving to her to be able to communicate to me," Abbott said. "If she wanted to stop at any time, I absolutely would have done that."

"Was it important vis-à-vis the passion that you just referenced, was it important because you were collecting more evidence of emotional instability, or was it important because of EO issues that you were anxious to pursue?"

"Objection!" Wendel snapped.

"So, I take a bit of offense at your statement of was I collecting emotional instability," Ms. Abbott said, with as much offense as she could feign. "Number one, I'm not a psychiatrist. Number two, I take my job seriously. I am concerned about employees; I care about people and I care about what to do! I act with integrity. And… I was going to investigate, but I needed to investigate with her. I was there to be an investigator and I absolutely try to connect with people so they know and understand that I am there to investigate appropriately and I don't take sides. That's not what I do. I act with integrity!"

Integrity my ass, Darby thought. Ms. Abbott did not operate well under the slightest bit of pressure, especially when her responses defied logic.

Chapter 62

She gobbled down a salad and within 45 minutes they were back in the room. Robert not only saw the light, but he was also blinded by it. Global's star witness was nothing of what he had thought her to be. She was inconsistent, lacked transparency, and the process that she purported to follow would not have received a departure clearance.

"Are you familiar with the term discovery, as that term is used in litigation?"

"I am, yep!" she said.

"Do you have those notes from your meeting with Ms. Bradshaw?"

"Everything I had went into my summary."

"So, the notes that you took on the safety report itself, you discarded that safety report?"

"I did. It was a copy that I didn't need any more, once I put everything into my summary," Abbott said.

What the hell, Darby thought. Abbott had testified that she had been involved in many legal cases. She was working directly with three attorneys, yet she threw away the singular document that could have supported Global's case beyond a 'she said/she said' from their side or would have proven Darby's. Abbott knew better. Therefore, there was only one reason that document went into the trash.

Robert continued to query Abbott on her and Darby's discussion during their meeting regarding safety concerns. That very discussion would be the connection to win her AIR21 case. Abbott admitted a couple of the safety issues they had spoken about, and other issues she simply couldn't recall. But confirmation of one point of safety was enough, and they already had multiple points verified. Abbot had been sloppy in her evil ways.

He questioned her on her fatigue concerns, yet Abbott was unable to determine if flying fatigued would be a safety concern. She simply wasn't familiar with flight operations. Then again Dodson had no clue about the legality of flying fatigued, and he was a Chief Pilot. He finished reading the event in which a B737 came within seconds of impact. Abbott confirmed that Darby had explained the concern with that situation.

Robert finally said, "Okay. It sounds frightening, though, doesn't it?"

"Yes! I don't like to fly, so it… I'll just leave it at that."

She's afraid of flying? Darby thought. That explained so much. The reason she did not sleep after their talk had nothing to do with being concerned that Darby thought someone in flight operations was out to get her. It wasn't that she couldn't sleep because of her concern for Darby's paranoia, she couldn't sleep because Darby had scared the hell out of her.

"Now, you spent three hours with Ms. Bradshaw in the hotel lobby on November 22nd, 2016. Correct?"

"Yes."

"And then you went to catch a flight, correct?"

"Correct."

"Did you make any effort to call Ms. Bradshaw's friends or family?"

"I didn't…" she said with a furrowed brow.

Here it comes, Darby thought, watching and waiting for Ms. Abbott to figure out what Robert was alluding to. *Come on... you can do it,* Darby thought. *Bingo!* The light bulb moment hit, and acknowledgement found Abbott's eyes.

She reached for the edges of her sweater and quietly said, "I did not."

"Did you call *anyone* at the company before you departed?"

"I reached out to Martha Jones."

"Yes, and you left her a message that you could not recall," Robert said. "But did you call anyone else on November 22nd?"

"At Global?"

"Yes," Robert said.

"No."

"You have testified that you were concerned for Ms. Bradshaw's wellbeing, correct?"

"Yes, very."

"Then please tell me why you did not get her help, and left her standing alone in a hotel lobby, with knowledge that she would be getting on an airplane the very next day."

"I object!" Wendel said.

Chapter 63

DARBY DID NOT even take time to change her clothes. She simply dropped her computer bag off at her room and rushed out the door. Robert was already in the restaurant and sitting at a table with a couple drinks in front of him when she walked in. She returned his wave and headed his way.

"I took the liberty to order you a scotch," Robert said. "This one is on me for having to spend three hours with that woman during your alleged safety investigation meeting. That was nothing but a hunting expedition."

"I hope it's a double," Darby said, sliding into her seat. "I really need this." She lifted her drink and sipped. "Seriously, did she really say, *I didn't get a promotion, only a 5% raise?*"

"I did not want to believe Abbott was involved in this, to this extent," Robert said. "A conspiracy was not the direction I'd planned to take your case." He shook his head and then tipped back his beer.

"And now?" Darby asked reaching into the bowl of nuts.

"She's definitely part of it," he said.

"Does that excuse your behavior today?" Darby asked, with a smirk. "I mean you did *offend* her." She tilted her glass toward him. "A proud moment by the way."

"That lying bitch offends me," Robert said with a laugh.

"You and me both." Darby popped a nut into her mouth.

"She was their key witness and we cracked her," Robert said reaching into the bowl and grabbing a handful of nuts. "She has nothing to offer."

"There was also not a notebook. She *only* had my safety report and wrote directly on that."

"The fact that she admitted to having it while she interviewed you, along with her discussing the instructor training issues should make our prima facia case."

"I thought it was funny that she alleged I was crying the entire time, and was so worried about me," Darby said, "But then she didn't call anyone to get me help."

"There are far too many holes in her testimony," Robert said. "If we had deposed her before our request for summary decision, we may have won it based on her testimony here today."

"Because she admitted we discussed my safety concerns in the report?" Darby asked.

"Yes, in part," Robert said. "What intrigues me is that she had conversations with attorney Wolfe before she met with you. Then she called Martha Jones immediately after, not the HR attorney who allegedly assigned her. Then, after hundreds of investigations with Global, this was the only time she did a pilot. Why now?"

Darby smirked at his choice of words *doing a pilot*. There was not one pilot that would do her with a ten-foot pole. Regardless, there was more than one reason for the selection of Abbott besides her ability to be bought—she was ignorant, believed management's safety propaganda, and she was afraid of flying.

"There was something else that was interesting," Darby said. "When you asked who she spoke to after our discussion, she said Martha Jones. But when you pushed what they talked about, she conveyed she didn't talk to her, she just left a message." Darby lifted her glass and jingled the ice. "Oh God, I would love to have that message."

"You and me both." Robert took a long drink of his beer, and then said, "The judge won't be pleased that she threw away material evidence."

The waitress arrived and told them the specials. However, having spent too much time in this restaurant, they knew the menu well and both Darby and Robert ordered the salmon, sautéed spinach, a side Caesar salad, and a glass of wine. The waitress walked away, and Darby stifled a yawn.

"We'll make this a short night," Robert said. "We've got Wolfe tomorrow, and he won't be an easy a target."

"I'm looking forward to meeting the slime bag," Darby said. "He's taken an overt interest in destroying me for some reason, and I would love to know why."

"Unfortunately, that's one of many questions he probably won't answer."

"I'm certain they won't want to press forward with this in court," Darby said. "Their shining star crashed and burned today. Do they seriously think *any* judge would believe her with all the neon signs flashing liar, liar, pants on fire?"

"Nothing is guaranteed," Robert said with a grin. "But I'm not sure how they can undo this damage."

Chapter 64

Joe Wolfe Deposition
February 20, 2019

They were scheduled to start in three minutes, but there was no sign of Global's legal team or Joe Wolfe. Darby walked to the coffee pot and poured herself a cup, despite promising herself to never drink depo coffee again. Unfortunately, the Starbucks line had been too long.

She added a packet of stevia and then some cream to the cup and sipped. Then with a shudder, she walked to the sink, dumped it down the drain, and tossed the paper cup into the garbage. Life was too short to drink bad coffee. She opened the fridge and grabbed a Diet Pepsi.

Laughter traveled down the hall with the entourage as they approached. Darby wasn't sure why that was irritating, but it was. She turned toward the door as the legal team walked in with Joe Wolfe, Global Air Lines Labor Relations attorney. Robert stood and shook Wolfe's hand from across the table as he introduced himself. Wolfe told Robert it was nice to meet him.

Darby, however, stepped around to the table and stood in front of him.

Wolfe extended his and said to her, "Joe Wolfe, it's nice to meet you."

She shook his hand and stared into his eyes, squeezing firmly, and said in the coolest voice she could muster, "Darby Bradshaw, I am certain it is."

His look of surprised was not missed. Wolfe attempted to pull his hand from hers. But she held firm just for a second, not removing her eyes from his. Then she released it.

The scummy little worm, she thought. She walked over to the credenza, grabbed a couple of napkins, wiped off his sweat from her hand, and tossed the paper into the trash can. He was nervous and deservedly so.

I definitely need to lose this attitude, she thought. She did not want to become a fury, a deity of vengeance. She was better than that and would not allow anything they did to change who she was. She had a great distance to travel before she became the angel of mercy. For now, someplace in the middle would suffice. Her friend had suggested she write a book, *Flight for Forgiveness.* Perhaps one day, but she was not there yet.

Wolfe pulled a chair out and sat. Now he avoided looking at her. She, however, had noticed he had a large spot in the front and center of his khakis, and it was not his manhood. He had slopped breakfast on his pants, and she thought about telling him but decided better of it.

Darby sat to the right of Robert and waited for Wolfe to look her way, but he wouldn't. He sat on the opposite side of the table and his eyes shifted from Robert then straight forward staring at the empty seat to Robert's left. He folded his hands on the table and tucked his fingers. He then pulled them to his lap.

Either he couldn't handle a firm handshake, or maybe it was the death stare that had scared him. Perhaps it was his guilty conscious of his complicit behavior in trying to destroy her. Insecurity was not a good trait for an attorney. Regardless, Clark made the decision and

Wolfe made it his duty to see to it that Darby would disappear forever.

Wolfe was sworn in, and once under oath Robert began with the preliminaries. He was nothing Darby had expected. There was no arrogant confidence like Rich Clark. Instead, he was a nerd who chewed his nails down the nubs. His sweaty palms and bleeding fingertips spoke volumes.

"And starting in 2012, in what department were you employed by Global?" Robert asked.

"Labor relations."

"So, during the entirety of your tenure at Global, you've been in that department?"

"Yes."

"Has your job title changed over the years?"

"No."

"Are you a pilot?"

"No," he said, narrowing his eyes.

"Have you ever been a pilot?"

"No."

Joe Wolfe had wanted to be a pilot in the Navy, but he couldn't cut it. Maybe that was the reason he took pleasure in taking out his aggressions against pilots. Whatever he had against her he didn't have the balls to look at her now. Contrary to Dodson who could lie while staring into her eyes with a smirk, or Clark glaring and watching her every movement, this guy avoided her.

"Are you familiar with a program referred to as SMS?"

"Generally familiar, yes, sir."

"Is the adoption of an SMS program required by the Federal Aviation Regulations, to your knowledge?"

"Yes."

"Could you describe your knowledge as to what the FARs require in terms of an SMS program?"

"I believe it was… uh, boy, it's been maybe five or six years ago… the FAA came out and said that we were going to… they were going to mandate carriers to adopt SMS programs, and then they…" he said, staring at Robert. "I think Global was one of the first carriers that implemented an SMS program and then over the course of four or five years went through all of the requirements that you need to satisfy to be certified as, you know, having an appropriate SMS program," Wolfe added. "I think that happened last year at Global if I'm not mistaken."

"What happened last year?" Robert asked.

"I think that Global was… I guess formally recognized for having a certified SMS program in place. I'm probably getting some of that terminology wrong but… there were stages."

Darby folded her arms and smirked as Wolfe talked about the four stages of SMS. She glanced at Wendel who was now watching her. This time she rolled her eyes and slowly shook her head with a grin, attempting to express that Wolfe did not know what he was talking about. She realized that there were a lot of idiots at Global, perhaps an entire village.

Global had an approved SMS program and with that approval, they were required to follow it. An airline was required to follow *any* approved program regardless of if it was an FAR mandate or not, so testified George Wyatt and Rich Clark.

Wolfe was attempting to build the case that her reporting safety information regarding SMS was not protected activity because Global's six-year program wasn't in place until last year, *after* she had reported. His testimony was contrary to Wyatt's and Clark's assertions. Apparently the million-dollar legal team did not brief him on the fact.

If that's all they have, they're toast, Darby thought.

Robert presented Wolfe with what they called the Action Plan in which Clark and Wolfe had determined who would investigate which events embedded within her safety report. What nobody at Global seemed to understand was those events in the report were simply examples to support failures in safety culture and SMS, with additional federal regulation violations thrown in. Much of it was examples of unsafe operations due to inadequate pilot training.

The events they deemed important enough to investigate at present time, because of some corporate asserted gender motivation, had all occurred and were reported at the time, years earlier. Yet they had never been investigated. Never was there a claim of gender discrimination either.

"Okay, prior to November 22nd, did you have a discussion with Ms. Abbott about the scope of her investigatory responsibility?" Robert asked.

"I didn't have *any* discussions with Ms. Abbott prior to November 22nd."

Gotcha, buckwheat, Darby thought. Abbott had said Wolfe was the *only* person she spoke to in Flight Operations prior to their meeting. One would have thought that they would have at least gotten their stories straight. Sloppy or arrogant, she wasn't sure. Robert reminded her often what his father had always said to him—*its better to tell the truth because the truth is easier to remember.*

"Did you have any correspondence with Ms. Abbott?"

"Well, I broke down… uh, I took the document, the assessment document… and just broke out a summary of the different EO claims that she was being asked to go and meet with Ms. Bradshaw on and clarify, you know, get clarification and understanding of exactly what was being alleged because at that point there were still … uh, it was still really just not clear.

"We knew she was trying to allege some things and had put some things on paper, but the company was trying to get just a better understanding of exactly what, who did this, when did they do it, add some context to it. So, I was just helping Ann out, just getting those things out of the document and sending it to her so she could take it and then have the ability to meet with Ms. Bradshaw on that."

"Do you know if Global Air Lines ever made a determination that Ms. Bradshaw had raised any of the issues cited in her safety report in bad faith?"

"I don't know what her motivations were for bringing the report forth. I'm not aware that Global Air Lines made any conclusions there. Like I said, they just found that, you know, either the safety, on the safety side, they just didn't have anything."

George Wyatt had said Darby had been a catalyst for change. Apparently, management was truthful about one thing—nobody was sharing their testimony with each other because everyone had a different story as to the facts. Or they simply did not understand the implications of false testimony. Darby wondered if there would be any implications.

"Do you recall having any discussion with Captain Dodson as to the reasons underlying the issuance of the December 15th Section 8 letter?"

"Yes, yeah, I'm sure that there was a discussion with Captain Dodson before he issued the letter, yes."

"A conversation that you had with Captain Robert Dodson?"

"Yes, I did. I talked with Captain Dodson."

"Did you explain to him at that time what the reasons were for the Section 8 letter?"

"Yes, I just explained that Captain Clark had made a decision to enter Ms. Bradshaw into the Section 8 process, and I just told him the reason is that, you know, based on some responses that she had given as part of the ongoing EO investigation, the EO investigator had met with her and had just provided some just very concerning responses."

"Did you describe with particularity what the responses were that gave the company concern?"

"I can't remember the specific conversation, but I wouldn't, uh… it sounds like something that we probably would have told Captain Dodson, what those responses were that triggered the Section 8, yes, but I can't remember exactly what I told him."

"Are you aware of any effort on the part of Global to review Ms. Bradshaw's job performance record prior to the issuance of the Section 8 letter?"

"Can you expand on what you mean by job performance?"

Darby found great humor in that response, being he was the Labor Relations attorney. She wished he would look her way, but he would not afford her that pleasure. Which might be serving her well.

"How she performed as a pilot," Robert said. "Let me give you a few categories. What her attendance record was, what her disciplinary record was, any failures."

"Oh, I would say no to that. I don't think the company took that into account at all."

Priceless, Darby thought. How the hell could they not look at a pilot's performance if they thought the pilot had mental issues? She was dumbfounded. Global's legal team appeared to be digging their grave deeper with each witness.

Global's excuse was that they had to do this because of the Germanwings pilot. However, that pilot had a documented history of psychotic and severe depressive episodes. His condition caused him to suspend his training for nearly ten months and undergo treatment. During this period, he was hospitalized and underwent nine months of psychotherapy for anxiety and suicidal ideations. He was prescribed multiple anti-depressant medications. He also had a history of poor performance in training. Not only did they not look at Darby's performance, but they never checked her medical history either.

"So, Ann Abbott had that interview with Ms. Bradshaw, and when did you first have contact with her after that?"

"A couple days after," he said.

"And it was just you and she on the phone?"

"Actually, we met in person. It was her and I, and then legal counsel was also there. Global legal counsel."

"Who was the legal counsel?"

"Martha Jones. And I believe Ann's supervisor, Julie Christy, was there as well, the head of the EO department."

"What did Abbott describe as having seen and heard?"

"She just described meeting with Ms. Bradshaw, and Ann was just very upset, just the meeting was very upsetting to her. She was very concerned about Ms. Bradshaw's mental state, her safety, just safety in general. She described Ms. Bradshaw as being very erratic, shifting back and forth between topics very rapidly, rambling," Wolfe said, placing his hands on the table, and then immediately tucking his fingers.

"She described her as making some statements that were really concerning to the effect that there were people at Global that were out to harm her, and Ann clarified that meant that were physically out to harm her. She relayed that Ms. Bradshaw had told her in the event that she was harmed, she had taken steps to provide her friend with documents I guess she had put them in a safe of some sort, you know, documents that she had created that her friend was to take to the press in the event that something happened to her."

"What documents?"

"Documents that she had created. I don't know what those documents were."

"And it's your testimony that Ms. Abbott said physically harm, she used the word physically?"

"That's what I remember, yes. And that, I guess, that along those lines that Ms. Bradshaw was day-to-day living in fear and feared for her safety."

Oh God, she wanted to smack him. Abbott never said she would be physically harmed. Contrary, Abbott had written in her report that she had inferred harm. Darby stared at Wolfe. *The only person who should be living in fear should be you for lying. And maybe Rich Clark.* Then she added a few more persons of corruption to the list. Perhaps the next book she should write was *Flight For Revenge*. That thought intrigued her.

Darby continued to stare at Wolfe, but he refused to look her way. Then she glanced at Wendel. He wasn't objecting today, proving that there was a first time for everything. Betty, however, was still living the dream, eating chocolate, and playing with her phone. Some things never changed. Karen was simply a non-event.

"And did she describe what Ms. Bradshaw referenced as the source of that fear?"

"Just that there were unnamed people at Global that she believed were out to harm her."

Unnamed people that everyone now knew to be, Rich Clark, George Wyatt, and you, you asshole, Darby thought.

She wasn't so sure where her irritation came from today, but she was going to need an attitude adjustment if she were to survive this deposition without going postal. Linda had said she would have days like this.

"Did you take notes at this meeting?" Robert asked

"I did not."

It was interesting how no notes were taken by any of them, and those that were taken, were conveniently thrown away. Darby quietly drummed her fingers on the table.

"Who made the first contact with Dr. Wood?"

"I think I did actually."

"Was that done by telephone?" Robert asked.

"No. Email. It was just a reach out to say hey."

"To say hey?" Robert said.

"Say, *hey, we've got an issue and we'd like to talk to you about it*. I didn't want to cold call him. It felt like the appropriate thing to do."

"Wait for a question to be asked," Wendel said.

Robert ignored Wendel and proceeded to question Wolfe about his discussions with Dr. Wood. He asked him why he had sent the safety report, her blog address, and copies of specific blog posts to Dr. Wood. Wolfe said that Wood had wanted them. Darby was unsure how Wood knew to ask for those documents, but the creative writing in Wolfe's story was becoming interesting.

Instead of being angry at his mistruths, she decided to let it go. There was nothing she could other than document his criminal behavior. Robert continued to question him about the documents that he and Dodson had provided Dr. Wood. Wolfe continued to assert that the doctor requested them all. It appeared that the doctor could request anything he wanted, but Global management couldn't push things to him.

After some basic questions about the meeting itself, Robert scanned his papers and then reached for a document and slid it in front of Wolfe. "I've handed you a document we've identified as Wolfe Exhibit 39, Bates stamped DW 525 through 541. Is this information that you sent to Dr. Wood on November 22nd, 2016?"

"Yes."

"Do you know what this information relates to?"

"Yes. This is what I told you earlier. He was very interested in understanding what communications were coming out of Global regarding the Air France, Air France 447 crash in... I believe 2009. And so, yeah, I went and managed to track down the information I could locate that was being communicated to the A330 pilots during that time."

Darby grinned and folded her arms. *So he was the idiot who did that,* she thought.

"Do you have a thorough understanding of the technical information contained here?"

"I wouldn't say a thorough understanding. I have a general understanding of, like I said earlier, that the incident was created, and it had to do with a pitot static system that was faulty that created issues with control of the aircraft that could lead to high altitude stalls."

"But why did you give him *this* information?"

"Because he wanted it."

There was no way Dr. Wood, could know to ask for those documents without knowledge of their existence. That information had never even been communicated to the pilots. The FAA and the airline took no action regardless of the incidents, and 228 people died. Darby was most certain that Wolfe's intent to remove her, overshadowed any common sense that he may have had in another life.

Chapter 65

San Quentin
February 20, 2019

BILL WALKED INTO the common area and glanced around the room. He spotted Drake leaning against the back wall watching television, grinning like a Cheshire cat. The announcement of George Wyatt for the FAA administrator position had just been announced. This announcement had something to do with Drake. Bill was sure of it. Drake glanced his way, and their eyes connected. Bill smiled and nodded, then headed his way.

"You look pleased this morning," Bill said.

"It's a good day," Drake responded.

"Think they'll vote him in?" Bill nodded toward the television.

"Absolutely."

"Hmmm," Bill said. "Not sure if that's such a good idea."

"Why not?" Drake asked with an amused look.

Bill shrugged. "Global owns the union and the local FAA. With Wyatt in D.C., they'll own the FAA at the highest level. You want to give all that power to one airline?"

"You have a problem with that?" Drake asked.

"Too much power to incompetent management is not normally the best idea," Bill said. "They always find a way to fuck something up."

Drake laughed loudly, and then nodded toward the door and began to walk. Bill followed him. They walked out of the community room and into the courtyard. The morning held the weight of damp grayness that emphasized prison life. Grayness that signified oppression. Bill followed Drake to the far wall in the courtyard, and they sat on their bench. Nobody else ever sat on that bench.

Drake turned to Bill, and said, "There are a few reasons we're putting him into that position."

"I'll bite," Bill said. "Why?"

"The first is to ground the Boeing 737MAX."

"I'm not following," Bill said. "The FAA already grounded the MAX after the second crash."

Drake looked his way. The look of *how much can I tell you?* churned behind his eyes. Plotting, planning, and playing games wasn't good enough if he couldn't tell someone what he was up to. That someone was Bill.

Bill waited patiently as he always did. The curious human sitting beside him couldn't help but brag about how much power he had. Bill had no doubt the real reason Drake had pulled Bill into a State prison with him was to have someone he could confide in. Bill understood his need for power and control more than most. Perhaps murder gave sociopaths a bond like none other.

Bill was different. He had a mission to protect the piloting profession at no cost. There were simply sacrifices that needed to be made. Drake, however, appeared to have other motivations.

"Global's CEO canceled all Boeing orders," Drake began. "But not before, let's just say his signing a very lucrative agreement with Airbus Industries. In the process they agreed the MAX would be grounded for an extended period of time." Drake leaned back and stretched his legs, crossing them at the ankles.

"You sold bad parts to Boeing, that would impact the MCAS system. Crashed a couple planes to give this Wyatt guy justification to ground the plane indefinitely? Airbus finances this deal and Boeing dies?" Bill stared straight ahead, trying to figure out the logic of this one. It had merit on some level, but how the hell would Drake profit?

"A beautiful plan, if I do say so myself." Drake said.

Bill leaned forward resting his elbows on his legs, then turned toward Drake feigning a look of confusion. He lowered his voice and asked, "What purpose does shutting down Boeing and making Global rich, exactly do for *you*?"

"I'm glad you asked," Drake said, his grin widening. "Airbus is the future of technology. Boeing enables pilots to interface with the plane. Boeing builds a plane any human can manage. You were right about training. The U.S. pilots could handle the stabilizer issue for the most part. This took far too long to get two crashes out of that failed system."

"Perhaps," Bill said. "But that was more due to experience versus the airline's shitty training practices."

"I couldn't agree more," Drake said. "Despite the FAA agreeing to look the other way, and allowing airlines to cut training to the bones, the accident rate is not what I expected. All we've been getting is a bunch of fucking ASAP reports that don't manifest into fatalities."

"Many pilots still have experience," Bill said.

"Or they're getting lucky," Drake said with a chuckle. "Regardless, we needed to give them a little extra push. Or we need to find a reason for them to retire early."

"Why not put the bad parts on the Airbus?" Bill asked. "Put a Bus pilot in Alternate Law and watch the accident rate go up even in the U.S."

"That's the problem, everyone wants immediate gratification."

"I'd like a little more gratification," Bill said with a smirk.

"Too much of a good thing will turn you soft." Drake smiled and patted his leg. He then leaned back and looked toward the sky. He closed his eyes for a moment, his face a kaleidoscope of thought.

God this man was so predictable. Bill hoped the time would come when he could use that predictability to his advantage.

"Boeing dies a sudden death and Airbus prospers, as does Global," Bill said. "What's your long-term plan?"

"Pilotless aircraft," Drake said opening his eyes. "My plan has always been to get rid of pilots. Airbus builds airplanes that are machine-centric, and pilots are nothing but high-paid programmers. My technology, Drake Industries, will take Airbus to the next level and remove pilots."

The industry had been building a case for automation for years. Bill simply had never imagined that the FAA and airline management were short-changing training on purpose to make that happen. A sobering thought crossed his mind. Perhaps he had been a pawn in their game without his knowing it. That did not please him.

"Shitty training leads to pilot error," Bill finally said.

"Precisely," Drake agreed. "As long as we can keep chipping away at training, enabling pilot error to continue, we'll continue to lay a foundation for when the time is right. Hell, that ASAP program was the greatest idea ever invented. It identifies, tracks, and documents pilot error. There's nothing to stop the direction we're headed. Inadequate training followed by pilot error will lead to pilotless aircraft. ALPO is assisting nicely in that area, and Wyatt will help lock this into place."

"The very reason Global tried to get rid of Bradshaw," Bill said half under his breath.

Darby had known where this trajectory was headed, but she was as naïve as the rest of the world to not realize airline management, manufacturers, and the FAA were part of this. The very reason they had to silence her. And Bill had almost done that for them.

"Did you read Bradshaw's book, *Normalization of Deviance*?" Bill asked.

"Hell, I don't have time to read. I was briefed. With Wyatt in place, it won't matter what the hell she writes, or who the hell she talks to," Drake said with a dismissive flick of his hand.

"Better make sure they don't fire her," Bill said.

"How's that?" Drake asked with a sideways glance.

"Global won't be protected by their social media policy if they terminate her."

"Accidents happen," Drake said. "For now, she's simply a distraction. A very useful distraction. They're keeping her busy and out of everyone's way with this litigation. Besides, Global has the largest and most powerful legal team. She has one little man from White Plains. Some bumfuck town in New York. I'm not worried."

"Should you be worried that someone else could bring that technology to market while you're locked up in here?"

"Nothing that a little viral pandemic can't stop," Drake said, with a chuckle. "Close the borders and distract the world. Just another reason for automation to control the skies. We are about to see an entirely new world emerge and Drake Technologies will be in the right spot at the right time."

A cool breeze worked under Bill's skin with the thought of a world pandemic. *What the hell was he up to?* Bill wondered. "You mentioned there were a *few* reasons you're making Wyatt the FAA administrator. What are the others?"

Chapter 66

Wolfe Deposition Continues
February 20, 2019

During lunch, Robert spent the entire time reviewing his remaining questions, deep within his zone. Darby ate a sandwich in silence and thought about how much Wolfe's testimony opposed that of Abbott's. They had clearly worked together but forgot to compare notes.

It appeared that Rich Clark, the Senior Vice President of flight operations, gave the order for her death sentence. Joe Wolfe, the Labor Relations attorney, was the executioner, and Wolfe had hired Dr. Wood, the company medical examiner, to pull the trigger. There were many supporting players as well. She took a bite and chewed on that thought.

After lunch, Robert questioned Wolfe on the series of communications with Rich Clark and he asked about the date that Darby was issued the Section 8 letter that removed her from duty. They had delayed a week from the date it was signed before they presented it to her. Their excuse was that Dodson, the Regional Director, needed to provide it in person.

"And why is it more appropriate to do it in a face-to-face meeting?" Robert asked.

"It's a significant event," Wolfe said.

"Why is it a significant event?"

"Well, you're removing a pilot from the line to go for a medical evaluation when their medical status is a prerequisite for their ability to fly. That's a significant event, and it's one that the company takes very seriously. So, it merits a face-to-face meeting. It merits giving the pilot the opportunity to have ALPO present to answer any questions and lend any assistance that they can lend."

"Did anyone meet with Ms. Bradshaw in person to provide her the bipolar diagnosis?"

"No."

"How was she notified?" Robert asked.

"I believe, uh… by a letter via FedEx, and I believe Dr. Wood also sent an email."

"Can a pilot hold a medical certificate with a bipolar diagnosis?"

"No," Wolfe said.

"It's permanently disqualifying for life, without any options for treatment, correct?" Robert asked.

"Yes, I believe that to be true."

"In your opinion, which would be a more significant event, a letter from the company placing her on full pay while she went through the process, or a letter from a doctor stating she would never fly again?"

"Objection!" Wendel snapped. "Don't answer that question. Argumentative."

Robert stared at Wolfe for a moment, until Wolfe looked away. Robert said, "The question stands. Understood, counsel advises you not to answer."

Nothing more needed to be said. Darby knew the truth and this would be something that she hoped Judge Geraghty would see through as well.

"Ultimately, it's the FAA that determines whether a first-class medical is issued, correct?" Robert said.

"Yes. The FAA is the one that grants the certificate."

"Now, is it your understanding of Section 8, that during the pendency of that process, the company medical examiner should not report his determination to the FAA?"

"That's what the… uh, yes, that's what the contract states, yes," Wolfe said.

"And what's your understanding of why that provision is in there, within Section 8?"

"Well, my understanding is it's twofold. Number one is that the process needs to run independent of the FAA. I believe this was something that the union and the company agreed on would be worthwhile for the sake of the pilot. The FAA not receiving negative information about the pilot, but also for the company to benefit because, you know, it could undermine the Section 8 process to have the FAA as part of that process," Wolfe said. "Again, it runs independent of whether the pilot has an FAA medical or not. So, it makes sense that nobody should communicate with the FAA until the process is complete."

"Has Dr. Marsh ever asked you for legal advice?"

"You know, I'm not really… uh, it depends. I mean it's… uh, I know this is a broad term, but it really depends on how we're going to classify legal advice."

"Has he ever asked you about how to interpret Section 8?" Robert asked.

"Yes, yeah, we've had discussions about Section 8."

"And did he ask you those questions in the context of Ms. Bradshaw's evaluation?"

"I don't recall having too many conversations with him about the Section 8, the entry. I think later on in the Section 8 process when an FAA medical, uh… I think she had communicated to Dr. Marsh that she had received an FAA medical after Dr. Wood had reached his determination, which was negative, I think there were some discussions about the process at that point."

"I'm sorry. When she got a negative evaluation from Dr. Wood?" Robert asked.

"Right. And then after that, she had communicated that she had received a medical certificate post Dr. Wood's determination and evaluation, there were some communications about, you know, Global's obligations at that point under Section 8 as well as the FAA's."

"Well, do you recall the nature of that exchange you had with him?"

"Vaguely but it's, uh… yeah, I mean, it was just, you know, essentially, hey, how… you know, Dr. Marsh was wondering how can, you know, she have this determination, you know, did she disclose this to the FAA before getting a medical," Wolfe said. "That's something that would go on the Form 8500 before receiving a medical. So, the question was, *was this disclosed*? And then, alternatively, if it was disclosed, the FAA, you know, has certain guidelines. And, you know, it became a question as to why is the FAA issuing a medical with this kind of a determination and also while the process is still playing out."

"Why was that a concern?" Robert asked.

"Objection," Wendel said.

"Why was that a concern of yours?" Robert clarified.

"A concern of mine?" Wolfe asked,

"Yes."

"I mean, it's just a general, uh… you know, the question was posed to me. I wouldn't really call it a concern of mine. My concern was to administer the contract. My concern was getting her through the Section 8 process.

"The fact that she had an FAA medical really wasn't particularly relevant to us... to the Section 8 process, but from a more generalized safety standpoint, it was a little unnerving to understand how at that point a medical could be issued," Wolfe said interlocking his hands, then moving them off the table to his lap. "But our primary concern, at least in labor relations, was to keep the process moving and get her through it, and the FAA issue was just something that wasn't particularly welcomed but, at the same time, really not much of an impact on the process itself."

"During the pendency of the Section 8 process for Ms. Bradshaw, did Dr. Marsh communicate to the FAA with respect to Dr. Wood's determination?"

"I think after that, I believe he did. I believe he asked them, hey, how could she have a medical with this determination. I believe he did."

"And did you direct him to do that?"

"I did not."

"Did he ask you whether it would be appropriate for him to do that?"

"We did have that conversation, and I left it to him," Wolfe said.

Robert pushed another document from the stack toward him. "We've now handed you a document that's marked as Wolfe Exhibit 4, and it's Bates stamped C-2303 through 2398, and are you familiar with this document?"

"Yes."

"What do you understand this document to be?"

"This is a report that was released from the Pilot Fitness Aviation Rulemaking Committee that was convened to examine mental fitness issues in the aviation industry."

"This was in the aftermath of the Germanwings accident?" Robert asked.

"That's correct, yes."

"And this was a committee put together by the FAA?"

"Yeah, I think it was a joint effort by the FAA and the industry, but certainly the FAA takes the lead on these in standing up a rulemaking committee, yes."

"What was the objective?" Robert asked.

"The objective is kind of… uh, is listed in here," he said turning the page. "It's really just to discuss and provide recommendations to the FAA on pilot mental fitness for duty."

"And you were a member of the committee?"

"Yes. I was an observer," Wolfe said.

"Does Global Air Lines attribute any standing or significance to this report?"

"I don't know how to answer that," Wolfe said

"Is it a report in your own view worthy of consideration in terms of setting Global policy in the areas that are addressed by the report?" Robert asked.

"I think it would really depend on what the policy is and what issue you are trying to address."

This was nothing but a cat and mouse game. Wolfe knew precisely that the report defended the rationale to *not* administer a mental health evaluation to all pilots and explained the procedural steps that airlines would take *in lieu* of assessing everyone. Most significantly that the company would investigate all reports prior to placing someone into a mental health process. In Darby's case, they not only did not investigate, but they also refused to tell her why they had pulled her.

"And were you an observer for Global Air Lines with respect to the committee?"

"Actually, the way it worked, there were certain seats for, you know, identified in the committee, and then there's an organization called Airlines for America that could bring in additional seats, additional observers. And so, I was I guess technically a guest of Airlines for America as part of the process."

"What is Airlines for America?"

"It's basically an organization in Washington, D.C., that advocates, you know, for... uh... basically for the airline industry," Wolfe said.

Advocates for the industry, my ass, Darby thought. That group is for one purpose only, financial lubrication for the company to stuff it to the flight crews where the sun didn't shine for pure profitability; safety be damned.

An hour later Robert asked, "Was Dr. Wood compensated for his participation in the teleconferences with you and the larger group?"

"I think *eventually* he was," Wolfe said glancing to Wendel.

"What do you base that on that he was eventually compensated?"

"I'm just basing it on the fact that we were asking him to perform a consulting function for us. So, I don't have any, uh... I don't remember cutting him a check right after the call, but I think it was probably lumped into his overall bill to Global."

"Overall?"

"Yeah, his bill for work, for services rendered to Global at the conclusion of the evaluation."

"Is he on a monthly retainer for Global?"

"No, he's not."

"You mean his payment for advisory services was lumped into his invoice for the work evaluating Ms. Bradshaw?"

"Sure."

Darby glanced at Wendel to see if he understood the implication of what Robert had illuminated. Wendel was reading something on his phone, his expression unchanged. He either wasn't listening, or didn't understand, but Darby did. Global had commissioned Dr. Wood from the onset. He recommended the evaluation in which he would be paid an extremely large sum of money to give Darby a medical diagnosis that would remove her from flying for life.

They had alleged Wood was employed for his opinion during the conference call, and only for that call. They then created the pretext that a month later they decided to employ him for the evaluation. But lumping the two events into one paycheck spoke volumes. Wolfe had in fact employed him, in violation of the contract.

Robert placed two additional documents in front of Wolfe.

"You've just been provided documents that we've identified as Wolfe Exhibit 19, and Wolfe Exhibit 20. Let's go in reverse order. Wolfe 20 shows that it's billed to you, and it's titled at the top, Invoice, Bates stamp KW1331. Is this an invoice that you received from Dr. Wood on or about December 18th, 2017?"

"I believe so, yes."

"And the total… uh, well, let's refer to 19. That's the Bates stamp 1098, 1099, with a KW marking, and here you are *not* listed as an addressee, but did you ultimately receive this invoice as well?"

"I saw it and, I mean, received… well… uh… these actually go to flight operations. Flight operations pays these invoices. So, when they came in, they were just routed down to flight operations, and they have access to the vendor system where they enter, you know, vendor information and W9s and all that kind of stuff," Wolfe said. "But, yeah, I was made aware of this and the other as well, but I don't have… I didn't take any action on that. I don't have a budget to do that."

"The primary issue is these two documents are authentic documents, correct?"

"Yes."

"So, this combined total of the 60,000 and 13,000 plus, how does that compare with other Section 8 invoices that you've seen from medical professionals?"

"I've never seen another Section 8 invoice, so I don't know," Wolfe said.

And why now? Darby wondered.

"Do you know why the second invoice came to you?"

"Probably just because Dr. Wood had been dealing with me a lot as far as in the process and… uh… well, you know, he was requesting documents, and I was one of the people providing them to him. So, I think he just sent it to me thinking that it will get to the right place."

"And it would be someone in flight ops, you're saying, that would have to approve these invoices?" Robert asked.

"Yes. It goes down to the admin arm of flight ops which is in flight ops, and then they, again, have access to the vendor system at Global which is how they're… it enables payment. They have to get entered in the system. They go through a somewhat elaborate process that's very bureaucratic to pay vendors."

Who the hell at Global would authorize close to $74,000 for this? Darby wondered. More questionable was that they labeled Dr. Wood as a vendor. The fact that Dr. Wood billed Wolfe directly made it personal.

Chapter 67

A NUMBER FLASHED across Darby's phone with an area code that she'd been anticipating. She slipped a note in front of Robert and asked if they could take a ten-minute break. He nodded, paused a moment looking at his notes, and then requested a break. They went off record.

Darby listened to the message as she left the room, and then stepped into their briefing room and closed the door. She pressed the number to return the call.

"Illinois Medical Board, how may I help you?"

"This is Darby Bradshaw, returning Ian Jones' call."

"Please standby."

"Darby, thank you for getting back to me so quickly," Ian said.

"Of course, what can I help you with?"

"As I stated in my message, I had been tasked to investigate Dr. Wood. To begin with, this guy's a nutcase. I've got a dozen reports on him, but unfortunately, only two are strong enough to go all the way. Yours is one of them. I can't thank you enough for the information you've provided."

"You mean each case does have to stand alone?" Darby asked.

"Yes, unfortunately," he said. "The other, I am not at liberty to state the name, but—"

"Let me guess, Captain Hill from Global Air Lines," Darby said sitting on the table.

"Do you know him?"

"I do," Darby said.

"The one thing I cannot figure out is how these agreements come about. I mean does the doctor solicit an airline and say, hey, I can be bought, or does the airline go searching for him?"

"That's one of the million-dollar questions," Darby said, wondering what she would find if she searched the internet for criminal doctors for hire. "But there are many in the medical industry who know that he's for sale; I suspect airlines do, too. Word gets around and they know who to call."

"This makes me sick," Ian said.

"You and me both. It turns out they flew both Hill and me quite a long way to see Dr. Wood when there were doctors available in our own backyards."

"I'm really sorry this happened to you," Ian said. "But we have a little problem. I was just notified that they are moving me to the cannabis department in a week."

"In the middle of an investigation?" Darby said, incredulously.

"Yes," Ian said, "but I promise you this. I'm not leaving with this report open. Even if I have to work 24-7 for the next week, I will finish it."

She thanked him and said goodbye. Darby could not shake the chill of what she'd just heard. The fact that her concerns against Dr. Wood were spot on, but they were pulling Ian from the case. That worried the hell out of her. Regardless, Wood was being investigated by someone who cared, and that gave her hope.

Ian held strong opinions regarding Wood's unethical behavior, and someone in his department did not like what he had to say.

Regardless, there was headway. She wondered once Ian's report was submitted if someone could bury it. There was nothing she could do about that and pushed the very thought from her mind. Darby headed back to the deposition.

Chapter 68

BACK ON THE record, Robert shifted subjects and asked, "Did you ever discuss with anyone within Global management the appropriateness of Captain Clark's consideration of the Section 8 referral on July 11th, 2016?"

"I did not."

Darby had not only discovered that Clark had planned this, but everyone involved knew about it. Wolfe knew that Clark had been planning this action four months before he created the pretext, as did Dr. Wood. Wolfe even provided that very email to Dr. Wood.

Robert circled back and placed the document identifying Global's 14 events regarding the Airbus pitot static system and airspeed events in front of Wolfe once again.

"Would this information that's attached be confidential information in terms of Global's proprietary interest?"

"Yeah, I mean, I think this is definitely nonpublic information, yes."

"And you gave Dr. Wood this document and numerous posts from Ms. Bradshaw's blog, correct?"

"At one point, yes, he did ask me to print them."

"How frequently have you visited Ms. Bradshaw's blog?"

"Other than a couple of times back during the Section 8 process,

I can't think of another time."

"Now, at some point did you provide Dr. Wood with information concerning a grievance that Ms. Bradshaw had filed?"

"I did."

"And why did you provide him that information?"

"Again, he asked for continuing communications, and I believe we told him that she had filed a grievance, and he asked to see a copy of it, and we sent it to him."

"You told him?" Robert asked.

"Yeah, we told him that, yeah, that was part of the continuing communications that he wanted to see, and we said, yes, a grievance has been filed over the Section 8 process, and he asked that he could see that."

"Dr. Wood specifically asked you to keep him abreast of any grievances?"

"Not abreast of any grievances no, but abreast of continuing communications with Global management and interactions… continuing communications and interaction with Global management."

"So, you determined that the grievance would fit within that category?" Robert asked.

"I believe I asked him if he wanted it, and he said that he would like to see a copy."

Robert then handed Wolfe another document. "And is this correspondence from you to Dr. Wood?"

Wolfe's color changed as he read the document. Then he said, "Uh… well… uh, Captain Bradshaw had written another book, and I just sent it to Dr. Wood just thinking… no real reason other than I thought he might be interested in it. I understood the case was over but thought he might be interested in reading it. Um… just because he had invested a lot of time in this case."

Darby wished the guy had the nerve to look her way. She glanced at her watch. He managed to spend six and a half hours without even a singular glance in her direction. Then she looked at Wendel and smiled.

"Would you agree with me that… or, well, let me just ask it. This reference: *FYI, here is the latest and greatest from Captain Bradshaw*, is that intended to be sarcastic in tone?"

"It was not intended to be that, that way, no, but it was the latest book that she had written. I know she had written a couple books, and that was something that as part of his review. I know Dr. Wood was very interested in, and I think at one point he had told us that he was reading one of her books. So… again, I think somebody flipped it to me, or I saw it somewhere and it's… uh, kind of pulled it up."

"Can you identify who sent it to you?" Robert asked.

"I can't. I can't."

"I've handed you an exhibit we've marked as Wolfe Exhibit 55, Bates stamp C-6828. It's a letter on FAA stationery addressed to Darby Bradshaw that an investigation substantiated a violation of an order, regulation or standard of the FAA related to Global. "Were you ever provided with a copy of this letter by anyone at Global?"

"No."

"Do you know what violation of an order, regulation, or standard of the FAA was substantiated with respect to Ms. Bradshaw's safety reports?"

"No."

Would you care if you did, dipshit? Darby thought.

It amazed her, that so far nobody in flight operations knew they were charged with a violation. Either they were all in denial or violations were buried in a pile of paperwork. The scum that floated to the top of the Global Pond was more than ridiculous, it was criminal.

"Under the collective bargaining agreement, Section 8, who is responsible for selecting the neutral doctor?" Robert asked.

"That responsibility falls on the company medical examiner, and the pilot medical examiner, to work together to come up with a mutually acceptable neutral doctor."

"And in the case of Ms. Bradshaw, did you become involved in the neutral medical examiner selection process?"

"I did."

How much cockier could Joe Wolfe be with his admissions of violating the contract. The very contract that was his responsibility to uphold. He had to know she would file grievances based upon those violations. *What the hell is he doing?* Darby wondered. His demeanor, however, was a complete contradiction of his open display of nerves.

"Now, my question is… on or about June 19th, 2017, did you communicate to Dr. Wood that Ms. Bradshaw had made additional safety allegations and was telling other pilots not to follow the training?"

"I think that must be accurate. I think that's around the time that she had… uh, well, they had a procedure that the company was implementing dealing with… basically, it's called the upset recovery procedure. So, I sense from this it must have come up in conversation," Wolfe said. "So, I was made aware, and, again, I just mentioned it to them offhandedly, I think. I think. That's my best guess as to why that's in there. I don't have any reason to dispute that."

"But you had some document in which Ms. Bradshaw communicated to other pilots not to follow Global training?"

"I believe I did. I must have. Again, I'm straining my memory, but I think I did, yes."

There was no document. Darby had, however, written to the senior leadership that Global's upset recovery training was against the FAA standards and unsafe. Despite management's marketing efforts to tell the pilot group that Global did not retaliate if concerns were brought forth, she knew better.

The noose was already around her neck, so she had submitted her concerns figuring if they tightened that rope it wouldn't matter. Hell, they had already kicked the box out from under her feet so what more could they do to her? The best Clark had in him was to send her a nastygram. He even stated in his deposition that he still had concerns for Darby's mental health because she reported another safety concern. Not the brightest statement he could have made in response to the AIR 21 statute.

Management shortly thereafter published a memo that their procedure was not a procedure but a strategy. Then they later changed that strategy to comply with federal regulations. What she could not figure out was if Wolfe was just pulling shit out of his ass, or if someone had told him she had written to the pilots and told them not to follow the strategy. Either way, it probably didn't matter.

"I'm almost done here," Robert said. "How about a five-minute break?"

Chapter 69

DARBY AND ROBERT walked out of the deposition room and stepped into their walk-in closet office and Robert closed the door. He turned toward Darby.

"I think we're done," Robert said. "It's been a long day. Do you have anything else you want to ask?"

"I would like to know if someone at Global told Dr. Gelder to drop me," Darby said.

Dr. Gelder was the forensic psychiatrist that Darby had planned on seeing prior to the Mayo Clinic. He suddenly had a conflict of interest and canceled their appointment days before she was supposed to meet with him. Despite his dropping her, he had been of great assistance advising her as to why Dr. Wood's report was inaccurate. She'd taken copious notes that found their way directly into the documents she provided the Illinois medical board.

"Do you have anything concrete for that request?" Robert asked. "Or are you fishing."

"One of my favorite pastimes," Darby said with a grin.

"Okay, then ... we'll see if he bites."

Darby had called Dr. Gelder for over a year to find out what that conflict was. He never answered her calls or returned her messages. Then she borrowed Kathryn's cell phone, in which he answered immediately. She advised him she was about to be deposed and she needed to be able to answer the question of why she switched from Dr. Gelder to the Mayo Clinic. He said that Global had hired him. She was not fishing, she simply wanted details.

They returned to the briefing room ten minutes later and settled into their seats. Wolfe was biting a pinky nail when they arrived, and his finger started to bleed. He wrapped a tissue around it and placed his hands into his lap.

They went back on record.

"Do you know who Dr. James Gelder is?" Robert asked Wolfe.

"I'm familiar with Dr. Gelder, yes."

"Have you had discussions with him, telephonic discussions, ever?"

"I've spoken to Dr. Gelder." Wolfe Glanced at Wendel, but of course, he was texting. Wolfe was on his own.

"Did you ever speak to Dr. Gelder about Ms. Bradshaw?"

"We retained Dr. Gelder on another case, and prior to that case he mentioned that he was in contact with a Global pilot, and he identified Ms. Bradshaw. And we told him, you know, hey, if you're going to do work for Ms. Bradshaw, here is the situation that could be a conflict of interest. So, we would like to retain you to consult on a case that we were working on. And we just said, It's up to you. Let us know what you want to do," Wolfe said, more rapidly than he had all day. "He called back a few days later and said that he was happy to work with Global. So, we retained him as a consulting expert in an arbitration that we were working on."

"Did Dr. Gelder advise you of any preliminary determination he had made with respect to Ms. Bradshaw?"

"Not that I recall. He said that he had seen… that she had sent him the report, but he hadn't engaged or taken any steps. And that's when we were, hey, are you retained or are you working for Ms.

Bradshaw, and he said that he was not."

"But you communicated to him that if he were to be retained by Ms. Bradshaw that he would not be retained by Global?"

"At that point what we told him is we believed it would be a conflict of interest and that we could just go, and we would be okay without him. It was completely up to him as to what he wanted to do, but we just felt like there would be a conflict there, and it wasn't worth engaging him."

Gelder, a top forensic psychiatrist in the United States, had not only read the report but they had talked on the phone for well over an hour. He had told Darby that she was not bipolar and gave her the rationale as to why not. At the time he canceled, he had told her there was a conflict of interest but would not disclose with whom. Nobody at the company knew she was planning on using Gelder, except for ALPO.

ALPO had even refused to provide Gelder her medical report when she'd asked, so he allowed her to send it directly to him. She scheduled an appointment, booked a hotel, and purchased an airline ticket. He was commissioned and one week later said he had to cancel.

There was no way that Global needed a forensic psychiatrist for a grievance and Gelder had told her she was fine. He would have conveyed that to Global as well and advised them there would be no conflict because he had found her fit and had planned to clear her. The only conflict would be if he had gone against Global's wishes. That would have been a huge conflict.

Why they feared having a forensic psychiatrist as her medical examiner was beyond her. Granted, he could have testified in court as an expert. Then she smiled, a broad smile, as she fully realized the reality of what happened. At that moment, she also recognized the legal team was watching her. Her smile drove a questioning look between Wendel, Karen, and Betty.

Global and ALPO had done her a huge favor. Had Global not interfered, she never would have gone to the Mayo Clinic. Furthermore, Dr. Wood would never have agreed to Mayo Clinic to fulfill the role as the neutral medical examiner. As it turned out the team at the Mayo Clinic provided far more strength than one doctor opposing Dr. Wood. Because of Global's interference, she had a vote of 10 to 1 in favor of her mental health. The real question was, why did her pilots' union advise Global management of her plans for Gelder?

Robert was done with Wolfe and glanced her way. She nodded. She too was done with him.

It was Churchill who said that nothing was as exhilarating as a bullet missing your head by two inches. That's exactly what had happened to Darby, yet she wasn't quite certain exhilarating was the best description of her experience. The truth was, that the bullet they fired had hit her and she had bled for two years. Unfortunately, using the justice system to ensure this would never happen to anyone again, was almost as bad as the first attack by the company.

She was bleeding badly and the pain this process caused was excruciating. Yet, they were getting close to the end.

Chapter 70

Oklahoma City,
Corporate Offices
February 21, 2019

CROFT WELCOMED GEORGE Wyatt warmly and closed the door behind them. "Can I get you a drink?" he asked.

"A Diet Coke would be nice," Wyatt said sitting on the couch.

"I appreciate you coming," Croft said striding across the room to his fridge.

"Of course. It's great being back."

Croft returned, and handed the can to Wyatt and said, "They're turning you in to a teetotaler I see."

"Goes with the job," Wyatt said with a grin.

Croft both understood and appreciated Wyatt's dedication. "It's really good to see you."

"You, too, sir," Wyatt said. He flipped the top on the can. "Looks like we're going to do this, doesn't it?"

"I never had a doubt."

"I'm surprised that that Bradshaw didn't make any noise when the announcement came out," Wyatt said.

"We'll slip under the radar with this," Croft said. "They've got her tied up in depositions and she's been flying a heavy schedule to pay for the process. Besides, she's battling Global, not you. Hell, you've been retired long enough that you'll be fine."

"I hope so," Wyatt said.

"I know so."

"So, what can I do for you today, sir?" Wyatt asked.

"We've got some friends who are banking heavily on you," Croft said. "I'm just the messenger today."

Wyatt nodded. His eyes never leaving Croft's. "I'll do everything I can."

"Good," Croft said. "When it becomes official, you will have to remain scarce around the headquarters. We won't have opportunities like this in the future."

"I understand," Wyatt said. He sipped his Coke and then set it on the coaster.

"I want you to ensure the MAX is grounded for many years," Croft said. "You'll also need to ground United's entire fleet of triple sevens."

"Both events are doable," Wyatt said.

"We're in the process of establishing an inhouse online internet service and phasing out Gogo Inflight. We'll also cutoff T-Mobile's free service. I'm going to need you to place a warning regarding 5G and then when we're ready, we'll prevent all telephones onboard. We need to control all airborne communications in the future. No person will be able to communicate with *anyone* on the ground unless we say it's okay. When we pull the plug, the skies will be silent."

Wyatt nodded. Understanding filled his eyes. "You'll let me know when?"

"The message will be sent loud and clear," Croft said, standing and walking to his bar. He poured himself a couple fingers of scotch then returned to his seat. He was drinking more than he should these days, but the warmth calmed his nerves.

When Croft returned, Wyatt said, "Anything else?"

"Yes." Croft sipped his scotch as the reality of the world they were headed into played out before him. "They want approval for commercial drones. FedEx and UPS at first. The public won't care about freight operators. Airbus has been developing an aircraft for single-pilot operations, and she's almost ready to go. When the pilot shortage is strong enough, you'll approve that plane for U.S. operators."

"Consider it done," Wyatt said.

Croft nodded and assessed him for a moment, unsure how far he would go. But as the adage goes, there's no turning back. He emptied his glass and then said, "There's one more thing that we need to discuss."

Chapter 71

Shanghai
February 25, 2019

Darby awoke to her phone ringing and glanced at the time. It was 0300, and she'd forgotten to silence it. She answered. "Hey Neal, what's up?" She asked rolling on her back and closing her eyes again.

"Where are you?"

"Shanghai."

"Sorry, want me to call you later?' he asked.

"Nope. I'm good," she said with a yawn.

"I got an update on Stan,"

"What did you find out?" she asked, not sure if she really wanted to know.

"Stan did have something he was going to tell you," Neal said, "and they were going to send him back into the program if he did."

"He was going to testify for me," Darby said. "He would not have killed himself for that."

"Well, he did kill himself," Neal said. "And I think there was more to it than telling you why ALPO didn't defend you. I don't know, but I think it was big. On that note, the threat of going back into the program would be enough to do anyone in. I think he might have already been on his second strike anyway, so if they nailed him, he would have lost his job."

"That wouldn't have looked very good for the program," Darby said.

"Nothing could make that program look good," Neal said. "But now we've got a dead pilot, a new HIMS Chairman, and we'll never know why he did it."

"I can't believe if he was going to take his life, why not write a note to explain why and rat them out. Especially if he was going to die anyway. None of this makes sense."

"We'll never know," he said.

"Thanks for the call," Darby said.

"When will you be home?"

"Tomorrow. We've got Croft's deposition on the 28th."

"I hope you give that asshole hell," Neal said. "Did you know he stays awake at night figuring out how to get more out of the pilot group."

Darby chuckled, and said, "Not much sleeping going on with Global management. Abbott stays awake worrying about me because of my fear that management's out to get me."

"They *are* out to get you."

"That's an understatement."

"Oh, wait. Before you go," Neal said. "What are you going to bid?"

"For next month?" Darby asked.

"No. For your new equipment," Neal said. "Didn't you hear? They're shutting down all the triple seven bases and getting rid of the plane. They're replacing them with A350's."

Chapter 72

Oklahoma City
Global Boardroom
CEO Walter Croft Deposition
February 28, 2019

THE VIDEOGRAPHER'S VOICE boomed with authority. "We are now on the video record. Please note that microphones are sensitive and can pick up whispering and private conversations. We ask that you turn off cellphones or at least place them away from microphones as they can interfere with deposition audio. Recording will continue until all parties agree to go off the record."

The first time they had deposed with the same videographer, his dramatic effect was non-existent. Today they were inside a Global boardroom instead of an office, and the deposition was the CEO of Global Air Lines.

Darby glanced at Betty Dickson, Global's in-house attorney. Today there wasn't a package of candy in sight, and she was paying attention. *Good girl,* Darby thought. At least Betty knew enough to remove temptation. In hindsight, Darby thought she should have brought a package of chocolate to slide in front of her.

The videographer introduced himself and then said, "The caption for the case is Darby Bradshaw, Plaintiff, versus Global Air Lines

Defendant. This case is filed in the United States Department of Labor, Office of Administrative Law Judges. The name of the witness is Walter Croft."

Introductions were made around the table and the Global team was sitting tall, in stark contrast to that of Croft who either had had a very long day or felt he was above this process. Darby suspected the latter. There was no sign of Global's lawyer, Von Dietrich, but only Wendel and the perky little miss Karen Sherwin, with Betty in tow. Darby hoped Betty's blood sugar wouldn't drop in the next three hours, because it wouldn't be pretty if she passed out.

Croft was clearly not pleased to be present. Darby was not pleased either, but if anyone could have prevented this, it would have been Croft himself.

Despite having to go through this monkey show, Darby knew with all her heart that after today they would be done. She smiled a slow smile knowing this would be the end. Once Croft learned the depth of deception among his people, he would not allow this to go to court. He would hold all those involved accountable. He owed it to the stockholders and every passenger who boarded a Global aircraft.

Croft was a revered CEO and today he would prove his worth in more ways than one. A good name is more desirable than great riches. To be esteemed is better than silver or gold—a proverb Darby held close to heart.

"What is your understanding of the AIR21 statute?" Robert asked.

"I have none," Croft said flatly.

Both Darby's brows raised. Was he serious? Darby thought as she glanced to Wendel who was nodding in encouragement to Croft. She would have thought at the very least his high-priced legal counsel would have briefed him on the law, if nothing else, to understand why his presence was required.

If Wendel and the legal team had not briefed the witnesses on the statute, then they were negligent. Darby wrote a note to ask Robert about that later. Global was not getting their money's worth from this group they called a legal team. The admissions from all of Global's witnesses continued to build Darby's case, simply because nobody understood the law. They didn't really need Croft at this point, but Darby wanted him to fully understand and end this because it was the right thing to do.

Those they had deposed had lied about things that had no relevance, yet they admitted to those facts that signed Global's fate. This was the most perplexing thing Darby had ever experienced. At least flying airplanes made sense—pull back go up, push forward go down. She glanced at Wendel and wondered if he understood the law.

"Did you review any documents to prepare for your deposition today?" Robert asked.

"I did."

"What documents did you review?"

"A small number of emails with counsel."

"And nothing other than emails?" Robert asked.

"Nothing."

"What is your current position with Global Air Lines?" Robert asked, removing his glasses.

"I'm the chief executive officer."

"How long have you held that position?"

"Three years."

"And before that?" Robert asked.

"I was the chief financial officer."

"For the record," Robert said, "I have handed you a document that is dated September 12, 2016. It is from Walter Croft to Darby Bradshaw with the subject line being Congratulations. Do you recall receiving this initial email from Ms. Bradshaw?"

"I do remember hearing from Darby. It was around the time of my appointment as CEO, yes."

"And you signed off on your response here—*Best. Walt*. Is that a common signoff for you in your email correspondence?"

"Often times," Croft said, and then he looked at his watch.

"And did you consider it inappropriate for Ms. Bradshaw to address you as Walt?"

"Not at all."

"Now, in your response you reference, or part of the response is, *Looking forward to many great chapters for us to write.* Can you explain what you had meant by that sentence?"

"I can't recall at the time," Croft said. "I presume that it is because she referenced that she had written books, and I was embarking on a new chapter for myself in Global as I took on the leadership of the company."

"Is there any written chain of command policy at Global that precludes a rank-and-file employee from emailing you?"

"Not that I'm aware of."

"Do you recall that in December of 2016, Ms. Bradshaw was referred for a Section 8 mental health evaluation?" Robert asked.

"I don't recall."

Darby's eyes went wide. He had a 30-minute meeting with Clark about her, the day she was meeting with Abbott. *How the hell could he not know?* He also had told Wyatt to brief him, who said he had, albeit in a general way.

"Did you at some time during your employment with Global, learn that Ms. Bradshaw had been referred for a Section 8 mental health evaluation?"

"I'm not familiar with Section 8 period. I was aware that there were some discussions, medical discussions, going on but no details at all."

"So, no details about the reason *why* Global— I just want to make sure I'm getting the foundation so I don't provoke an objection. You knew at some point in December of 2016 that there were medical concerns related to Ms. Bradshaw?"

"No," he said. Then he added, "I don't recall the timing."

"Okay," Robert said sliding the Section 8 letter in front of him. "I would like you take a look at—"

"I don't ever recall seeing this document," Croft said dismissively.

"Well, wholly aside from the document," Robert said, "did you learn at some time that there were expressed concerns within Global management with respect to Ms. Bradshaw's mental health?"

"I was aware that there was a medical situation regarding Ms. Bradshaw that flight operations management was working on, but that is the extent of my knowledge."

"And when did this knowledge come to you?" Robert asked.

"Sometime in the last three years. I have no recall of dates."

Nice trait for a CEO, Darby thought.

Croft's arms were folded on the table. He appeared irritated, clearly annoyed for having to sit through this. He was not the polished executive he portrayed during planned interviews.

"Okay. Putting mental health conditions to one side," Robert said, "do you have any recollection of other issues related to Ms. Bradshaw that were brought to your attention by Global management representatives?"

"Not that I recall."

"Do you know a man named Fred Oliver?"

"Yes."

"Do you remembering having a conversation with him regarding

Ms. Bradshaw?"

"Not that I recall."

"Do you know a man at Global named Peter Jackson?"

"Yes, I do."

"Did you have any discussions with Mr. Jackson related to Ms. Bradshaw?"

"Well, Peter is our general counsel so I'm not sure if that is relevant," Croft looked a Wendel and said, "Counsel?"

Wendel looked up from his phone and said, "You can answer whether or not you had a conversation, but not anything that was said during the conversation."

"I recall having a conversation at some point," Croft said. "I can't put a time on it."

"What was the subject matter of that discussion?" Robert asked.

"Objection," Wendel said.

"Just to reassure you, I'm not looking for anything other than what has been identified by Respondent's own privilege log. I'm just looking for the general subject matter."

"Is the question asking whether or not the subject matter was Ms. Bradshaw or something else?" Wendel asked.

"No, beyond that. What the subject matter was. What was the general subject matter as it related to Ms. Bradshaw?" Robert asked.

"I don't think that that can be answered without divulging privileged information," Wendel said, "so I have to direct him not to answer that."

"Okay. We may come back to that," Robert said, as he sorted through his papers. The delay irritated Croft more so than it did Wendel.

Darby stared incredulously at Walter Croft. She had believed in him. But now he hid behind the shield of a protection order.

Fred Oliver was the executive vice president of marketing and Peter Jackson was the executive vice president of corporate legal. Croft was both evasive and dismissive, and his contradictions brought a chill into the room.

He was part of this, Darby thought.

At the very least, he was fully aware of what had happened, and he had allowed them to proceed. If Global was innocent in their actions, then why not divulge the content of their discussion? Far more was at risk than her career, the safety of everyone at this airline and for all those that flew on their aircraft were in jeopardy if the CEO had been complicit in this action.

Robert handed Croft a document of his correspondence with Fred Oliver, Peter Jackson, and the Chief Financial Officer, with the subject line—Bradshaw. Update.

"Does this refresh your recollection with respect to having discussions with Fred Oliver in October of 2016 related to Ms. Bradshaw?"

"It does not." Croft stared at the document.

"Have you been… has anyone ever provided you with information about Ms. Bradshaw's social media activity?"

"No."

"Do you have any knowledge of Ms. Bradshaw ever being subject to discipline while employed at Global?"

"No."

"And do you have any knowledge of Ms. Bradshaw having engaged in misconduct while employed at Global?"

"No."

"Have you ever complained to anyone about Ms. Bradshaw's conduct?"

"No."

"Did you consider any of her correspondence with you to be in violation of Global's rules of conduct or Global's policies?"

"No."

"Did any of her correspondence to you ever cause you concern about her mental health?"

"No."

"Did you ever complain to anyone concerning Ms. Bradshaw's correspondence with you?"

"No."

"Did you consider any of her correspondence to be annoying?"

"No."

Sullen would be the best way to describe him now. With each response, he looked down and answered quietly and calmly. And he was the first witness that could actually say the word *no* instead of *I don't recall.*

"Have you provided copies of her correspondence to you to other persons?"

"No. Well, I mean, let me rephrase that. I certainly forwarded certain emails, but not copies, which was your question," Croft said.

"Do you recall which emails you forwarded?"

"There were some that we reviewed this morning."

"Do you recall the subject matter of any of the emails that you forwarded?"

"No."

Robert's questions were presented methodically and slowly. Croft leaned forward, arms on the table, except when his hands spread and bounced for emphasis on occasion. His head was in a permanent tilt sideways toward Robert. With lips closed, his mouth retained a straight line.

"Do you know the reason why you would have forwarded any of the emails to others?" Robert asked.

"The reason, as I recall from seeing the emails this morning, was that Darby had raised some concerns around safety," Croft said.

"Do you recall what those issues were?"

"No. I was not aware of them."

"Now, are you familiar with the acronym SMS?"

"Safety Management Systems," Croft said. "I believe."

"Are you familiar with what SMS refers to?"

"I'm not a pilot or a technician, but I understand it is one of our core systems by which we measure the safety of the operation and monitor it and make improvements," Croft said with a smile for the first time during the deposition.

Oh, my God, Darby thought raising a hand and covering her mouth. Being a pilot or technician had nothing to do with a person's knowledge regarding SMS. Mr. Croft didn't know what SMS meant, and she doubted he knew his responsibility to the program either. This was not going to end well.

Chapter 73

CROFT WAS NOW ill at ease, as he should be, by his lack of knowledge. The smile was a defense mechanism for his ignorance. Darby felt embarrassed for the man.

"What is your understanding of the components of SMS?"

"I don't know the components off the top of my head," Croft said shaking his head. "I have no idea."

"Would you have had a superior knowledge of SMS and or its components in the year 2016?"

"A superior knowledge?" Croft asked, confused by the question.

"Yeah, more knowledge than you have right now," Robert replied.

"I don't know," Croft said shaking his head again, this time tightening his lips.

"I mean, how would you describe your current involvement with Global's SMS program?" Robert pressed.

"SMS is a broad acronym. There is a lot that falls under that relative to safety metrics. So, we measure and track an awful lot of safety measures for the system," Croft said, spreading his hands and bouncing them in the air with each statement for emphasis. "You can talk about SMS, and I think the clarity of what you're talking about gets into the metrics itself."

Frustration emerged with each word he spoke. His hands finally found a home when he was done, folded together on top of the table.

"I'm asking you what *your* personal involvement is in SMS compliance?"

"I don't have one," he said with a shake of his head, looking at the table.

What the hell? He was the accountable executive of the SMS program until the time Darby filed her AIR21 complaint. Shortly thereafter they removed Croft as the accountable executive to eliminate his liability. But at the time he held that position. They also forgot sanitize the manuals and in many places he was still listed as the accountable executive.

"I understand that answer to be with respect to today," Robert said. "However, was there a time when you did have some participation?"

"I'm not qualified as either a pilot or a flight operations leader to actually have responsibility for the development or the tracking of SMS," Croft said, his hands spreading wide assisting with his effort to explain. "That would be outside my specific range of expertise," Croft said with a grin. This time his smile was as mocking as his tone.

"But my question is, was there a time during your tenure at Global where you had more involvement in SMS compliance than you have today?"

"No," Croft said shaking his head. "Not that I recall."

Robert reestablished the date of Croft becoming CEO, and then asked, "Do you have any role currently, in promoting flight operations safety culture?"

"Absolutely."

"What is that role?"

"Safety is our priority across all aspects of our business. It is our number one priority."

"And what role do *you* play?"

"As the company's chief executive, I put it at the very top of my list as one of the most," he said with a sardonic smile raising his hands, "the most, not one of most, but a very important thing that we do for our employees as well as our customers and communities."

"Week to week, what activities do you engage in that promote flight operation safety, if any?" Robert asked.

"Again, I don't focus specifically on flight operations. I focus on the safety of the entire operation. I will be involved in meetings. I will get reports. I will be in town halls with employees to talk about the importance of safety, both personal as well as operations."

"Weekly meetings? Daily meetings? How frequently?" Robert asked.

"I will give weekly reports on the safety of our operations."

"And that is a compendium report including all aspects of the operation?" Robert asked?

"No. It is a summary report."

"So flight operations is in those reports with—"

"All other operations, yes," Croft said interrupting Robert.

Croft lifted a hand and adjusted his glasses. Then he began to say something but gave an audible sigh and folded his hands on the table in front of him. His discomfort with this line of questioning was noted.

"And is SMS discussed in weekly reports?" Robert asked.

"I can't recall if SMS is specifically but, again, all the metrics that SMS measures are tracked within it, yes."

"And aside from the reports, are there face-to-face meetings with department heads regarding safety issues?" Robert asked.

"Yes."

"How often do you have meetings with flight operations representatives concerning safety?"

Croft hesitated. He looked at the table and put some thought into his answer. "My meetings with safety, again, are for all aspects of safety, not just flight ops. So, I meet with our safety lead at least once a month to go through it."

Seconds ticked by while Robert wrote a note, and then gathered the next document. Croft adjusted his glasses again, sighed and then placed the palm of his hand against the side of his face supporting his head. His eyes flashed to Robert's movement of documents.

Robert handed him a document, and Croft lifted his head and accepted it, then held it with both hands. His lips shifted from a straight line to a bit of a downturn as he silently assessed the document, clearly perplexed. His face reddened.

Chapter 74

CROFT'S GLANCE FROM the document to Wendel did not go unnoticed. Darby wished she could be a fly on the wall when this was over. Someone was about to get ripped a new one.

"I have handed you a document which is identified as Global Exhibit 6," Robert said. "It is on Global letterhead with the title Corporate Safety, Security & Compliance, Safety Management Systems. And under that, a subheading of Revision Log. I want you to refer, if you would, please go to the sixth entry at line 16, Revision 26.

"If you will look at the fourth bullet point which reads—*Accountable executive changed from CEO to COO* throughout the document. My question, with that background, is prior to January 14, 2017, would you agree that you functioned as the accountable executive for the SMS program at Global?"

During Robert's question, Croft's hand had gone from the document to pushing his glasses up on his nose and then touching his nose and back to his glasses.

Robert identified that Croft had, in fact, been the SMS accountable executive, and Croft simply smiled and said, "I… uh…" and then he looked at Robert with a closed-lipped smile and fell silent.

Wendel came to Croft's defense after moments of uncomfortable silence while the CEO was left twisting in the wind, not knowing what to say. What Darby found funny was that Wendel brought a rubber hose to a gun fight with his reply.

"Objection. You can answer the question if you know the answer."

Clearly, he can't answer, Darby wanted to tell Wendel.

"I'm not familiar with the specific reason why this was changed," Croft finally said with an uncomfortable smile, "but as I said earlier, you don't delegate accountability for safety within the company. As the top officer of the company, safety *is* my priority."

Croft's grin never faded, but his face reddened with embarrassment that he had been the accountable executive of a program that he knew nothing about. *Why hadn't they told him?* Darby wondered looking from Wendel to Betty, and finally to Karen. Then she chided herself for the stupid question.

"But my question is…" Robert began. Then he looked to the court reporter and said, "Could you read back my question?"

The court reporter read the record as Croft flipped through the pages, looking for something that would save his ass, or give him anything to grab onto. He looked for anything that could be used as a lifesaver. There was nothing.

After the question was reread, Robert said, "I would like to add to that prior to January 14, 2017."

"Objection. You're asking him to interpret a document that—"

"No, I'm not. I'm asking if he knows whether, prior to January 14, 2017, he was the accountable executive for the SMS program at Global?"

"Bad question," Wendel said, "but you can answer that question."

Croft said, "No."

"I'm sorry. You don't know?"

"As I said, my responsibility for safety is all aspects of safety throughout the company. I'm not the direct, responsible, leader for

SMS in the company," Croft said with a forced grin.

"Okay. So, I'm just trying to understand your answer. Is your answer that you don't know… or that you were not the accountable executive?"

"My answer is I have never seen this revision log! So, I would need… so it's pretty hard for me to answer your question."

"Let's not reference the revision log. Were you at any time the accountable executive for the SMS program at Global?"

"I'm not sure what accountable executive means," Croft replied.

Chapter 75

NEVER IN HER life had Darby been more surprised than when those words—*I'm not sure what accountable executive means*—came out of Croft's mouth. If she hadn't heard it herself, she never would have believed it. The CEO of the largest airline in the world didn't know what accountable executive meant.

Her dismay shifted toward anger. Mostly because she had been a fool to believe in him. Now she wanted to know who was pulling this puppet's strings.

Who the hell is running this company? she wondered. Darby now realized that Walter Croft did not have the level of intelligence to run an airline. She thought Robert's jaw was going to hit the table. But instead, he began sorting through documents, allowing those words to hang in the air. Darby glanced at the camera. *For the world to view,* she thought.

Croft's face continued to redden as the reality of what he had said became clear. But Wendel, the quirky little man, nodded his head rapidly toward Croft as if he was agreeing that was a good answer. Darby shifted her attention to Wendel in disbelief.

Robert finally slid a document across the table toward Croft and a copy to Wendel.

"Was this document produced in discovery?" Wendel asked

referring to Exhibit 6. "It doesn't have a Bates stamp."

"I'm pretty darn confident it was. I know it was used in a prior—"

"We can make a note to check," Wendel said.

"We used it in the motion that got us here," Robert said.

"I think that may be true," Wendel said, "but that is not the same as producing it, but, okay."

That document was the memo that Global had provided them in discovery, albeit in the initial group that was not Bates stamped. If it was not Bates stamped now, then they had removed it. She never would have known about Croft and Wyatt's meeting if these attorneys had not been so sloppy. Now Wendel identified his intent to knowingly violate the court order and hide discovery.

Robert ignored Wendel and pushed another document toward Croft.

"All right. I have now handed you a document that is identified as Exhibit 7," Robert said to Croft ignoring the first document for a moment. "It is on FAA letterhead from the Office of Audit and Evaluation, addressed to Darby Bradshaw." Robert provided him the letter that substantiated a violation of Global.

"My first question is, were you ever provided a copy of this September 8, 2016, document?"

"No."

"Were you ever provided with knowledge that the FAA had substantiated a violation of Federal Aviation standards based on Ms. Bradshaw's reports?"

"No."

Robert returned his attention to his list of questions and began scanning through them. Walter Croft, however, balled one hand and placed the other over the top of it, and brought them to his mouth. He stared, looking at nothing but was deep in thought. Then he pulled his hands away, rubbed them together, and folded his arms on the table. Then one hand went to the side of his face again and he reached for the document Robert handed him with the other hand.

"I have provided you a document that we have marked as Exhibit 8. This is an email thread, first page, from Darby Bradshaw to Walt Croft. Would you look at the first page and tell me if you recall receiving this email correspondence from Ms. Bradshaw?"

"I don't have specific recall of this, no," he said staring at the document.

"Now, if you look at the last paragraph, the first sentence reads—*Research indicates that the CEO must be notified if risk falls into a red category on the ICAO risk matrix, and we have a few areas that do.* Are you familiar with the acronym ICAO?"

"I am."

"What does ICAO stand for?" Robert asked.

"International ummm… Audit Organization. I don't know exactly what it stands for. I know who it is, it's a safety organization," Walt said.

Darby folded her arms and an eyebrow raised involuntarily. ICAO was the International Civil Aviation Organization, not an audit organization. She was dumbfounded at how ignorant Croft was to aviation and everything associated with it. He was nothing like Croft's predecessor, Lawrence Patrick, who had worked his way up through the airline and understood the business from a safety perspective to efficiency.

Darby sighed. Passengers' lives were in his hands… and yet, Croft was nothing but an empty suit.

"Reading this now, we do understand Ms. Bradshaw to be communicating that there are compliance issues with regard to flight operations that she was concerned about, correct?"

"Reading this now, I will tell you that Darby, her *personal opinion* was that she had some concerns," Croft said.

"Concerns related to what?" Robert asked.

"Related to the red category," he said with a smirk. "I'm not sure what they were."

"Did you ask anybody what she meant, or what red category on the ICAO risk matrix signified in terms of flight operations?"

"As I can see on the same document, I forward it along to uhhh… the… I actually saw in an earlier email in prep that I forwarded this along to Captains Wyatt and Clark."

"Why did you forward it to them?"

"Because any employee that is mentioning a concern around safety requires it be assessed and evaluated."

"Now, there is a reference here to—if we move up one paragraph, the prior paragraph reads—*Coincidentally, I submitted a lengthy report to Captains Wyatt and Clark last month with my concerns as to flight operations culture, (safety culture), that is not in alignment with our core values and most important behaviors. Unfortunately, we have current practices that also do not support the 2018 Safety Management Systems (SMS) mandate. As a follow up to my report, I have been asked to deliver an SMS presentation, April 4th, 10:00 a.m., in Oklahoma City which will focus on safety culture.*

"At this point did Global have an SMS program in place, do you know?"

"I believe so," he said rubbing the top of his hand.

"And would you agree with me that under The Federal Aviation Regulations, Global was required to have an SMS program in place?"

"Absolutely," Croft said.

"Under the Federal Aviation Regulations, Global is required to comply with its SMS program, correct?"

"Correct."

"Now, you appear to have responded just up from the paragraph I read—*Thanks Darby. I would appreciate seeing the report and will be sure to follow up. Walt.* Did you receive a copy of the report that she was referencing?"

"I don't recall."

"Did you follow up with her?"

"I didn't follow up with Darby. I followed up with sending the note along to Captains Wyatt and Clark."

"So, if you look at the second page, the second email is from Walter Croft to George Wyatt and Rich Clark—*If you guys could brief me. Thanks. Walt.* The response is—*Will do.* Is that the exchange that you had with George Wyatt and Rich Clark concerning Ms. Bradshaw's communication?"

"Yes," Croft said, staring at the paper.

"And did they? Did either Captain Wyatt, or Captain Clark or both ever brief you with respect to the SMS issues and ICAO risk matrix issues?"

"I don't recall."

Chapter 76

AND THEN IT began—*I don't recall*. There was no way they had not briefed him. Darby stared at Croft who refused to look her way. He placed his face into the palm of his hand again and stared at the table. God, she wished she knew what was going through his mind. If anything.

"I have handed you a document that has been marked as Exhibit 9," Robert said. "At the top of the page, it is from Bill Thomson to Joe Wolfe. Just for the record, it is Bates stamped GLB 22038 to 20239. Moving down the page, there is an email from George Wyatt to Rich Clark, subject line Safety Culture, that reads—*Thanks Rich. We'll need to brief Walt and also draft a short reply. I'm fine with you briefing him, but we will see how he wants to handle. Will calendar on Monday.*

"Does this refresh your recollection as to whether Captain Wyatt and or Captain Clark briefed you with respect to the issues raised by Ms. Bradshaw?"

"It does not," he said, removing his hand from his face and placing it on the table.

"Did you provide input to Captain Wyatt or Captain Clark in terms of how you wanted them to handle the issues for Defendant Bradshaw?" Robert asked.

"Only other than the note that you saw that asked for a briefing, and when I suggest briefing, that implies that I want them to evaluate and to the extent I need to be updated, to update me."

Darby's mouth opened. She wanted to object and force him to clarify what he had just said. But her lips closed more quickly than they opened. She did not want him to be part of this, and her heart sank deeper with every word he spoke.

"Did you ever get an update from either of them?"

"I don't recall."

"I have provided you with a document I have identified as Exhibit 10. The subject is *Darby Bradshaw Update. Location Walt's office. Start Wednesday, November 23, 2016, 4:30 p.m. and Wednesday, November 23, 2016, 5:00 p.m. Recurrence, none. Meeting status, accepted. Organizer, Walter Croft, Rich Clark, Peter Jackson.* Would you agree that you initiated a meeting with respect to Ms. Bradshaw for November 22, 2016?"

"No. I don't know how to organize meetings," he said with a smirk. "I assume my secretary must have done this."

Darby stifled a laugh at the thought—*of course, a CEO who doesn't know what accountable executive means could not possibly know how to organize a meeting.*

"Did you ask your secretary to organize a meeting regarding Ms. Bradshaw?" Robert asked.

"I did not. Again, not that I recall."

Darby wasn't sure how Robert was maintaining his composure. But she felt humiliated for Croft. She wondered if he would ever read his deposition and realize what an incompetent fool he came across as. Then she remembered the camera. He may not be able to read, but he could watch the movie.

"I've provided you with a document that is identified as Exhibit 11. The title at the top is Assessment of Global Air Lines Flight

Operations Safety Culture, Bates stamped C-178 through C-220. You received this document, correct?" Robert asked.

"I don't recall seeing this document."

"I'm sorry," Robert said a bit incredulous. "You don't recall ever seeing this document?"

"I do not."

"Do you recall anyone within Global discussing with you, safety and or compliance issues that Ms. Bradshaw had raised in her written report?"

"I do not recall that, no."

Darby had hoped more than anything that she could prove everyone wrong, and that Walter Croft had been played, and was not part of the problem. Instead, it appeared that she had been a fool to believe in him.

"If you could turn to the fourth page of the document that I have given you. I'm asking you to read down towards the bottom, just above where the series of five bullet points occur, and starting with the line—*Statements from Global*. Do you see where I am?"

Robert proceeded to read through the list of statements, one by one, that Darby had conveyed in her report. The last being, *if there was a better way, we would already be doing it.*

"Would you agree that these statements are not in compliance with Global's SMS program?"

"It is not compliant with our culture. I don't know about specific to SMS or not."

"Would you agree that safety culture is a core component of SMS?" Robert asked.

"Safety is core to our culture, period."

"Yes," Robert said. "But that is not my question. My question is would you agree—"

"SMS is a tracking vehicle," Croft said interrupting him, now frustrated. "Culture is about safety. The priority for our airline is about safety."

"Would you agree that the promotion of safety culture is a core component of SMS?"

"I'm not familiar with what SMS includes," he said exasperated, "but I can tell you that safety is core to the operation of our airline."

Wow, Darby thought. If anyone needed SMS training it was Croft. He didn't have a clue what SMS was. He thought it was a tracking program. He had no knowledge of the very program he was the accountable executive of, which made most of Robert's questions irrelevant. Furthermore, he was was oblivious to aviation safety.

The good news was that his deposition would be done sooner than later. The bad news was that the CEO was illiterate to SMS.

Croft uttered nothing but buzz words about safety being the highest priority. The man was clueless as to what safety meant. Darby now understood how Clark was able to bullshit his way through meetings, because nobody in charge knew otherwise.

"You also said you're not familiar with the Section 8 process?"

"I am not."

"Are you familiar with any specific cases involving a pilot's referral for mental health evaluation other than that of Ms. Bradshaw?"

"Objection," Wendel said. "Foundation."

"I don't understand," Robert said to Wendel.

"There is nothing in the record that he is familiar with anything having to do with Ms. Bradshaw either, so the question was, there was no foundation for the second part of the question."

"I think you may have misunderstood my question," Robert said. "Putting Ms. Bradshaw to one side, are you familiar with any specific cases of a pilot being referred for a mental health evaluation?"

"Not specifically, no," Croft said.

"Do you recall ever having been briefed about a pilot's mental health issues?"

"I don't recall, no."

"And do you recall ever being briefed with regard to safety or compliance issues made by a specific pilot?" Robert asked.

"We talk about safety and opportunities to improve all the time, so it is a pretty open-ended question."

"I meant it to be very narrow. Let me try again. Do you recall being briefed on safety issues raised by a specific individual pilot in the past?"

"Not specific to a pilot, no."

"I've handed you an exhibit number 14," Robert said. "I refer you to the third paragraph thereof which reads—*Maybe she didn't understand that the IAAS conference she was attending was a safety conference? But glad to meet with her anytime. Probably good to engage HR again at this point given this latest email to Dodson as I believe we could find ourselves being accused of inappropriate wrongdoing by her and we need to start the tracking for this phase. I also think we should consider whether a Section 8 is appropriate. While I'm sure she would find issue with that course of action, if she cannot embrace and understand the reasons behind our actions, it stands to reason she might not be able to make appropriate decisions for the safe operation of a flight as a crew member.*

"My question is, Mr. Croft, were you advised by Mr. Clark or any other management representative of Global that a Section 8 referral would be contemplated for Ms. Bradshaw in July of 2016?

"No."

"I've provided you with a document which has been marked Exhibit 8 from George Wyatt to Rich Clark dated July 16, 2016, and proceeds to an email exchange between George Wyatt and Clark, and then down to another email exchange between Wyatt and Clark," Robert said. "I want to read as background says—*Here we go. Just FYI. I will brief HR and handle this with kid gloves. She could be a candidate for a Section 8 after this goes through. She continues to see herself as the victim and refuses to accept that she cannot just use proprietary information as her own as well as Global pictures and intellectual knowledge. Will keep you informed.*

"Were you ever advised that these Global managers were considering a Section 8 referral four months prior to the pretext in which they submitted her to a mental health evaluation?"

"Objection to the form of the question," Wendel said. "You can answer."

"No, I wasn't."

But you know now, Darby thought folding her arms.

Chapter 77

WHILE ROBERT'S GOAL was to gather information from Croft critical to the case, Darby simply wanted to expose him to the truth. Despite all the signs that he had previous knowledge, Darby still wanted to believe that Walter Croft was a good man, albeit ignorant, and would do the right thing once he knew all the facts. If he wasn't involved, he would end it. Unfortunately, his refusal to admit that he'd spoken to Clark and Wyatt was a concern.

Darby wondered what he would do now, even if he had been part of the plan. Now that they had presented him with the evidence to hang his managers, would he do the right thing? There was no way he could allow this to go to court. No way he would want his deposition and admissions to become a public record. Admissions that proved two things—Global retaliated against her for reporting safety concerns, and that Walter Croft, the CEO of Global Air Lines, was incompetent.

Either way, if he knew or did not know, there would be no benefit of going to trial, only complete and total embarrassment in the public's eye. Croft was not doing well under this scrutiny, and Robert reading the questions in silence was infuriating him.

They had all professed that Croft was a busy man and had places to be. The reality, however, was they were experiencing this deposition hell because Croft lacked any leadership skills and had no courage to deal with Rich Clark. Darby wondered what leverage Clark had over the leadership team.

Croft's hands went to his face, then they clasped, seconds later he folded his arms on the desk. His expression shifted from grim, to bored, and then to immense anger. He reached for a bottle of water and took a long drink, and then recapped it, and Robert finally provided him another document.

"I have handed you exhibits that we have marked as 16 and 17," Robert said providing him the invoices. My question to you is, were you aware that charges for Ms. Bradshaw's psychiatric examination directed by Global cost over $73000?"

"No."

Darby could not determine if he was lying. But he showed no sign of surprise. His face remained somber now and he appeared bored. His expression did not shift with the exorbitant sum. He didn't even look up from the document. He just stared at it.

"Who in the flight department would be authorized to approve such an expense at that dollar level, do you know?" Robert asked.

"I don't know what the specific authorization levels within flight ops are."

He's so full of shit, Darby thought. He had been the chief financial officer. If anyone knew who was authorized to pay these invoices it would be him. She wished Robert would ask him if he would have had greater knowledge as the CFO.

"Were you ever told that Ms. Bradshaw's subsequent analysis by the Mayo Clinic cost $3300?"

"No," he said, clasping his hands together and placing them in front of his mouth.

Croft denied ever seeing a copy of her safety report. He denied seeing the copy of her presentation she gave to divisional leaders, despite her sending it to him with a personal note. That note ended up in her medical report by Wood. Someone in the company had given it to him.

"I have handed you an exhibit identified as Exhibit 20 on the letterhead from Dr. Wood, MD, entitled Psychiatric Evaluation, Darby Bradshaw. If you would turn to the second page, you will see there is a cut and paste of an email from you to George Wyatt and Rich Clark. It says—*if you guys can brief me. Thanks. Walt.* And below that, Darby Bradshaw's email to you starting off saying—*Walt, I just finished taking your Global culture survey. Thank you.*

Robert then took him to a portion of her medical report.

"If you go down the page from there, the third line when we get to the typewritten material states—*She was told to never go outside of the chain of command.* And at the bottom, at the end of the paragraph, starting a new one-sentence paragraph, it reads—*Also note that she addresses Mr. Croft as, quote, Walt. Undue familiarity associated with mania.* Were you ever advised that her reference to you as Walt contributed to the psychiatrist's adverse psychiatric evaluation of Ms. Bradshaw?"

"Objection," Wendel said. "Foundation. You can answer the question if you understood it."

"I had no knowledge of any of this evaluation."

But you know now, Darby thought again. Her arms were still folded as she watched him and slowly drummed her fingers.

He now refused to look her way. He also had knowledge that she was diagnosed for using the open-door policy that *he* promoted, and referring to him as Walt, when he encouraged everyone at the airline to acknowledge him on a first name basis. Yet, he stared without reaction to the information before him. Darby wondered if he even noticed that Dr. Wood had spelled undue influence as *undo*. *Excellence at its best,* she thought.

"Now, if you could turn to the next page, Bates stamped C 00491, and there is a handwritten note that begins—*Walt, we have one of the most successful airlines in the world.* At the bottom, *Darby, CA 757.* Did you provide this handwritten note to the psychiatrist, Dr. Wood?"

"I never recall seeing this, sir."

"You don't recall ever seeing this?"

"Huh-uh," he said shaking his head.

"You have to answer yes or no," Wendel said.

"And the question is?" Croft asked.

"I will withdraw the question," Robert said.

"Well, he answered it," Wendel said. "He didn't say yes or no, so—"

"I'm satisfied," Robert said.

"Uh-huh is not an answer," Wendel said. "I would like him to verbalize it."

"I didn't realize that," Robert said. "I was fine with that he said he has never seen this note."

"I think the court reporter will show you, it is uh-huh. Could you verbalize what your answer was to the last question when—"

"I don't recall what the question was," Croft said.

Chapter 78

This was beyond ridiculous. The court reporter read back the question, and Croft said he didn't see it. Wendel was now trying to prove his worth. He had allowed Croft to be hung out to dry. Regardless, Wendel should learn to pick and choose his battles. Unfortunately, he held the emotional maturity of a two-year-old, and Darby wondered, once again, which partner's daughter he was married to. He could not possibly remain with this firm based on performance alone.

"Do you recall anyone ever approaching you and asking you to authorize the transfer of any correspondence or notes from Ms. Bradshaw to a psychiatrist?"

"I don't know," Croft said.

"We have provided you a document that we have identified as Exhibit 21. I want to direct your attention to the fourth to the last page. You can look at the pagination at the upper right and turn to page 78?

"Go down to line 22 which reads—*And so we eventually, we sought the assistance of an outside auditor. We felt that would be a healthy process for us to go through at that point in time. And the catalyst for that, frankly, I think we would have done it anyway but certainly a catalyst for it was the meeting with Darby.* My question is, did Captain Wyatt or anyone else ever advise you that Ms. Bradshaw was a catalyst for bringing in an outside auditor for Global's flight operation practices?"

"Objection," Wendel said. "Foundation. I mean, I have let these go, but you haven't... the witness—"

"I understand there is an objection based on foundation," Robert interrupted. "I would rather we avoid some coaching here. And if you want to direct him not to answer, that is—"

"I don't want to waste everybody's time," Wendel said.

"Well, there is an order from the judge here that allows us to go into SMS issues, training issues, protected activity, and—"

"You know, the Court gave you three hours, but he didn't require you to use the three hours and just take the time up of Global's CEO."

"I won't if he can come to a conclusion."

"That question is—there is no foundation for that question," Wendel said. "You showed the witness the document. You haven't identified what the document is. You haven't identified whether the witness has ever seen the document. You read some language in the document and asked a question."

Perhaps Wendel had noticed Croft's shift from boredom to irritation, and the reason for his interaction. Regardless, after his antics, Wendel allowed Robert to continue.

Robert queried Croft about company surveys, various executive responsibilities, and Global's *first-ever Safety Day* that occurred days after Darby was sent into the Section 8. Darby glanced at Betty, who was paying attention for the first time in all the depositions. Proving one thing—she could survive longer than an hour and a half without sugar.

"And would you agree with me that this reference bullet point that I read previously raises an FAA compliance issue?" Robert asked.

"I don't know," Croft said propping up his face again.

"You would agree with me that if Global forces a pilot to fly after she advises she is fatigued, would be in violation of Global's FAA approved policy?"

"It certainly would be counter to the culture of our organization," Croft said, still leaning into his hand. "I would have to reference the specific FAA fatigue policy to answer your question in any detail."

"As you sit here today, you don't know whether it is contrary to Global's FAA approved fatigue policy to force a pilot—"

"We certainly do not force pilots to fly fatigued. I think there is some judgment that is required of that, and evaluation," Croft said dropping his hand. "You're asking me the policy specifics and I'm not familiar with those details."

"You're not knowledgeable as to whether Global has a written FAA approved policy that prohibits its managers from coercing a pilot to fly fatigued?" Robert asked.

"I'm saying our fatigue policy complies with the FAA requirements," Croft said.

"Yes," Robert said. "But I'm asking about the contents."

"I have not seen the fatigue policy in quite a long time."

"So, you don't know sitting here today whether that policy prohibits a flight manager from coercing a pilot from flying fatigued?"

"Objection," Wendel said. "You can answer."

"Again, I answered the question already. I think that would be inconsistent with the value of the corporation and the safety culture we discussed. However, you would have to ask the specific manager the background on the topic in order to evaluate indeed is it a fatigue situation or not. I don't know what the answer is," Croft said.

"Could you read back the last question?" Robert asked. The reporter read the question and then Robert said, "Your answer to that is I don't know?"

"My answer would be that it would not be consistent with our policy. You're getting into a specific detail that I don't have any information to impart," Croft said, defiant on answering what had actually been asked.

"My specific question is, would that be in violation of Global's FAA approved fatigue policy?"

"To coerce a pilot to fly fatigued?" Croft asked.

"Yes," Robert said maintaining his patience.

"We would not do that, no," Croft said.

"That is not responsive to my question," Robert said removing his glasses.

Darby felt Robert's pain. He was simply trying to get Croft to admit to protected activity. Croft had either been briefed not to admit this, or he was more ignorant than Darby could have imagined. Everyone should know that management coercion to fly fatigued would be contrary to *any* policy, let alone the FAA's.

"Asked and answered," Wendel said. "Move on. The record will reflect his answer. You can move on and make a note if you don't like the answer, but ask another question."

"Are you directing him not to answer that question?" Robert asked.

"He has answered it five times," Wendel said.

"What he has never done is answer the question—"

"Watch your tone, sir," Wendel said.

"What he has never done," Robert said softer, "is that tone acceptable to you?"

"It is," Wendel agreed with a smirk.

"What he has never done is answer the question as to whether a manager's coercion of a pilot to fly fatigued is in violation of Global's FAA approved fatigue policy."

"That is your opinion and you can certainly take that—make

that opinion known," Wendel said.

"Are you directing him not to answer that question?" Robert asked.

"He has answered it already. If you want to ask it again, it is your deposition," Wendel said. "If you want to ask him the question again and see what the witness responds, you can certainly do so. That is within your rights. I'm not directing him in any way."

Darby watched this volley game as they slammed attacks over the net with an open hand. Back and forth. Bottom line, Croft was refusing to admit that management coercion was in violation of their FAA-approved program because Global would be in violation of protected activity.

"Very good. Thank you," Robert said. "Sir, would you agree with me that it is a violation of Global's FAA-approved pilot fatigue policy to coerce a pilot to fly while fatigued?"

"No," Croft said. Then he added with emphasis with his hands, "No meaning we would not coerce a pilot to fly while fatigued."

"So, it would be a violation of that FAA approved—"

"We would never coerce any employee to operate in a fatigued manner!" he snapped.

Darby wanted to yell—yes you have! As has been admitted by Dodson, Clark, and Wyatt. Not to mention, that Global received a violation from the FAA for doing that very thing.

"I'm asking whether you know if that would be a violation of Global's FAA approved fatigue policy?" Robert pressed.

"I'm not specifically familiar with our—the details of our fatigue policy. I would have to reference it. As I answered about five times, we would never coerce an employee to operate equipment of any variety in our airline under a fatigued setting."

"Okay," Robert said with a sigh. "Again, it is not my question whether Global would do it or not. The question is whether that act—"

"If you bring me the policy, I can answer it specifically," Croft snapped. "It would be inconsistent with our culture is what I'm saying."

Robert stared for a moment and then said, "So you don't know—"

"I don't know what that specific policy states, but it would be inconsistent with how we operate this airline."

Chapter 79

OH MY GOD, this was crazy. The incompetence of Croft is unmatched only by Dodson. Darby wanted to tell him to just say yes, or that he could not recall.

Robert leaned back in his chair and stared at Croft for a moment and then he turned to Wendel. "I was about to propose cutting a lot of questions and it might be time efficient if we took a ten-minute break. He can replace the video and I can try to reduce this outline."

"If the goal is to end earlier than the allotted three hours, I certainly agree to that," Wendel said.

Darby and Robert went to the briefing room and Robert closed the door. He turned to Darby and said, "That man is incompetent."

"So now what?" Darby said.

"I had to cut more than half of my questions because he doesn't have the requisite knowledge to answer them," Robert said, placing a hand on his hip. "I simply cannot believe he is running the world's largest airline."

"I'm good if we cut it short," Darby said. "But I am curious about a couple things."

Darby conveyed to Robert what she wanted brought to Mr. Croft's attention, and then they returned to the briefing room.

"That helped reduce the number of questions," Robert said

entering the room. "I will apologize in advance because these last couple questions are random. But two more and we will be done."

They went back on the record and Robert asked, "Has anyone advised you that the Illinois Medical Disciplinary board has referred Dr. Wood to the prosecution board of that state?"

"Objection!" Wendel snapped. "Foundation."

"I'm just asking if he has knowledge of that."

"Okay," Wendel said.

"I have no knowledge," Croft said.

"Is there someone assigned to open your mail other than yourself?" Robert asked.

"My assistant can, yes."

"Would she have the authority to discard mail from pilots without alerting you to the content?"

"Not to discard," Croft said. "Maybe to forward and send elsewhere in the company but not to discard."

"So there might be email communications—"

"I get thousands of emails a day, okay?" he said, a bit too abruptly. "I wouldn't have time to sit here for three hours with *you*, if I didn't have someone help me with my emails."

"That is fortunate for me," Robert said calmly.

"Yes, it is," Croft retorted.

"So, is that a common practice, then, in your operation, to have emails directed to you read by your assistant without disclosing the content to you?" Robert asked.

"If there was something I needed to know, she would certainly let me know but, yes, she does that all the time."

"And do you have any knowledge—if you would refer back to Exhibit 18. I will ask you to turn to the second page. This is the Safety Culture Ethnographic Study of Global Air Lines. Is this the type of document, if it were received by your assistant that she would have the authority to forward to others without disclosing the content to you?"

Croft stared at the document. "I don't know, but she could have."

"Pass the witness."

Chapter 80

Oklahoma City
Corporate Offices
Feb 28, 2020

WALTER CROFT STORMED into his office and pulled the door closed firmly. He walked directly to his credenza and removed a glass from the shelf, then poured three inches from the closest bottle not caring what the hell it was. He took a long drink.

There was an expected knock at the door. "Come in," he barked over his shoulder. Kowalski, Clark, and Wolfe entered. He turned toward them and extended his hand toward the seating area. "Sit. Please." He took another long drink, closed his eyes for a moment and shook his head, then breathed deep.

"You could have prepared me." Walt turned away from the group and set his glass on the desk. He paused, and then turned toward the men. Embarrassment did not cover how he felt. Mortified would be more accurate. He stood with his hands on hips looking down at Wendel Kowalski. "You led me to the wolves," Croft said.

"Robert Allen is looking for anything to make this case fit the law. You gave him nothing," Wendel said, with a dismissive flick of his hand.

"I came off looking like a fucking idiot!" Walt snapped. "Why the hell didn't you tell me I had been the accountable executive of the SMS program? It would have been nice to have been prepared."

"There was no way of knowing what he was going to ask," Wendel said. "Our team is just as surprised as you. However, we are done with depositions. We did good. You did just fine."

"We'll be ready for trial," Wolfe said.

"You think we should go to trial?" Croft asked turning toward Wolfe and then back to Wendel. If his testimony ever got out, he would be a laughingstock. "Would that video become public if we went to trial?"

"That video will never see the light of day," Wendel said. "There are laws in place to protect you. We can assure you of that."

"Very good," Croft said, relaxing for the first time since he walked out of the deposition. "Then let's bury her in trial." If he could financially drain her for embarrassing him as she did, he would have some sort of vindication.

"Of course, it's up to you," Wendel said. "But our firm does not recommend trial."

"Because we won't win?" Croft asked, folding his arms.

"Winning is not the issue. I believe we could win on a technicality. But the testimony overall does not paint a positive image for Global," Wendel said. "And at that point, your deposition would become part of the trial. It would not be released to the general population, but it would be presented in court and become public record."

"If we settled, would it be sealed?"

"It would," Wendel said. "We would see to that."

"What time is your flight?" Walt asked, having had enough of Wendel Kowalski for the day. This was supposed to be the best firm in the industry, and they had paid dearly for them. He wasn't so sure anymore. Wendel should have protected him. And where the hell was Von Dietrich? he wondered.

"An hour or so," Wendel said glancing at his watch.

"Then you'd better get going," Walt said, dismissing him.

Wendel stood holding tight to his briefcase and headed toward the door. He turned the knob and then looked back toward Croft. "Like I said. You did good today, sir. You gave them nothing."

Walt nodded, and Wendel left the office.

It was after 5:00 p.m. and he had already sent his secretary home for the day. Croft walked over to the door and locked it, then turned.

"Was it that bad?" Clark asked.

Croft flashed a glare Clark's way. "You should have told me about the SMS change and that I had been the accountable executive. What the hell was that all about?"

He walked over to his desk and tipped back his drink, emptying the glass. If it hadn't been for Clark, they would not be in this position, cleaning up his mess. He strode around his desk and sat heavily.

Wolfe stood and walked across the room and sat in a chair across from Croft, Clark did the same, reluctantly.

"I'm sorry, sir," Clark said. "I simply did not realize the CEO was the accountable executive unless we redesignated it. Hell, I didn't know there was one. Not until Bradshaw mentioned it, did we look."

"Our only option was to take you out of the heat," Wolfe said. "I had no idea that the notice of change would be present."

"You'd better fix that process," Croft said. "We demand the ability to change procedures and adjust policies as necessary online and without record."

"It's in process," Clark said.

Historically any changes to their policies or manuals had to be approved by the FAA. With online manuals, this process was bypassed and Global changed anything they wanted. One day it was simply rewritten without record, and the way they liked it. The *change record* had become a problem.

"What can I do to help?" Wolfe asked.

Croft steepled his fingers and placed them to his lips for a moment and closed his eyes. *Nobody makes me look like a fool,* he thought. He blamed Darby Bradshaw.

He opened his eyes and looked between the men. "When Wyatt is in office, I want Bradshaw gone. I want her and her airplane to disappear. Make it to look like she flew it into the ocean, and intentionally killed everyone. I want the world to see that we were correct, and she should have been grounded."

Croft had already agreed that he would sacrifice one of Global's aircraft in a total hull loss to open the door to U.S. pilotless aircraft. That would be Wyatt's message to approve of Airbus' autonomous aircraft. They would prove that technology was safer than pilots who were prone to error. In this case, the pilot would be Darby Bradshaw. There would be no better ending or vindication that he could think of.

Chapter 81

Oklahoma City Airport

THE OPENING AND closing of any life event should be held in celebration. Within minutes Darby and Robert were at the airport. They stopped at a bar between their gates, and each ordered a scotch and Darby ordered a large plate of fries for them to share. Their flights would depart in 43 and 55 minutes.

"That man simply astounds me," Robert said after the waitress set their drinks and fries on the table. "To think he is the leader of the world's largest airline is stunning. Simply amazing."

Darby couldn't agree more. She stuck a fry into the paper cup of ketchup and swirled it around. She had hoped for so much more from Croft. Disappointment did not explain the extent of her feelings. He was incompetent, insincere, but now knew the truth about everything. If he hadn't known before, he did now.

"You can dress up a pig and put lipstick on him," Robert said, "but he's still just a pig."

"Well, I hope that pig doesn't survive."

"My Dad always said *bears make money and bulls make money, but pigs always lose in the end.*"

Darby chuckled. "I think my dad said, *Pigs get fat and hogs get slaughtered.*"

"If that's the case, then let's hope he's a hog," Robert said raising his glass.

"I'm surprised that he's as ignorant as he is, having been a CFO," Darby said. "Did he *really* say he didn't know what an accountable executive means?"

"He did," Robert said with a nod while reaching for a fry. "What I cannot figure out is what the hell his legal team is doing. Not that I'm complaining, they gave us the win. But this is borderline negligence on their part. They should have advised him better than they did."

"How could they have known what you were going to ask?" Darby asked.

"It was in the discovery *they* gave to us," Robert said.

Darby laughed. "Kind of like the giving us his memo meeting with Clark." She grinned. "At least they'll end it now."

"That they will," Robert said, and raised his glass in a toast. "I'm quite surprised they allowed him to go through that fiasco in the first place. I'm embarrassed for the man."

"Me too," Darby said, clinking her glass to Robert's. "But thank God this is over. I want to do a happy dance. I cannot believe we've found the end of the nightmare."

"I suspect we'll hear an offer by tomorrow," Robert said. "Will you sign an NDA?"

An NDA was a non-disclosure agreement in which the company was willing to pay off the employee, and in agreement be able to hide their wrong doings. The only reason Darby traveled down this path was to create change. Despite all the programs Wyatt said that Global instituted because of her report, nothing had changed. Employees feared coming forward, and the CEO was unwilling to hold anyone accountable. If she took money for her silence, she would be no better than those who were paid to look the other way.

"No," Darby said. "I'd keep their payment silent, but not what they did. Somebody must be held accountable for what happened, or change will never occur."

They rehashed the highpoints of Croft's testimony as they finished their drinks. Robert glanced at his watch and said, "One more?"

"Absolutely!" Darby said. "I can't determine if this is a celebration that it's over, or a wake for the death of the man I thought Walter Croft to be."

Robert ordered the drinks while Darby went to check their flight status. She called Tom on her way, and his phone went directly to voice message. Then she called Kathryn who answered on the first ring.

"How'd it go?" Kathryn, asked.

"Our CEO is beyond incompetent," Darby said, searching the board for their respective flights. "But there is no way in hell they are going to court."

"Oh sweetie, I am so happy for you!" Kathryn said. "It's over."

"That it is," Darby said, confirming their gates and looking at her watch. "I've got to get back and finish my second celebratory drink, but just wanted to tell you the good news."

"When are you coming home?"

"My flight leaves in 30 minutes," Darby said. "Lunch tomorrow?"

"Hell no," Kathryn said. "We're having a celebration. I'll call Jackie and Linda. Dinner at my house at five."

Darby said goodbye and returned to the table. "Good news for you. Your gate moved to right there," she said, pointing across the hall, as she sat. Then she lifted her glass and said, "Thank you. I could not have done this without you."

Chapter 82

Global Corporate
March 1, 2019

WOLFE KNEW THAT the other side of fear would be freedom. He was not, however, looking forward to this meeting he'd been ordered to take. He had no idea what to expect, but he'd learned to be open to anything. He glanced at his watch, just as his secretary buzzed.

"Your eleven o'clock is here."

"Thank you. Please send her in."

He stood, took a deep breath, and walked toward the door as it opened. "Mrs. Branson, thank you for the visit. I'm attorney Joe Wolfe," he said. "Please join me over here."

They sat at his briefing table, and he poured her a cup of coffee. His secretary had brought in cookies. "Please let me tell you how sorry we are for your loss," he said handing her the cup.

She nodded and stared at the cookies. "Thank you."

"So, what can I do for you," Wolfe said. "We are here for anything you need."

"I'm here for one reason only," she said, blotting under her eyes with a handkerchief. "Your HIMS program is broken."

"What do you mean?" Wolfe asked with feigned empathy.

She stared at him for a moment and their eyes locked. She looked away first and opened the purse that sat perched on her lap. Removing an envelope she said, "Stan left a suicide note." She pulled it to her chest, and fresh tears began to flow. "I'm sorry," she finally said placing it on the table and reaching for her handkerchief again.

Wolfe dropped his eyes to the envelope. This was what he had feared. His heart beat rapidly. His urge to grab it and run was replaced with pouring Mrs. Branson a glass of water.

"Don't be sorry," Wolfe said softly. "You've been through far too much, and I wish there was something I could do to help. I worked closely with Stan in the HIMS program. He was a good man. He cared about the program. If it's broken, we'll fix it."

"That's why I came to you. He mentioned you often. And being an attorney, you would know the liability of what I'm about to give you." She lifted the envelope. "He'd asked me to give this to the media. I'm disrespecting his wishes because I don't want the program to be shutdown, I simply want it fixed."

Wolfe nodded, his heart about to break from his chest. "I understand," he said. "And if it's broken, I want that too."

"I'd hoped as much," she said, and pushed the envelope across the table.

He reached for it. "May I?"

She nodded and Wolfe opened the letter and began to read. He intentionally furrowed his brow, displaying deep concern as he read, when all he wanted to do was vomit. He finished the first page, and then scanned the remaining pages.

When done reading he folded the papers and set them on the table, and said, "I had no idea." He dropped his eyes and brought back the memory of his grandfather's death when he was four. When he looked up, the tears were real.

"I suspected as much," Mrs. Branson said, closing her purse and standing. "Helping to get Stan sober was the best thing that could have happened to him. The HIMS program is essential, but something must be done about that," she said pointing at the letter.

Chapter 83

Once Mrs. Branson was gone. Wolfe called Rich Clark. "I need to see you. Branson's wife just left my office. I'll be right there."

Wolfe walked down the hall and gave a quick knock at Clark's door and opened it without an invitation.

"What is it?" Clark said.

"A suicide note," Wolfe said, "Handing him the envelope."

Clark opened the envelope and removed a dozen pages and began to read.

Dearest Barb, I am sorry that you had to find me the way you did. I am nothing but a coward, not the decorated man they portrayed me to be. I have lived a life fighting demons within. The violence I have bestowed on everyone will now be directed on me. Please know that I am not taking my life. This is an execution of a person who deserves more than a life sentence.

In the program I was expected to make amends to those I have harmed. That list is too long, and a simple apology would never suffice. I knowingly cost pilots their jobs. I knew of many pilots who were accused of relapse that did not, and I did not help them. Some have taken their own lives. Others have unjustly lost their hard-earned careers.

Global utilizes the HIMS program to control pilots. They use the dry blood spot PEth test to check for alcohol of those they want gone, because that test produces false positives. They do not host this program because pilots drink, but to control them. Pilots in the program fly fatigued, work sick, and they keep their mouths shut knowing that if they step out of line, they will be removed from duty accused of being a drunk, even if they gave up the bottle.

Global has placed a pilot into mental health evaluation claiming she was a risk to aviation safety using the Germanwings crash as a fear-based tactic to get rid of her for reporting safety concerns. Yet, another captain has reported a pilot for placing a gun into his mouth, and the company has done nothing. I had planned on meeting an attorney tonight to tell him all I know. And in response I was warned I'd be returned to the program. Once an addict, always an addict.

Please know that I did not do this because of fear of returning into the program, or that I would lose my job. I did this because I deserve to be punished appropriately. I believe in capital punishment. I have harmed far too many people in the HIMS program, and I cannot undo that. Anything I could say would be silenced by those in charge of the program. Ironic because I was supposedly in charge of the program, but it was in title only. They would claim all that I had to say was drunk talk. I cannot bring back and/or help those who are unjustly terminated because of what I did. Or those who took their own life because of this program.

The only thing I can do now is to make a grand gesture. That being the Chairman of the HIMS program committing suicide and the reason why will be newsworthy. I'm asking you to take this letter to the media. That is the only way we can impact change. That is the only way my death will have meaning. The following pages list names and events of those that have been harmed on behalf of the HIMS program. Please take this to the media. They will do the rest.

Please forgive me. I love you forever, Stan.

Clark finished reading and glanced at the remaining pages and looked up. Wolfe looked as if he had witnessed his own hanging. Clark knew they had just escaped a death sentence.

"We dodged a bullet," Clark said. "Who else has seen this?"

"Nobody, that I know of," Wolfe said.

"Good."

Clark walked over to the credenza and lifted the pitcher of water and poured it into the potted plant. He returned to his desk and set the pitcher in front of him. He placed the pages inside the container and opened his desk drawer and removed a package of matches. He ripped one off and struck it until it popped into a flame. He stared at the match for a moment, then placed it to the corner of a page, and then to another corner and another. He then dropped the match into the center of the burning pages.

"Problem solved," Clark said.

Chapter 84

Seattle Washington
March 2, 2019

Darby squeezed Tom's hand in the assurance that he wasn't going to be on the menu. They walked hand in hand up the path to Kathryn's front door. It took some convincing for him to join them for dinner. She knocked once and then opened the door.

"Hey Kat, we're here," she called.

They removed their coats and found Linda's husband, Niman, in the living room with John. Darby said hello to the guys, gave them each a hug, and left Tom with them, then headed to find the action.

"Hey, ladies," Darby said as she entered the kitchen.

Kathryn was peaking under the foil of a very large prime rib. Jackie was tossing a Caesar salad, and Linda stirred something on the stove. They all welcomed her, and Darby walked over and placed a hand on Linda's back and peered into the pan. "This smells amazing."

"Mushroom wine gravy," Linda said, lifting a bite for Darby to taste.

"Oh my God, this is so good," she said. "Now what can I do to help?" she asked, as Jackie handed her a glass of wine.

Kathryn hugged Darby and then placed a potato masher in into her free hand. "I saved the best job for you. They're in that pan.

Butter and milk are in here," she said as she pressed the 40-second button on the microwave

Darby laughed. "You had ulterior motives, didn't you?"

"You know me so well," Kathryn said with a grin.

"Here's to the power of visualization," Darby said raising her wine glass in a toast, and then sipped. Peering into the pan at the potatoes she said, "And I can see George Wyatt, and Clark, and Wood, and Marsh, and Ms. Abbott, oh, and there is Walter Croft hiding behind them all." She raised the masher and plunged it into the pan, and everyone laughed.

Within no time they were all seated at the dinner table, a feast like non-other was displayed before them. Kathryn said, "Thank you all for joining me in this celebration dinner. This is finally over."

"Thanks, Kat," Darby said. Tom held her hand and squeezed, and everyone raised their glasses.

"Here's to Darby's success and survival of Global's attack on her," Kathryn began. "Not only surviving the process of that offensive mental health evaluation, but also the Christmas Eve bipolar diagnosis that would have done most people in. Darby never lost her medical, and she also never lost her faith and fortitude. She found her way back into the sky having not flown for two years, but only to face months of reliving the horror of Global management's depravity."

Kathryn then looked directly at Darby and said, "Here's to a really good settlement. I know nothing will ever make you whole, but perhaps Global will hold those involved accountable, and the healing can begin."

"Amen," Tom said, and they all lifted their glasses.

John sliced the prime rib, and bowls and platters were passed between then. Plates were filled, and everyone told Kathryn how delicious everything was as they discussed the case.

"Did Global's legal team state a settlement would be forthcoming?" Niman asked, slicing his beef.

"Not yet," Darby said. "But we only had to prove causation, the judge agreed that I gave them protected activity in good faith and that a mental health evaluation is considered retaliation. The discovery we gathered proved that this was premeditated, and the depositions were the dessert."

"They won't want this to see the inside of a courtroom," Tom said. "If nothing else, because of the CEO's deposition."

Darby grinned. "He actually said he didn't know what accountable executive meant."

Jackie choked her wine. "He didn't."

"Oh, he did," Darby said, and then she proceeded to tell them all about the Croft deposition as they emptied their plates and reached for seconds.

"My, my," Niman said. "Now I understand why a settlement will be forthcoming. Good for your attorney by the way. Not many people could pull a CEO into a deposition."

"Did they ever find any information on that murdered pilot?" Jackie asked.

"It was suicide," Tom said. "Not murder. But the timing was an oddity."

"I wish we knew the why," Darby said. "It had something to do with what he was going to tell me. The interesting thing was that he was the chairman of the HIMS program."

"HIMS?" Niman said.

"The pilot alcohol program," Darby said. "The company uses it to control pilots. Alcoholics Anonymous is a great program for those who need it. But our HIMS program groups everyone into the same category, and the treatment is the same for all—don't drink."

"They don't address why the person is drinking?" Linda asked.

"Oh, they make everyone come up with an excuse. It's always someone else's fault or an issue in their childhood," Darby said. "But the treatment is the same regardless."

"That's horrible," Kathryn said. "What about those who drink to hide depression?"

"My thoughts exactly," Linda said. "You take their crutch and don't solve the problem; most wouldn't be able to survive."

"They use the dry blood spot PEth tests that generate false positives," Darby said. "From what I hear, it's a way to terminate pilots they want to get rid of."

"Those tests are not even FDA approved," Linda said. "What's wrong with your company?"

Darby shrugged. "The worst part is that pilots who could benefit from the program will avoid it to not get nailed by a false positive."

"We've got a broken world," Niman said patting his wife's hand.

"Speaking of broken, what's going on with the MAX?" Darby asked John.

John took a bite of prime rib delaying his answer. But Darby was patient for this one. "I'm hearing rumors that the MAX may be grounded for many years," he finally said.

"Why?" Darby asked

"Because people died," Jackie answered. "You can't just let them keep flying."

Darby hesitated before she spoke. Everyone at this table had been touched by death and lost someone they loved in an airplane, and Jackie was no exception. Darby gave her a moment before she responded.

"Because the fix is simple," Darby finally said. "Mandate a second pitot tube as a backup, create a new type-rating, and train the pilots."

"That will never happen," John said. "This happened because the airlines didn't want to spend the money to train them in the first place."

Darby added a small scoop of potatoes to her plate and said, "What happened to me was for the same reason. I guess that might be the underlying problem—failure to train properly."

"Speaking of training, when do you start?" Kathryn asked.

"What training?" Jackie asked.

"A350," Kathryn said. "Global is getting rid of their triple sevens and Darby's bidding the A350."

"Why am I always the last to know about this stuff?" Jackie said, with a sideways glare at John.

"Kathryn, did I tell you how wonderful this meal is?" John said, and everyone laughed. Then he said, "I'm sorry honey. I knew about the cancellation, but not where Darby was going next."

"My fault," Darby said. "I just learned they were getting rid of my plane and decided to go for a new type-rating. We hadn't had a chance to talk yet."

"That's what tonight is about," Linda said, and Jackie nodded.

"I'm just dealing with toddler exhaustion," Jackie said in apology. "There should be a law about women having kids outside of their twenties."

"Maybe John could help with that one," Tom said with a grin, and wiped his mouth. "Absolutely delicious, Kathryn."

"If I could go back in time," John said with a grin, and Jackie jabbed an elbow into him.

Darby laughed. They made wonderful parents despite the fatigue-driven strain. Besides, Kathryn's twins loved babysitting her, and Jackie's son loved the twins being there. It was a win win for all. Especially for them to be able to have a meal without kids.

"John needs to create a law to prevent removal of pilots from the flight deck," Darby said with a smirk. "What I want to know is what's going on with Bill and Drake in prison together?"

Kathryn and John exchanged a glance, and then John said, "I'm not exactly sure."

Darby decided to not press the issue. There was more to every story, and this was not the time to ask. "Okay. What about Wyatt becoming the FAA administrator then?"

"He's the top contender," John said. "However, he was not exactly forthright on his statements regarding his history and your whistleblower action."

"We were talking about how to keep him out," Linda said. "What if the aviation senate committee learned of his involvement?"

"That might help," John said. "That's one more reason Global would not want this public with a trial."

"This is the most perplexing company," Niman said. "I often wonder who is running it."

Darby raised her glass to him. "My thoughts exactly!"

It was difficult to believe that this had been ongoing for three years, and why it happened in the first place. One thing she and that sociopath Bill Jacobs had agreed on, was that the industry was killing the pilot job. But nothing in life happened by coincidence.

There was a reason that Bill and Drake were in prison together. There was an underlying motive as to why Global attacked her for presenting a safety report. There was also a hidden objective as to why the FAA did not ground the MAX with the first crash, but waited until the second. There was also a reason management fought Darby so adamantly instead of just fixing the problems that appeared so simple to solve. Unfortunately, Darby could not put her finger on the reason.

Stan did not kill himself because of depression and she suspected that his death had everything to do with what he knew. She also doubted he would kill himself and not leave a note. Tom had assured her that none was found. Then there was Wyatt, the leading contender for the FAA administrator, and the old administrator was sitting on Global's Board of Directors.

Darby sipped her wine, pushing everything from her mind, and smiled. Listening to the chatter of her good friends with a wonderful meal was the perfect ending to the chaos that had become her life. She was thankful this was over.

Reaching out to Tom, she placed her hand on his and squeezed. Then gave him a warm smile. She had found love again with a man she could trust. Darby looked forward to going to the A350 and putting this all behind her. She would continue to help make the industry safe. But she would never be naïve again. There was a purpose and reason for everything, and she would pay attention to the chess game they played and would move her pieces carefully.

A phone rang and Darby said, "That's mine." She pushed back from her chair. "I told Robert to call the minute they gave him the settlement offer."

"Good luck Darby," Kathryn said, placing a hand to her chest.

Darby rushed to get her purse. She grabbed her phone and answered. She listened as she returned to the table and sat. Tears filled her eyes and then she said, "Thanks. Can I call you tomorrow?"

"It's that good?" Linda said.

Darby raised her napkin and dabbed under each eye. She slowly shook her head. Then she smiled and looked at all her friends' expectant faces and said, "We're going to trial in twenty-three days."

Epilogue

Seattle Washington
March 3, 2019

Clement Stone once said, "Truth will always be truth, regardless of lack of understanding, disbelief or ignorance." Darby sat at her desk in disbelief. Trial was three weeks away. She could not believe they were going forward with this. Nobody could. If Croft would have honored his charity donation and had met with her, this could have ended before it began. Regardless, she would have bet anything after his deposition he would have ended it.

Darby had no intention of doing anything beyond simply providing the information to leadership. If they chose to toss her report, that would have been their choice. She simply felt obligated to share what she knew.

Never had she been more disappointed in someone than she was in Walter Croft. She had believed in him on many levels. He'd once said in an interview that it was his mother's guidance that drove his decisions to become a servant leader. He was not a servant leader, he simply plagiarized Herb Kelleher's statement from Southwest Airlines. One thing Darby knew, his mother would be rolling over in her grave if she knew what her son had been involved in.

The fact they were going to trial was surreal. There was no possible benefit for Global management to take this path. They did not have a case. *What the hell are they thinking?* she wondered. None of this made sense. There had to be more to this than any of them could imagine. Regardless, she was done giving Walter Croft the benefit of the doubt. Darby sipped her coffee as she thought how to begin. Then she set the cup beside her computer and began to type.

Dear Mr. Croft,

I am writing directly to you because of your stated position during your deposition, that it was okay to do so. The reason I placed a silent bid of $4000 to have lunch with you, shortly after I was involuntarily placed into the Section 8 mental health evaluation, was to have the opportunity to speak with you to avoid where we are today. I won the auction, but I was denied my lunch.

I reached out after I returned to work. Denied. I reached out after the OSHA ruling asking to meet so we could avoid court. Denied. My attorney insisted on your deposition because of Dr. Wood's purported reliance on my safety-related communications with you to reach his determinations that I suffered from bipolar disorder. Your testimony, however, assisted in disproving this contention.

I hoped that an ancillary result of the deposition would be a resolution of the litigation that I have always pursued with mixed feelings. I was confident that you had not been informed about the facts of the case—that I had brought forward legitimate flight safety issues substantiated by the FAA and I was subsequently forced into a compulsory and degrading psychiatric examination.

I was certain that you would be shocked and want to resolve the matter. I knew that once the facts were brought to your attention you would put an end to this. However, apparently, the facts didn't matter. This saddens me because I wanted to believe in you.

It didn't matter that I brought critical flight issues forward in good faith and that my report was a catalyst for change, as confirmed by Captain

Wyatt's sworn testimony. It didn't matter that Captain Clark had been discussing the strategy of forcing me into a Section 8 evaluation many months prior to his doing so and had advised multiple people. Yet despite those facts, Clark remains in the position to which you promoted him.

It doesn't appear to matter that Corporate Legal, Labor Relations, Flight Operations, Human Resources and the DHS were all involved in this action in a manner that made a mockery of our corporate guidelines and ethical compliance.

The only question is why did this happen? If I ran a company, I would love to have all of my employees care as much as I did for the future of the airline and make such an effort to help.

You've encouraged people to come forward if they see something. I did, and this is what happens. This is very sad. I did not criticize my employer's safety deficiencies on social media, nor did I complain to the FAA. Instead, I tried to work within the company and, because of that, suffered through the worst three years of my life. One of the many lessons from this unpleasant experience is that in the future, I must go directly to the FAA with my safety concerns.

In that you've made it clear you have no intention of honoring your obligation for the lunch you donated three years ago, and/or holding the people accountable who participated in this action against me, I respectfully request a refund of my donation. I no longer want to have that lunch. I also believe that the charity should not suffer for your lack of commitment. Rich Clark had emailed me the option of a refund in lieu of your following through a year ago. This will be the best option.

After the letter was complete, Darby typed Walt.Croft@Global.com, and then copied and pasted her letter into the body of the email. Hesitating a moment, she thought of the many creative things she could write in the subject line but settled on *Charity Lunch*. With a big sigh, she pressed send.

If they wanted to go to court, that's what she would do. She once read that the only way to become a champion was by fighting the next round. When things got tough, you had to just keep stepping into that ring. Global management had knocked the wind out of her many times over the years, and she kept getting back up. She would be ready for the next round.

AIR21

THE WHISTLEBLOWER LAW

THE AIR21 STATUTE is the Whistleblower Law more formally known as The Wendell H. Ford Aviation Investment and Reform Act for the 21st Century.

This law protects employees from retaliation when they report safety concerns (protected activity) to their employer or the FAA. The name "Whistleblower" implies that the employee is blowing the whistle on their company to the FAA. However, while the law does protect an employee for reporting to the FAA, more employees are retaliated against in response for internal reports to their company. Mechanics who write up maintenance concerns, pilots who critique substandard training or object to flying fatigued, and so much more.

AIR21 is a discrimination law and belongs in federal court. Your union representatives may encourage you to file a grievance instead. However, the judicial system understands that safety cannot be held in the hands of an arbitrator—a businessman whose livelihood depends upon his next paycheck—and therefore this law allows a pass of the grievance process. The FAA may also lead you to believe that filing a report on their website suffices for the AIR21 complaint, it does not. You must also act immediately because there is only a 90-day statute of limitation period—the shortest of any statute.

Once filed, the FAA and OSHA begin their respective investigations. OSHA can take 2-3 years or longer to rule, and often rules on behalf of the company, regardless of whether there was substantiation of an FAA violation. You also do not have to be correct that your company violated a regulation, you simply must report in good faith that you believed it to be so. Either the company or the employee can appeal an OSHA decision. The appeal will take you to federal court with an Administrative Law Judge (ALJ).

There are four requirements to win an AIR21 complaint: (1) the substantiation of a violation identified as protected activity (2) brought forward in good faith that (3) resulted in an adverse action, where (4) a causal link connects the reporting to the adverse action.

If you want to learn more or need legal advice, contact attorney Lee Seham at ssmplaw.com. Lee Seham knows the law and he is an attorney that you can trust to guide you in the right direction.

Pilots and Alcoholism

If you are a pilot who has experienced an event with alcohol, your career is not over. The FAA requires the following steps to obtain a special issuance:

1. *Substance abuse assessment*
2. *28-day (preferably in-patient) treatment program*
3. *Establish a peer and company sponsor*
4. *A 3-month intensive outpatient follow up (IOP)*
5. *Heavy involvement in AA*
6. *Establishment in regular aftercare*
7. *Psychiatric and neuropsychological evaluations by a HIMS-trained addition specialist.*

If you are required to get a Dry Blood Spot PEth test (DBS PEth), know that this test produces false positives. Even one false positive is a life altering event if it's yours. Immediately go to a hospital and get a whole blood PEth, plus a fingernail and/or a hair follicle test to counteract a potential false positive, so you do not become a statistic. PEth is not FDA certified; there is not enough data, and this test has caused more harm than good with the associated false positives. The question remains—why hasn't ALPA denied the application of this test when there are so many other options available?

Acknowledgements

Life happens when we least expect it. I want to thank my team for their last-minute assistance in bringing this novel to market in 2022. Their phenomenal help will never be forgotten.

Dick Petitt, my husband of 40 years, not only read this book multiple times but he lived the story by my side. We can laugh, shake our heads, and wonder why…but at the end of the day there is always a story to be told. I cannot thank him enough for standing by my side throughout this journey called life. He is forever encouraging my dreams, always accepting of my failures, and he is my greatest supporter.

Carol Singleton began the journey with *Flight For Control* many years ago, and she is still flying strong with me after all these years. She is a talent beyond belief who has gifted me her valuable time to assist in editing this book on short notice. My heartfelt thanks go out to Carol for assisting me to make my novels the best they can be. I have made a promise to her for the next novel that I will fulfill… anyone who might not approve will just have to get over it. Carol is touched by aviation as she worked in the heart of flight operations for a major airline for several years, then she decided to take to the skies again and return work as a flight attendant. Her son is a pilot at a major carrier. Carol has a passion for aviation safety and I'm grateful she has joined my journey.

NATHAN EVERETT HAS been involved in the *Flight For* series from the beginning. As the owner of Elder Road Books, he is a prolific author and editor, and has helped me to bring my books to market. Nathan also has the patience to assist me in learning the structural art of crafting the book itself. I am thankful for Nathan's assistance in every area. If you need help bringing your books to life, contact Nathan at: ElderRoadBooks@outlook.com

INDIVIDUALS MAY INADVERTENTLY resemble characters in this novel. Authors write about what we know, and we develop characters from our experiences. While *Flight For Discovery* is a novel, and therefore fiction, I want to thank any attorney, airline executive, chief pilot, FAA representative, medical professional, ALPA representative, friend or acquaintance who may have inspired a character and the associated actions and dialogue in this novel.

ADDITIONAL WRITINGS

Novels

Flight For Control
Flight For Safety
Flight For Survival
Flight for Sanity
Flight For Truth
Flight For Discovery
Flight For Justice (February 2023)

Non-Fiction:

Normalization of Deviance, A Threat to Aviation Safety
Based on the dissertation:
Safety Culture, Training, Understanding, Aviation Passion: The Impact on Manual Flight and Operational Performance
https://petittaviationresearch.com

Flight To Success Be the Captain of Your Life.
For everyone who wants to master their life and achieve their dreams

I am Awesome, the ABCs of being me
To inspire your little ones to find their passion and see how passion can apply to what we do in life

CPSIA information can be obtained
at www.ICGtesting.com
Printed in the USA
BVHW031509200222
629557BV00005B/9/J